Books by
JOHN UPTON TERRELL

The Arrow And The Cross
Shawnee Chronicle
The Plains Apache
Indian Women of the Western Morning
(with Donna M. Terrell)
Pueblos, Gods and Spaniards
Apache Chronicle
American Indian Almanac
The Man Who Rediscovered America
Traders of the Western Morning
Journey Into Darkness
Zebulon Pike
Estevanico the Black
Faint the Trumpet Sounds
Pueblo de los Corazones
Sunday Is the Day You Rest
Land Grab
Bunkhouse Papers
The Navajo
La Salle
The Six Turnings
Black Robe
Furs By Astor
War for the Colorado River
Plume Rouge
Adam Cargo
The Little Dark Man

(Thirteen titles for younger readers not listed.)

THE ARROW
AND THE CROSS

A History of the American Indian
and the Missionaries

JOHN UPTON TERRELL

CAPRA PRESS
Santa Barbara
1979

Jacket design by Mary Schlesinger.

LIBRARY OF CONGRESS CATALOGING IN PUBLICATION DATA
Terrell, John Upton, 1900-
The arrow and the cross.

Bibliography: p.
1. Indians of North America—The West—Missions.
2. Missions—The West. 3. Indians, Treatment of—
The West. I. Title.
E78.W5T47   266'.00978   79-9293
ISBN 0-88496-132-X
ISBN 0-88496-133-8 pbk.

CAPRA PRESS
Post office box 2068
Santa Barbara, California 93120

CONTENTS

The tree and the rock speak.
The river talks.
The wind talks.
We hear the earth's song.
We are of all things.

AUTHOR'S NOTE

After more than four centuries of unrelenting effort, and the expenditure of enormous sums of money, zealous missionaries of both the Protestant and Catholic faiths have failed to achieve any significant progress in converting Indians to Christianity. Indeed, it can be asserted that this is especially true of apostles stationed in missions of the American West.

Lest it be assumed by some persons that this work is an anti-religious diatribe, let me forcefully state at the outset that it is and, as the BIBLIOGRAPHY AND NOTES confirm, a product of diligent research. Moreover, I am not an Athiest.

The material presented relates only to early missionary endeavors in the Southwest, the Rocky Mountains, California, and Oregon. I have imposed this geographical restriction chiefly for two reasons. Organized and legal religious persecution of American Indians was inaugurated in one of these regions, the Southwest, and was next practiced in another, California. And in these vast colonial empires, men of the cloth, unremittingly striving to destroy the Indian's resistance to Christianity, applied pressures, both mental and physical, that in their degrees of cruelty have no counterparts in the annals of other missions established within the present boundaries of the United States.

By some mystical course of reasoning, innumerable devotees of the Christian persuasion believe that they are endowed, presumably by their Creator, with an inalienable right to engage in proselytism. They labor under an indestructible conviction that, inasmuch as the Jehovah of heaven depicted in their bible is the only true God, it is their earthly duty to force down the throats of persons of conflicting faiths all biblical admonitions, tenets, and fables as unvarnished and infallible gospel.

It is interesting to note that in the Indian way of thinking, religion has never been acceptable as a cause for armed conflict. Unlike Christians, Indians have never engaged in religious crusades. Indians have never tortured, maimed and slain antagonists in the name of some supernatural. An Indian people has never invaded the domain and destroyed the property of other Indians because their beliefs and ceremonials differed from those they themselves harbored and performed. And Indians have never attempted to force white persons to disavow their own faiths, of whatever nature, and revere Indian deities.

Taken individually or together, the segments of this book reflect upon a subject to which some historians, regrettably, have not given the attention it deserves. I believe it to be inextricably woven into the history of the long and continuing conflict between American Indians and Christians, and that negligence in treating with it precludes a comprehensive understanding of that history.

JOHN UPTON TERRELL

CHAPTER ONE

THE TEMPEST

With the end of the earliest major Spanish conquests—those of De Soto and Coronado—in the unwritten lexicons of American Indians, from coast to coast, the words *Christian* and *Christianity* had become synonyms for *disaster* and *death*. Symbols vividly illustrated the accuracy of the definitions: the gun, the sword, the lance, and the cross.

Christianity came to the western Indians with Coronado, but the plants that sprouted from the seeds sown soon shriveled and died. As he marched on with his powerful force across New Mexico, the panhandles of Texas and Oklahoma, and the plains of Kansas[1], leaving a trail of blood, destruction, devastation, and death behind him, the dissemination of religious doctrine was a labor that inspired him not at all and to which he gave little attention. Uppermost in Coronado's thoughts, indeed paramount in every hour of wakefulness and the subject of his dreams, was a seemingly irrepressible obsession that he would find treasures greater than those discovered in the Andes of South America.

It was enough for him that tribal leaders whose peoples were threatened with annihilation accepted his King as their master.

It was enough that Indians whose homes had been destroyed, whose food and possessions had been confiscated, pledged obeisance to his God. It was enough that terrified men, women, and children, tortured and starved, crawled in their nakedness before the cross and lifted arms in supplication not alone to him but to the mysterious majesty he and his men elevated to celestial glory.

There may have been eight or nine friars with the Coronado Expedition, but the names of only six have come down in history. Acting in the capacity of Father Provincial of the company was the Franciscan, Fray Marcos de Niza. (The other identifiable friars: Fray Daniel, Fray Antonio de Victoria, Fray Juan de Padilla, Fray Luis de Escalona, Fray Juan de la Cruz. The last three were martyred.)

The year before, in 1539, Fray Marcos and the intrepid Moor, Estevanico, had led an expedition into the unexplored territory of northern Mexico. With the blessing of the Viceroy, Antonio de Mendoza, they pushed northward from Culiacan, with Indian guides, in search of the rich provinces believed to exist in that region. Indeed, they thought they were on the trail to the legendary Seven Cities of Antilia which purportedly had been founded by seven Spanish bishops who had sailed westward when the Moors invaded Spain.[2] Belief in the riches of these fabulous domains had inspired, and would continue to inspire, ill-fated explorers in the New World.

At Easter time, while Fray Marcos gave himself to devotions, he sent Estevanico, who was not a Christian, ahead to reconnoiter. He never saw him again.

The irrepressible Moor had refused to wait for Fray Marcos to catch up to him, and on a May day Estevanico opened the southwestern gateway to the future United States.[3] Probably early in June, after crossing eastern Arizona, he reached the ancient Zuni pueblo of Hawikuh in northwestern New Mexico. (Coronado and his army would not arrive there until a year later.)

The explanation Estevanico gave for his exploration aroused

suspicion and fear in the Zuni leaders. He told them that following him were men in flowing robes who would instruct them in divine matters and tell them about a supreme God, creator of all things on earth and in the heavens. After three days of questioning him intensively, the Zuni elders remained convinced that they were not being told the truth and that he had come among them with some ulterior purpose which they had failed to discover.

Of all Estevanico's statements, they considered most unreasonable his assertion that in the country from which he came the inhabitants were white, yet he, a black, was serving as their ambassador.

They killed him.

Although the Zunis undoubtedly knew that both white and black men existed—the knowledge would have reached them by the trail over which for centuries had passed the commerce between the Pueblo people and the Indians of tropical Mexico—it is certain they had never seen one of either race. Some of the Zunis apparently feared that Estevanico, even though he appeared in the form of an ordinary man, may have dwelt in the favor of some powerful deity, and that his slaying might bring upon them some kind of economic disaster or physical punishment. Evidently there was considerable discussion of the subject, and in the end the majority found acceptable the proposal that inasmuch as the black was dead, proof that he was not a man with friends in the sky, but nothing more than flesh and blood like themselves, might be obtained by cutting his body into small pieces. The test was successful, and after being dried in the hot New Mexico sun, bits of bone, skin, sinew, and hair were distributed among other tribes with a warning to kill any other intruders, either black or white, who might appear.[4]

It was good advice, but was inseparably related to an objective impossible to achieve. For bows and arrows and clubs, deadly in prehistoric inter-tribal warfare, were quickly relegated to uselessness by the firepower of guns, by lead missiles, steel lances, and armor. With the advent of Coronado and his horde of gold-crazed adventurers, the Iron Age supplanted the Stone Age in the land that would become the American West.

Fray Marcos was in southern Arizona, probably not as far north as the Gila River, when Indians brought him word that Estevanico had been slain by the Zuni.

Pedro de Castaneda, a soldier in Coronado's army, would eventually write that Fray Marcos lost no time gathering up his skirts and fleeing back to Mexico. But the priest would claim that when the *wretched news* reached him he was only three days' journey behind Estevanico and that he had gone on until from a distant hill he had seen Hawikuh, the pueblo in which Estevanico had died. It was, he reported to Coronado and Viceroy Mendoza, a city *larger than the city of Mexico,* and was in his opinion the *greatest and best of all that have been discovered.* Indians, he declared, had told him that farther on were even larger and better cities, one called Totonteac *with so many houses and people that it was without end.* After taking possession of the country for Spain and naming it the Kingdom of St. Francis, he had started back to Mexico *with more fear than food.*

Fray Marcos swore that he had gazed on Hawikuh about the middle of May. He was back in Compostela, Mexico, where he met Coronado, about five weeks later. The distance by trail between the two places was more than fifteen hundred miles. Perhaps by some miracle he had acquired wings for his sandals. To have completed the journey in such a short time he would have had to travel in excess of forty miles a day on foot over high mountains, across formidable deserts, and through torturous canyons.

When the Coronado Expedition set forth in 1540, the soldiers' imaginations had been fired by the tales of great cities told by Fray Marcos. Three brief statements suffice as a foundation for the fury of Coronado and the advance guard of his army against the priest.

When they gazed for the first time on Hawikuh, said Castaneda, *such were the curses that some hurled at Friar Marcos that I pray God may protect him from them. It is a little, crowded village, looking as if it had been all crumpled up together.*

To make a long story short, Coronado wrote the Viceroy, *I can assure you that Friar Marcos has not told the truth in a single thing he has said, for everything is the opposite of what he related* . . .

Some documents state that Fray Marcos had become ill and thought it best to return to Mexico City for treatment. Castaneda wrote bluntly that Fray Marcos went back *because he did not think it was safe for him to stay, seeing that his report had turned out to be entirely false, because the kingdoms he had told about had not been found, nor the populous cities, nor the wealth.*

Word of Estevanico's death had not yet reached Mexico City, when Francisco de Ulloa, a sea captain in the pay of Cortes, began a voyage up the Gulf of California, ostensibly searching for a water route to the Seven Cities. Near its head he was confronted by dangerous shoals which he believed to be impassable and so he turned back. The relative freshness of the outgoing tides and the types of debris they carried should have indicated that immediately ahead beyond the shoals was the delta of a large and powerful river. It was the Rio Colorado, not then known to exist.[5]

When Hernando de Alarcon, with three vessels laden with supplies for Coronado, sailed up the Gulf of California in the summer of 1540, he was able to pass through the shoals and against the raging current of the Rio Colorado in small boats. It was his hope, if not his belief, that the river came out of the province of Cibola, in which, he had been told, lay the great, rich, walled cities Coronado had set out to conquer.

Alarcon and his sailors were the first white men to ascend the Rio Colorado from its mouth. They went upstream until they had passed the site of Yuma, Arizona. From Indians they learned that Zuni lay several hundred miles to the northeast, beyond deserts through which travel was extremely difficult.

Alarcon had no friars with him while traveling up the Colorado, but he told the Indians of the all-powerful Christian God in Heaven. Little crosses his sailors fashioned were distributed among them, and several large ones were erected on the river bank. He led his men in religious ceremonies and taught the Indians to clasp their hands and kneel in prayer.

The Yuman people Alarcon encountered knew that within the past few weeks Coronado had sacked the Zuni pueblo at Hawikuh where Estevanico had been killed. Alarcon pleaded with the Yuman to guide him overland to the expedition, but they refused, giving as a reason their fear that they would be endangering their own lives by taking more invaders to the land of Zuni. In September, Alarcon went back downstream to his ships in Gulf and sailed for Mexico.[6]

Thus, as contemporary narratives and official documents would reveal to the world in time, the swiftness with which reports of Coronado's conquest were carried on foot great distances across mountains and deserts and plains was nothing less than remarkable. It is improbable that more than three weeks had elapsed before every pueblo in New Mexico, as well as the Yuman people of the Rio Colorado, four hundred miles to the west, and the Plains Apache of the Llano Estacado, an equal distance to the east, had been informed that the Zunis had been conquered. And, as the days passed, tales of the disaster would have continued to spread with similar rapidity to the Indians of southern California, to those who dwelt on the seas of short grass in eastern Colorado and western Kansas, and undoubtedly to the tribes of the Great Plains through which the Missouri, Platte, Arkansas, and Red Rivers cut their courses.

In April 1542, his army tattered and exhausted, and himself a dispirited, sick man, Coronado gave the order to start back to Mexico. A little more than two years had passed since they had ridden northward from Compostela on the coastal trail along the Pacific, pageantry and splendor rivalling the glory of their dream.

In this way Christianity came to the Indians of the West. They had been confronted by only a few of its confusing principles, and they had known only a few of the elements of the civilization associated with it, but tales of what had been seen and learned and of their sufferings and their losses would be told and retold about countless thousands of campfires for years after the last of the armored men who called themselves Christians had vanished over the horizon.

The things that the Spaniards coveted were as incomprehensible to the Indians as the doctrines the Spaniards preached. One question always remained unanswered in their long councils and discussions, always left them baffled and disturbed—and they would find no satisfactory explanation of it in centuries to come, when more hordes of white invaders had descended upon them.

Why, the Indians would ask and always wonder, *if you loved Him and adored Him, did you inflict such great cruelties on Him? Why did you beat Him and stone Him and crucify Him, if you worshipped Him? Why, if you revere Him now and He is your Great Spirit, your Supreme Deity, do you talk always of the terrible things you did to Him, and picture Him in His death agony? How can He help and protect you after you have killed Him?*

A question with many parts, but actually only one question.[7]

The material things that were for the Indian symbols of the white man's faith—the fire and noise and acrid fumes and missiles of guns, the armor against which arrows shattered, the sound of horses' hooves beating the earth and the peculiar odor of their manure, the clanking of spur chains and swords, the banners and plumes, the crucifixes and crosses and brilliant vestments—had existed for only two years after they had first appeared. The Indians who had known them in reality could live once again as they had always lived, with their own kinds of warfare and their own kinds of peace, with the fruits of their own labors and with the security and comfort they were able to provide for themselves.

They could never forget the magic and the wonders they had witnessed, the tragedies and terrors they had suffered, and their only recourse was to pray to their own gods to spare them from recurrences. They could hope, always hope, that Christian invaders would never come again but they could know no reassurances. Hope was not enough nor was faith in their own deities enough to keep them from gazing apprehensively each day to the horizon.

Yet, as the years passed they found some reason to be encouraged, for two new generations would be created among them after Coronado went away before they again would see horses and men in armor and again hear the sound of guns.

CHAPTER TWO

Indian Religion:
The Unity of All Things

It is improbable that in all of recorded history any people of any race on earth was guided more by religious tenets than primitive American Indians. Their beliefs influenced very nearly everything they did and thought, day or night. They devoted more of their time to spiritual worship, contemplation and ritual than to any other aspect of their way of life.[1]

The earth was the church of the Indian and the sky was its roof.

It was inconceivable to the Spanish that Indians were capable of maintaining an orderly society in which religion was vitally important to the effective functioning of government and to social control. Nor could the Spanish accord to people they looked upon as backward heathens an ability to merge cultural and spiritual elements into an efficient instrument, an impregnable contrivance such as that in which the doctrines of the Roman Catholic Church were walls and roof enclosing the social, economic and legal beams of Spain's monarchal structure. As for Americans, if constitutional provisions commanded against such an alliance of powers, their attitude toward the Indians' spiritual beliefs and socio-economic system was no less intolerant. Indeed, neither American Protestants nor Catholics, blinded by bigotry, not only toward Indians but to each other as well, made an attempt to be indulgent or understanding; forthwith they condemned Indian practices and philosophies, both spiritual and temporal, as degenerate and therefore unworthy of their consideration.

Ethnologists, archaeologists, anthropologists, and other scholars have shown that every part of the Indian life cycle was attended by appropriate religious ritual. Ceremonies ranged from a prayer uttered by an individual in private to a song or dance in which hundreds of men and women participated and which might have continued for several days and nights. Each ritual, from the simplest to the most complex, usually adhered to a rigid formula. Each dance was performed strictly as prescribed by tradition. Songs, prayers, and chants were memorized and recited verbatim. Any deviation was not only forbidden but aroused the fear that it would render the ceremonial ineffective.

No decision was made in council, no project was authorized, no act was committed without a plea to some supernatural for guidance and success. Some appeals were no more than a gesture, such as blowing smoke from a pipe to the Four Directions, and some involved a complicated series of supplications, such as those performed to effect cures, drive away evil spirits, bring bountiful crops and good hunting and victory in war.

Anthropomorphism and animism were essential attributes of Indian religion. Indians interpreted animals and plants and trees and even inanimate objects in terms of human and personal characteristics. They attributed conscious life to all things of nature, and they believed in spiritual beings and in the existence of spirits separable from bodies. They gave characters and personalities to the members of their hierarchies of deities, endowing them with physical powers and weaknesses, good and bad temperaments, kindness and ill will, joviality and surliness, and other qualities that were to be found in themselves and the beasts and birds and insects about them on earth.

Most white persons are inclined to ridicule the powers of Indian medicine men and to decry the efficacy of their practices. However, many cures were accomplished and some must properly be included in the realm of psychotherapy. Since Indians believed that diseases were controlled by Spirit Beings who had in some way been offended, they also believed that by ritual and prayer angry Spirits could be appeased and sickness removed from a suffering body. But a large number of drugs were used as well, and the extent of the Indian's familiarity with them is indicated by the inclusion of more than two hundred drugs that Indians used in the *Pharmacopeia of the United States* and the *National Formulary*.[2]

The medicine man was not merely a figure to be summoned for illness or bodily injury. His calling was a part of Indian religion, and he was usually a person of political power who ranked high in the priesthood and who was respected for his leadership as well as for his erudition.

Primitive Indians, striving to achieve some understanding of the phenomena of life and nature, assumed that every living body and object of their environment possessed a degree of magic power. This force or dynamic energy was called by numerous names with varying shades of significance in the many Indian languages, but one name, *Orenda,* serves with appropriate expressiveness.[3] In English a definition of this power would include *mysterious, immortal* and *wonderful,* but these adjectives fall short of connoting the full meaning and functions of *Orenda* as it was conceived by the Indians.

Indians believed that *Orenda* was transferable, and that it could be attracted and suppressed. If they would obtain even the simplest necessities, if they would know health and prosperity, if they would be successful in achieving their desired goals, if they would escape undue hardship, avoid suffering, prevent disastrous conditions from descending upon them, they must win the favor of innumerable gods, major and minor, all of whom were capable

of exercising *Orenda* in some form. These benefits and advantages were obtainable, if they were obtainable at all, through the
media of prayers, of propitiatory acts, of specific ceremonials, of
sacrifices. Seldom a day passed in the life of an Indian in which he
or she did not pause, at least briefly, for the performance of a
supplicatory act.

Without exception, the origin myths of all Indians relate that an
orderly universe existed *from the beginning of time*. And ever
since the mysterious advent of this cosmos there were continual
changes—metamorphosis in all things, both animate and
inanimate—brought about by inexplicable but obviously insuperable forces, the functioning of *Orenda*.

No less subject to these magical transitions than any other
natural entity, Indians eventually reached the surface world after
imprisonment for immeasurable ages in various older regions.
Some of these older regions were *below,* locked in eternal darkness, and some were *above,* in the illimitable realms beyond the
visible sky.

There is a striking similarity in the cycles of Indian genesis
myths in the respect that most of them speak of several worlds.
Some of them treat of six worlds surrounding the mid-world on
which Indians dwelt, one in each of the four directions, one
above, and one below. A color is assigned to each world.[4]

To Indians it was the height of irrationality to believe, as missionaries asserted, that woman was made from the rib bone of a
man. The natural processes, unceasing in their functioning, ne-
gated the allegation that one sex could have been created without
the other. How, they asked, could it have been otherwise? For all
living things—every man, every plant, every animal, every fish
and fowl, even the smallest insect—come into being only after
completion of the cycle that makes their respective lives possible.
Indians adhered to the doctrine that the female of their kind was
created simultaneously with the male. For apparent reasons, each

was endowed with peculiar qualities and sensibilities, neither was accorded supremacy, and each was made dependent upon the other for existence.

Despite this conceptual practicality, no sacred narratives, no allergorical expressions, were more imaginative, more fabulous, more permeated by mysticism, than those of the Indians. Brief consideration of the origin myths of widely separated tribes supports this assertion, and serves to illustrate, as well, the universal belief of Indians that they emerged from various worlds through transformations caused by super-natural processes.

In California, the Shoshoneans attributed their origin to the North, whence a great divinity, or captain-general of a pantheon of six (or seven) deities, some of them female, led the people to their permanent earthly homes. A sister of four brothers, all members of the pantheon, was made pregnant by a lightning flash, and gave birth to a boy who spoke when his navel string was cut.

The Juaneno and Luiseno people of California believed that the first things in the universe were the Sky and the Earth, brother and sister. From their union was born soil, sand, stone, flint, trees, in that order, and, finally, the deities who produced a race of beings that became men.

In the Mohave cosmogony, Sky and Earth, male and female, touched far in the west across the sea, and from them were born all men and beings.[5]

Turning to the Great Plains, in the cosmic hierarchy of the Lakota Sioux there were four major groupings of gods, comprising sixteen in all. Each god represented a manifestation of Wakan Tanka, the Great Mystery. In the Lakota origin myth, creation began with Wizinya, the Old Man, and his wife, Wakanaka, who lived together beneath the earth. They produced Ite, the most beautiful of women, who married Tate, the Wind God, and gave birth to quadruplets (again the number *four*), the North, West, East, and South Winds. Here once more it is related that mankind first emerged from an underworld.[6]

The Tewa believed that in the beginning they, their supernaturals, and animals all lived together in a dark underworld that lay beneath a large lake far to the north of their present Southwestern homeland.[7] Among supernaturals were their first mothers, Blue Corn Woman, or Summer Mother, and White Corn Maiden, or Winter Mother. The mothers asked one of the men, who would become known later as Mountain Lion, or Hunt Chief, to explore the realm above and find out how the people might leave the darkness.

Hunt Chief made four unsuccessful explorations, one in each direction, but on his fifth trip he came upon *tsiwi* (predatory animals and carrion-eating birds). They treated him badly at first, then declared they were his friends and gave him a bow and arrows and a quiver, dressed him in buckskin, and tied feathers on him. Thus, Hunt Chief became the first *Made* person.

Six pairs of brothers called Towa é were sent out. Each pair was a different color. The blue, yellow, red, and white pairs discovered mountains in each of the cardinal directions. The dark pair saw a large star in the eastern sky. The all-colored pair saw a rainbow. The people made three attempts to emerge from the darkness, but on each occasion were afflicted with serious defects in their characters and cultural structure, and were forced to return. At last, on their fourth journey, they found themselves qualified to cope with life on the surface world. Led by Summer Chief and Winter Chief, and watched over by the four pairs of brothers standing on four mountains in the four directions, the people began to move southward along the Rio Grande.[8]

Particularly interesting is the origin myth of the Osage, a Siouan people who dwelt mainly in the woodlands and prairies of Missouri, for it related that some of their tribe was indigenous to earth, the Sacred One, living there long before the others descended from the sky to join them. Befuddled and frightened by

the manifestations of the Great Mysteries, and me
Sacred One's anger and whims, the people from th
themselves the Little Ones. They had floated down i
tree, and in landing they had loosened acorns whi... ᴄᴌattered
among the leaves. Walking upon the Sacred One, the Little Ones,
Children of Grandfather the Sun, divided into three groups, calling themselves People of the Water, People of the Land, and
People of the Sky. It is not known when they found the Isolated
Earth People who had preceded them.[9]

In the Navajo genesis, both men and women evolved through
four underworlds before reaching the earth's surface. These
nether regions and the sunworld were portrayed as superimposed
hemispheres, the skies of which were supported by deities.

In the first Navajo underworld there were four clouds, which
embodied the prototypes of males and females. First Man was
created when two of the clouds met in the East, and First Woman
was created when the two other clouds met in the West. Although
First Man and First Woman lived together, they did not produce
mankind, for they were merely prototypes, and not in themselves
human beings. But it was predestined that human beings should
be, for First Man and First Woman planned their creation, and,
with the cooperation of many other types of beings—that is,
animate natural entities among whom they dwelt—they also
planned all other developments for the surface world on which
human beings eventually would live.

The emergence of human beings was slow and difficult. In the
second underworld the Navajo prototypes fought with Bird Beings before moving up to the third underworld. There they encountered Holy People and other kinds of beings. It was in the
third underworld that a miraculous event took place. There the
emerging people found the prototype of Changing Woman, who
represented fertility and life, its regeneration and recession with
the seasons.

But the third underworld was not without misfortunes. The sexes were temporarily separated, with the result that Monster Beings were born. Water Monster produced a flood that drove all other beings upward to the fourth underworld. After a hard struggle, the sexes were reunited, but Monster Beings continued to make the fourth underworld a fearful place, and at last First Man and First Woman led everyone up to the fifth world, the surface.

All the prototypes of animate and inanimate objects, which were both male and female, also were brought up to the fifth world, and there assumed the forms in which they would forever remain. And in accordance with the cosmic plan formulated in the lower worlds, the sun, the moon, and the stars took the places assigned to them and so night and day and spring and summer and fall and winter were established.

The Holy People went to live on four sacred mountains that marked, one in each direction, the boundaries of Dinetah, the home of the Navajo.[10] And ever afterward, when the Holy People wished to take a journey, they traveled on sunbeams, rainbows, and lightning. And Changing Woman, who was blessed with eternal youth and incomparable beauty, went to dwell in a great house beside the western sea.[11]

Speaking in general terms, Indian religious philosophies suppose that every object on, below, and above the earth belongs to one great system of all-conscious and interrelated life. Degrees of relationship are sometimes determined by degrees of resemblance. The Zuni, for example, believe that if an organism resembles man, it is related to man, and correspondingly mortal. If an organism is mysterious, it is believed to be removed from man, and more advanced, powerful, and immortal. Lightning may be taken as an illustration. It flashes through the sky in the zigzag motions of a serpent, but the serpent is mortal and less mysterious than lightning. Yet, because of its zigzag movements the serpent is believed to be more closely related to lightning than man, but at the same time more closely related to man than lightning because the serpent is a mortal organism and not a mystery.[12]

The dogma of missionaries proclaimed that only a person who had unreservedly embraced the Christian faith could possess the immaterial entity that was superior to the body, the spiritual essence called the soul. Thus, customarily, enslaved Indians dying of malnutrition and unbearable toil, and Indians to be executed for their defiance of civil statutes, were hastily baptized and prayed for by religious emissaries. This ritual it was asserted would establish a link, although perhaps tenuous, between a heathenish victim and holy salvation. The final decision regarding admission of a soul to the heavenly realm, of course, was a prerogative of God. All an earthly ecclesiastic could do was beg that it would be saved and hope for a favorable response to supplications.

Contrary to enunciated Christian doctrines, fundamental principles of Indian religion involved relations between life and the incorporeal soul. These relations were based on three mental processes: the power to act that is resident in a living body but distinct from the existence of the body; subjective sensations connected with imagery; and objective impressions made by memory images. Still another Indian concept of the soul was based on the associations of the phenomena of will power. These associations were expressed in beliefs having to do with animals, inanimate objects, and guardian spirits that carried out the wishes of their respective owners.

The power of acting concept was applied either to a whole body, parts of a body, or to no more than a single organ of a body. Many Indians believed they possessed several souls. The loss of one might cause sickness; the loss of another might cause disability of limbs, mental deficiencies, or transformations in personality; and loss of all, or only the principal one, could result in death. Some Indians believed that a departing soul took on the form of a living but invisible object.

It was almost universally conceived by Indians that souls continued to exist after leaving a body, living in the land of the dead. The mythology of very nearly every tribe included a detailed description of this land, and some believed that it was near by, while others placed it far to the west, beyond a great river. The greater number of Indian peoples identified the living soul of a deceased person with the owl. In the land of the dead the seasons came in reverse to those of the land of the living, and in it night prevailed when the sun was shining on earth.[13]

Christian theologians might take note that very few Indian religions proffered a conception of two hereafters, such as the Heaven and Hell of the Christian doctrines. Some Indians held the notion that those who died violent deaths, such as persons killed in warfare or perhaps while hunting, went to the sky, and those who died in sickness went to a place especially designed for them. There was more than one world in the hereafter, but no land of the dead was a fearful place. Quite to the contrary, the abodes of the departed were blessed realms in which their spirits would forever rest, but not without periodically returning, manifested in symbolism the living understood, and they would return as the bearers of beautiful thoughts and promising messages from the supernaturals who shaped the destinies of all creatures. If there was grief, there was also inspiration in fancies, in imagination, in dreams, and in memories.

Indians built no temples of wood and stone. Their shrines, their holy places, were designed and constructed by the forces of nature, secluded lakes and springs and remote mountain crests, and their altars were rock columns and pillars and caves and open windows in walls through which the sky could be viewed, and strange formations, carved and colored by the inexhaustible energy of the mysterious elements.

Indians saw themselves as inextricably woven into the natural scheme of things. *We all move along with the earth, keeping time with the earth,* they sang.[14] Indians did not think of themselves simply as bone and flesh and the possessors of certain faculties. They were also of the sands, the winds, the stars, the waters, the plants, the thunder, lightning, rain, snow, the sun and the moon and the seasons, the animals, and the rocks and hills, the birds, the mountains, the forests—everything that was made, everything that was born and lived and died in the eternal, unvarying, and always balanced pattern of the universe.

CHAPTER THREE

Beyond the Rim of Christendom

There were several reasons why the obviously immense land mass north of Mexico had been neglected for forty years and why the Spanish colonial government, in all that time, had given little thought to exploring it. However, the fact that Coronado had failed to find treasure there was not the basis of the official lack of concern. Mexico itself had become a land of turmoil. Indian uprisings, political controversies, the discovery of rich silver mines, the opening of vast new grazing and farming areas, defiance of royal decrees and other forms of lawlessness had created internal problems that required the full attention of the provincial authorities, if not higher officials in Spain. The frontier had pushed steadily northward from central Mexico. Towns had mushroomed, convents and missions had been established, and soldiers had been sent to protect them, crush rebellions, keep order and enforce laws. Although they fought desperately to defend their homes and their resources, the Indians of Mexico were crushed by the insuperable pressures, and, in violation of colonial statutes, uncounted thousands were enslaved. If this was a problem which greatly vexed the King and the Pope, and perhaps some other high officials of both State and Church, it was not one easily resolved. The slave trade was too lucrative to be halted, and many powerful and prominent men derived advantages from it, buying healthy young Indian men and women to labor for the barest necessities in mines, on farms, and in mills and other private commercial enterprises. Missions, as well as private projects owned by men of political influence, were granted permission to operate *encomiendas,* a type of peonage system.[1]

The stampedes and wild, uncontrolled growth in northern Mexico had prompted the Spanish Court to enact new laws prohibiting the exploitation of natural bounties and the establishment of towns and missions without royal sanction. The statutes also contained the provision that only persons of good character, known to be devout Christians, and who could be relied upon to treat Indians with kindness and justice, would be authorized to lead expeditions of discovery. There were few men on the frontier who could qualify for such undertakings under the new code, except priests, and it was required that even they must be accompanied by soldiers if engaged in such a venture. Sending padres and soldiers into the wilderness was expensive, and the provincial government was not enthusiastic about such proposals, despite repeated urgings from Madrid to expand Spanish power in the New World in line with official Church and State policies. Under existing provisions, the cost of an expedition—food, clothing, equipment, wages of the military and other participants—had to be borne by the colonial treasury, which seldom if ever contained sufficient funds to meet regular obligations.

Fray Augustin Rodriguez, who had served for a number of years among the Conchos Indians of Nueva Viscaya, (now the Mexican state of Chihuahua,) was the first missionary after the Coronado debacle to be granted permission to carry the word of God to lost souls who, his neophytes assured him, dwelt far to the north in a land unknown to white men. Two other experienced friars, Fray Francisco Lopez and Fray Juan de Santa Maria, were authorized to go with him, and Captain Francisco Sanchez Chamuscado, a veteran frontier officer, was assigned to accompany the three padres with a military escort.

The Rodriguez-Chamuscado Expedition, which started from Santa Barbara, Nueva Viscaya, in June 1581, would break a new trail to the future American Southwest. Besides the three missionaries, the little company was comprised of eight soldiers under Chamuscado, nineteen Indian packers and wranglers, ninety reserve horses, and some six hundred head of livestock. The duty of keeping accounts and writing a diary fell to Chamuscado's aide, Hernan Gallegos. The purpose of the journey, Gallegos would record, was to go "where God our Lord was pleased to direct them, in order that His holy faith might be taught and His gospel spread throughout the lands which they . . . might thus discover in His holy service and in the service of the royal crown."[2]

That undoubtedly was the chief purpose of the missionaries, but Chamuscado, Gallegos, and the other soldiers harbored another hope that had no relation to the work of spreading Christian gospel and converting Indians.

The route followed took the company down the Rio Conchos to the Rio Grande and northward along the latter river. Above El Paso del Norte they passed through totally unexplored country until they crossed Coronado's trail in northern New Mexico.

(Details of their experiences, descriptions of the country pueblos and natives written by Gallegos, while of great value to scientists and historians, are not within the scope of this work.)

By late summer they were in the Galisteo Valley, just east of the Rio Grande, where, at a Tewa pueblo, according to Gallegos, "we asked if there were many minerals in the vicinity, showing the natives the samples we had taken along for that purpose and requesting them to lead us to the place where such riches might be found. They immediately brought us large quantities of different kinds, including some of a copper steel-like ore. This material appeared to be rich . . . . The others assayed less. When we asked them where they obtained the ore, they gave us to understand that there were many minerals near the province and pueblo . . . . We went to investigate and discovered mines of different ores. The natives indicated that the Indians in the region of the buffalo had given them a part of the ore."

This is the statement showing that the expedition was looking for gold as well as souls to save, and further study of the Gallegos report leaves no doubt that they made a practice of wandering about the New Mexico mountains and deserts searching for minerals. Some of these investigations purportedly were successful, but the extent of their findings remains uncertain. Gallego's description of one area suggests that they reached the Magdalena Mountains, considerably west of the Rio Grande. In this range, he noted, deposits were "in a very fine locality with abundant water and timber; the veins are rich and well provided with supporting walls. In the opinion of all our men—who were nearly all miners—the deposits were excellent."

It was the tale heard from the Tewa that some of their ore had come from Indians of the Great Plains that brought the decision "to find the buffalo and to explore the land in which they lived." Fray Juan de Santa Maria, however, balked at the proposal. He announced that the others could search for the land of native cattle if they wished, but he intended to return to Mexico "to give an account and report of what had been discovered to his prelate, and to his Excellency, the Viceroy."

Everyone was astounded and "condemned the decision as inadvisable . . ." But Fray Santa Maria's mind was made up, and on a September day he started back along the trail—alone.

The company was gone for a month, wandering, lost some of the time, on the buffalo plains. They found just what Coronado had found, nothing but cows, seas of grass, and sky. When they returned to the Galisteo Valley they learned that Fray Santa Maria had been killed.

It is probable that their Mexican Indian servants obtained the sad information, but that is a matter Gallegos does not explain. He simply states that when the Tewa saw the friar riding away alone "they became alarmed, believing he was going to bring more Christians in order to put them out of their homes . . . . They followed the friar and killed him after two or three days of travel."

The expedition went on westward as winter approached, following Coronado's trail from the pueblos of the Rio Grande to Acoma and Zuni. The Indians were unfriendly, and on several occasions serious trouble was narrowly avoided. The richness of the field inspired the two friars, and they announced that they intended to remain and carry on the work of God. In deference to their demand that peaceful relations be maintained at all costs, the soldiers studiously sought to prevent open clashes, and, as Gallegos put it, "relinquished our rights."

The snow lay deep over the high country of northern New Mexico when they began their return march eastward from Zuni. The new year had begun when they reached the Tewa pueblo of Puaray on the frozen Rio Grande. (In New Mexico, the Tiwa, and Tewa, Jemez and Piro are divisions of the Tanoan stock.) Fray Augustine Rodriguez and Fray Francisco Lopez had selected it as their headquarters, and on the last day of January 1582, the two padres stood in their tattered robes before the Puaray gate, made the sign of the cross, and waved good-bye to their companions.

Captain Chamuscado, more than sixty years of age, died in terrible suffering on the return journey. On Easter morning, Gallegos and the other soldiers rode into Santa Barbara, where the expedition had started nearly nine months earlier. Gallegos soon left for Mexico City under somewhat mysterious circumstances.

How much of the contents of his notebooks was made public

before his departure is not known. He probably revealed very little regarding the company's discoveries, but someone—most likely the soldiers—engaged in loose talk. Whatever or however much was disclosed it was enough to give birth to rumors that the expedition had found fabulous quantities of gold and silver and other metals, that the friars left behind had taken possession in the name of the king of an immense unknown territory that not only held no end of treasures but contained limitless grass pastures, lush valleys, endless forests, millions of wild cattle, and an incalculable number of heathen Indians, all of whom were eager to become Christians. Gallegos, gossip had it, slipped away to Mexico City to give the Viceroy incredibly rich samples of ore— and that part, at least, was true, but the fact would not be known in Santa Barbara until much later. It did not matter. What was known there, or rumored there, was more than enough to fire the blood of any adventurer.

Undoubtedly a number of men of means contemplated forming expeditions, but the first definitely known action resulting from the glowing tales was taken by Antonio de Espejo, a Santa Barbara mine owner and cattleman with an extremely bad reputation, which included extortion and being found guilty of murdering an employee. Ten years earlier, when only twenty-nine, he had been sent out to Mexico from Spain as a confidential officer of the Inquisition. The post was lucrative, and offered opportunities for blackmail, of which he took full advantage, but he was consumed with an ambition to make a much greater fortune than was possible by exposing, or threatening to expose, heretics and officials disloyal to the church. After a short period in Mexico City, he went to the Santa Barbara region, where he soon became wealthy.

Espejo's criminal record precluded him from obtaining authorization to conduct an expedition of discovery, but luck played into his hands. When he learned the Franciscans were deeply concerned about the safety of the two priests who had remained at

Puaray, he offered to organize and finance what he euphemistically termed a rescue mission.

The churchmen of Nueva Viscaya were eager to accept his generous proposal, but they hesitated to circumvent the statutes governing such matters. Fervent letters requesting permission to make the investigation were sent to Mexico City, but months passed without their communications being answered. At last, disgusted with the red tape and delay, Fray Bernardino Beltran, who had been chosen by the Franciscan Order to go on the venture, declared that he would obtain the necessary permit by other means. How he accomplished the feat is uncertain. One account indicates that he got it from higher church authorities. Another relates that it was issued by the lieutenant governor of Nueva Viscaya. Still another states that a high military officer not only sanctioned the plan but approved the formation of a military escort composed of soldiers who wished to volunteer their services, all wages and expenses to be paid, of course, by Espejo.

In any case, issuance of the permit was not in compliance with the law, but that was a point the Franciscans apparently chose to overlook. Nor was Espejo concerned with this phase of the problem, for the permit did not bear his name. If there were repercussions, the onus would be on the Franciscans, and it seemed doubtful that they would be penalized for trying to find out if two of their colleagues were alive or dead.

The start was made shortly before the middle of November 1582, from the Valle de Allende, not far from Santa Barbara. Espejo had hired fourteen soldiers and a number of Indians to care for a small supply pack train and a herd of one hundred horses. It was a company prepared to travel with speed, and it did.

Diego Perez de Luxan, an educated officer who was Espejo's chief aide and who would exhibit great loyalty to him, kept a journal of the journey.[3] Following the trail taken by Rodriguez and Chamuscado, down the Rio Conchos and northward along the Rio Grande, by February the Fray Beltran-Espejo Expedition had reached the country of the Tewa Pueblos. There they were told by means of signs that Fray Rodriguez and Fray Lopez had been slain.[4]

Some of the men wanted to turn back, and some advocated that a fort be constructed and that seven soldiers remain in it while the others went on to verify the sign statements of the Tiwa. Espejo, who had been elected leader, refused either to return or to divide the company. Rescuing the friars, he declared, had been only one purpose of the journey. He had become excited by Indian tales that rich mines were to be found both to the east and to the west, and he had already obtained samples of ores. "This is a good opportunity for me to serve his Majesty, while incurring no expense to him," he told the others. Later he would reveal his hope that his discoveries and explorations would influence the court to grant him a pardon for his crimes and induce the King to give him permission to develop the northern country of the Pueblos.

The Tiwa were telling the truth. When the company reached Puaray the deaths of the padres were fully confirmed.

No attempt was made to capture and punish the murderers. Fray Beltran sang mass and bestowed upon Puaray the name of Paula de los Martires. The company reached Zuni late in March, finding there, still standing, crosses erected by friars who had been with Coronado. Espejo wanted to go on to the Hopi country to search for mines, but Fray Beltran refused, announcing that he would return to Mexico. After a heated argument, a compromise was reached: Espejo and nine soldiers would continue westward to explore, and Fray Beltran and the others would wait for them in Zuni.

Espejo came back to Zuni in May and announced that he intended to travel eastward to the buffalo plains. Fray Beltran refused to accompany him. The discussion grew violent, with pushing and a struggle over possession of a flag. Fray Beltran, six soldiers, and several Indian servants unceremoniously departed for Mexico. Espejo and the others went on to the Llano Estacado along the Rio Pecos in eastern New Mexico.[5]

Six of the first twelve missionaries who carried the banners of their church into the wilderness morth of Mexico were slain by Indians. Their deaths occured in widely separated localities: from the central Great Plains in Kansas to the Rio Pecos in eastern New Mexico to the pueblos in the upper Valley of the Rio Grande. Each killing was a cold-blooded, premeditated murder.

These factors make certain conclusions unavoidable. In the minds of the Indians—and with good reason—Christianity was inseparably associated with extreme violence. Therefore, its apostles, either the priesthood or the laity, were deadly antagonists. If the doctrines of the Christian faith, as interpreted by the invaders, remained beyond the comprehension of Indian medicine men, they readily recognized in them two menacing elements: (a) derogation of the spiritual beliefs of the peoples they served, and (b) a conjunctive depreciation of their influence and the high levels of their individual positions.

These were threats that the medicine men refused to endure beyond the occurence of circumstances that proffered opportunities to terminate them with little or no danger to their authority and welfare. The killing of a lone, helpless, unarmed, white missionary by conspirators inflamed by his vilification of their own gods was an act which medicine men construed as a religious triumph. They could not envision any possibility of it engendering reprecussions injurious to themselves. But this situation, at the time so advantageous to them, would not long prevail.

For fifteen years after the Espejo Expedition no missionaries were stationed in the American West.[6] However, the sixteenth century would not end before more of them would be there, and their assignments would take them, extending like a wheel's spokes, for hundreds of miles across mountains, deserts, and plains. More of them, many more, would be slain. Western Indians would know turmoil and suffering of unprecendented dimensions and intensity, created by a chaotic and unalterable blending of the laws of Christians and the tenets of Christianity.

CHAPTER FOUR

The Southwest:
Colonization

In May 1598, Indians dwelling in pueblos along the Rio Grande in central New Mexico gazed in wonder and fear at a great dust cloud moving slowly northward along the trail skirting the west bank of the river that sustained them. Many of them gathered what possessions they could carry on their backs and fled into the hills, but a few were bold enough to stay in their homes. Now they were stunned by a sight that not only surpassed anything they had known, but anything the wildest imagination was capable of conceiving.

The awe-inspiring cloud darkening the sun was caused by nearly a hundred heavily loaded wagons, troops of horsemen, and an unbelievably large herd of more than seven thousand animals strung out in a ragged pattern for more than four miles. In the column were one hundred and thirty families, men, women and children clinging to the sacks and bales and crates piled on the creaking vehicles. There were two hundred and seventy single men—soldiers, craftsmen, farmers, hopeful young adventurers—eleven Franciscan friars, sandaled and wrapped in flowing robes of Zaragoza cloth, and scores of Mexican Indian and Negro servants, vaqueros, and camp tenders. Leading the long parade, and the most impressive and colorful of its segments, was a group of men on fine horses, all splendidly arrayed in shining armor, plumed helmets, silk and lace shirts, and Cordovan boots with tasseled spurs.

As early as the summer of 1583, King Philip of Spain had made known his wish that practical measures be taken for the founding of a permanent colony in the immense region that had been discovered north of Mexico. In a royal cedula, he had stated the belief that the best procedure, and perhaps the most economical, would be to contract with some responsible person to undertake the conquest, a man who was not only wealthy, devout, and of good repute but who could be depended upon to obey the laws controlling colonization and the conversion of Indians, and who had demonstrated his ability to serve as the first governor of the new province, which would be called New Mexico.

It was asking a great deal, for only a saint could have come close to meeting the specifications, and there were not many identifiable flesh and blood saints in Mexico. However, there were any number of men who, if their records for integrity and responsibility were somewhat stained, could qualify as being wealthy and prominent, and anyone could swear to uphold the laws and attend mass on holy days.

Once the king's desires became known, proprietors of great estates, mine owners, magnates of commerce, political and military officials—indeed, the affluent and distinguished in every part of Mexico—became embroiled in a feverish competition for the coveted post. Both because they feared royal displeasure and because they were far more cognizant than the soverign in far-off Seville of the tremendous organizational, legal, monetary, and political complications of such an immense project, high church and state officials in Mexico City were careful to make no hasty decisions. In fact, they continued to engage in such prolonged deliberations, were so extremely cautious, and argued so much among themselves, that nothing at all was accomplished for twelve years.

At last, in 1595 the appointment was awarded to a man of wealth, distinguished lineage, and the nature of a beast. He was Don Juan de Onate´ of Zacatecas. It took three more years to organize the expedition.[1]

It was hardly surprising that Onate´, accompanied by an army of such great size and power, met with no resistance as he marched on from pueblo to pueblo. Events which took place in July at the ancient walled town that would be given the Spanish name of Santo Domingo were typical of the councils with Indians that marked the founding of the first colony of a European country in the future American West. A record of the meeting, prepared by His Majesty's Notary Juan Perez de Donis, preserves for posterity outstanding examples of the hypocrisy, humbuggery, and dishonesty employed by Spanish officials and countenanced by Spanish priests on such occasions.

After attending Mass at Santo Domingo, Onate´ addressed the assemblage, made up of several hundred Indians and their leaders who had been summoned from surrounding pueblos. According to the notary's report, the Govenor-General told the large audience that he had been sent to them "by the most powerful king and ruler in the world, who desired especially to serve God our Lord and to bring about the salvation of their souls, but wished also to have them as his subjects and to protect and bring justice to them, as he was doing for other natives in the East and West Indies. To this end he had sent the Spaniards from such distant lands to theirs, at enormous expense and great effort. Since, therefore, the govenor had come with this purpose, as they could see, it was greatly to their advantage that, of their own free will and in their own names and in those of their pueblos and republics, and their captains, they render obedience and submission to the king, and become his subjects and his vassals . . . By so doing

they would live in peace, justice, and orderliness, protected fro
their enemies, and benefited in their arts and trades and in their
crops and cattle. One could easily see and understand that they
were very pleased with the coming of his lordship. After delibera-
tion they spontaneously agreed to become vassals of the most
Christian king, our lord, and as such they immediately rendered
their obedience and submission. The governor explained to them
that they should realize that by rendering obedience and vassalage to the king our lord they would be subject to his will, orders,
and laws, and that, if they did not observe them, they would be
severely punished as transgressors of the commands of their king
and master, and that, therefore, they should reflect on what they
wished to do and what to answer. They replied that they understood and that they wanted to submit to his majesty and become
his vassals. They insisted that they spoke the truth, without deceit
or reservation."

Spanish swords and lances, glistening in the sunlight, and
troopers bearing loaded guns, made a menacing ring about the
council scene, as Onate continued, telling the Indians "that since
they were rendering obedience and vassalage to him of their own
free will, and had seen that he had caused them no harm or
allowed the soldiers to do so, they should fall to their knees, as a
demonstration that the Spaniards and they were now all one
people."

They knelt on the ground, and Onate "explained to them that
the main reason which had moved the king to send him to this land
was the salvation of their souls, because they should know that
their bodies had also souls which did not die even though the
bodies did. But if they were baptized and became good Christians,
they would go to heaven to enjoy an eternal life of great bliss in the
presence of God. If they did not become Christians, they would go
to hell to suffer cruel and everlasting torment. He told them that
this religion would be explained to them more at length by the

most reverend father commissary and the friars, who were present and who came in the name of his Holiness, the only universal pastor and head of the church, the Holy Father at Rome . . . therefore it was important that they should acknowledge God and his vicar on earth . . . and kiss the hand of the father commissary . . ."

The Indians obeyed, and the notary wrote that they declared they understood what Onaté had said to them. If they did, surely a miracle of linguistic communications had occurred. Onaté went on up the valley of the Rio Grande, holding similar councils in other pueblos, and three days later rode into the Tewa town of Ohke, which stood on the east bank of the river above the mouth of the Rio Chama. He announced that Ohke would be his capital. After the occupants had pledged themselves to obey him and revere God, he unceremoniously ordered them to vacate their houses. The Spaniards moved into the pueblo, and the Tewa were driven into the country.

The name Ohke did not please Onaté, and he promptly changed it to San Juan de los Caballeros. Everything in the pueblo was confiscated. While the former inhabitants sought refuge among neighbors, Onaté, his military guard and servants, and the priests lolled in the plaza of San Juan. They had gone ahead of the main expedition, which was forced by the animals and wagons to travel at a slow pace, and while they waited for it to catch up to them, they enjoyed the scenery, the pleasant weather, and the bountiful supplies found in the San Juan granaries and storehouses.

When the entire force arrived, the immense herds quickly turned the fields of San Juan into barren ground, but there was grass in plenty on the surrounding ranges, and the thousands of horses, cattle, sheep, oxen, goats, and mules were soon fat and contented. Such was not the case, however, with the Spaniards, now overcrowded in the small pueblo. Onaté moved his capital to a much larger Tewa town, Yunque, a short distance down the Rio

Grande. Yunque, which contained more than four hundred houses (apartments), was situated on the left bank of the Rio Grande at its confluence with the Rio Chama. The inhabitants were ousted. Once again dissatisfied with an Indian name, Oñate changed Yunque to San Gabriel. Here the first Christian church in the American West was built. It was made of stone, adobe, and lodgepole pines. Completed in a few weeks, it was dedicated in lengthy sermons, religious services, and pageantry.

Except on the south, New Mexico was a province without established boundaries. Tribes existed which would not be encountered and given names for years to come. Thus, when Oñate established seven mission districts, the size of each was necessarily vague, and the numbers and identities of Indians in them remained to be determined. Oñate's assignments to the priests were:

1—The Jemez and all the Indians of the neighboring sierras and settlements to Fray Alonso de Lugo. This district contained the Navajo, of whom almost nothing was known.

2—The northern pueblos of Picuris and Taos, and all the Apaches from the Sierra Nevada toward the north and east, to Fray Francisco de Zamora. These were Plains Apache tribes. The Spaniards at this time had never heard of Utes, Comanches, or the many Caddoan tribes.

3—The great pueblo of Pecos on the Rio Pecos in eastern New Mexico and others of the surrounding region to Fray Francisco San Miguel.

4—The Keres pueblos of San Felipe, Santo Domingo, Cochiti, and others to Fray Juan de Rozas.

5—Zia, Acoma, Zuni, and the Hopi people to Fray Andres Corchado.

6—Pueblos in the Bernalillo area to Fray Juan Claros.

7.—San Juan and other Tewa pueblos to Fray Cristobal de Salazar and Fray Juan de San Buenaventura. The Father Commissary, Fray Alonso Martinez, and Fray Pedro de Vergara also were instructed to make their headquarters in the first capital.

These ecclesiastical duties completed, Onate gave full attention to fullfilling the dream which had brought him to New Mexico, the dream of discovering treasure. In the ealy fall, he sent a nephew, Vincente de Zaldivar, to investigate the plains east of New Mexico. A few weeks later, with a hundred men, he set out with the intention of making an extensive exploration to the west. Another nephew, Juan de Zaldivar, was left in command at San Gabriel with instructions to follow him as soon as Vincente had returned from the region of the "cows."

In the next few months the Indians would learn how much protection and justice, promised them by Onate, they would receive, and how they would be enlightened and guided to a paradise in heaven by the priests whose hands they had kissed.

At the pueblo of Acoma, which, standing in its age-old wrinkles on a high table land, would come to be known as the Sky City, Onate and his company were liberally furnished with maize, fowls, robes, and other articles. After a brief rest, they went on to Zuni and Hopi Villages, in each of these communities being given more supplies, including warm blankets made of yucca fiber. The Hopis told Onate that mines could be found some distance to the southwest, and he sent Captain Marcos Farfan de los Godos and eight soldiers to search for them. The day after Farfan departed, Onate started back to Zuni, planning to wait for him there.

Farfan was gone three weeks. He brought back samples of ore from which silver was later obtained in assays.[2] It was now December, the weather was bitterly cold, the snow lay deep over the mesas, and Juan de Zaldivar had not arrived as planned. Onate decided to return to San Gabriel and in the spring resume his explorations. He had been traveling back toward Acoma only three days when he met several soldiers who were looking for him. They brought bad news.

Obeying orders, Juan de Zaldivar had set out from San Gabriel with thirty men as soon as his brother had returned from the buffalo plains. Reaching Acoma on December 1, Zaldivar demanded that his company be furnished with blankets, robes, clothing, and provisions for the journey to overtake his uncle. The leaders of Acoma refused his requests, for after supplying Onate with large quantities of such things only a short time earlier they had scarcely enough to meet their own needs through the winter.

When Zaldivar sent soldiers through the pueblo to confiscate the articles he wanted, the Indians attempted to stop them. In the ensuing fight, Zaldivar, two captains, eight soldiers and two servants were killed. The others managed to escape down the narrow, twisting trail from the high mesa and rejoin the men who had remained on the plain below. After dark the survivors divided into two groups, some starting back to the capital and others being sent to find Onate.

It was a sad holiday season in San Gabriel. The people of Acoma, declared Onate with tears running down his face, must be punished, not only to avenge the death of his beloved nephew but to teach them and all other Indians the folly of defying the Christian representatives of the Spanish king.

In the first few days of the year 1599, long and exhaustive judicial proceedings were held during which the testimony of the survivors of the battle of Acoma was recorded in minute detail. To complete the record, which would be sent to the Viceroy, Onate asked the Father Commissary for his opinion on what consitituted a just war, and what disposition could be made in a just war of the vanquished and their property.

Fray Martinez responded that a just war, first, required the authority of a prince with supreme power, such as the Roman pontiff, emperors, or the kings of Castile, who enjoyed the imperial privilege of not recognizing a superior in temporal matters. No private individual could declare war, as this required the organization of armies, which was an exclusive function of a prince. Second, a just war required a just cause, which might be any of four: (a) to protect the innocent who suffer unjustly and whom the prince must defend whenever he can; (b) to restore goods unjustly seized; (c) to punish transgressors of the law, if they are the prince's subjects, or transgressors of the laws of nature, even if they were not his subjects; (d) lastly and above all to attain and preserve peace, which was the main purpose of war.

The vanquished, stated Fray Martinez, as well as their property were at the mercy of the conqueror. If the cause of war, he continued in his opinion, should be the punishment of the delinquent and guilty, they and their goods would be at the mercy of the victor, in accordance with the just laws of the victor's kingdom, and so long as they were the victor's subjects. If they were not his subjects, the victorious prince may force them to observe the divine and natural law, using all means that he may justly consider expedient.

When he was asked by Onate to comment on the matter, Fray Claros added that while Fray Martinez's ideas were generally accepted, it should be remembered that in compelling guilty heathens to observe divine law the task must be accomplished by admonition and persuasion. Fray Claros thought Fray Martinez's opinion regarding an offensive war correct, provided that at all times consideration was given to the level of intelligence of the offenders. This should be done, declared Fray Claros, so that decisions against them could be rendered in accordance with the seriousness of their offenses. However, in a defensive war no authority to act was needed from a prince or from anyone else, for under natural law anyone individually or in common with others was entitled to defend himself from those attempting to injure him.

Fray Martinez proffered a supplement to Fray Claros's statement, remarking that self-defense was blameless, *cum mod-*

eramine inculpata tutela, and whether self-defense was performed by one or many it finally devolved on the individual or private person.

Oñaté had the support of the priests, who believed that his retaliation against the people of Acoma constituted a just war. Vincente de Zaldivar was accorded the honor of commanding the punitive expedition. On January 21, 1599, he arrived before Acoma with seventy soldiers.

Two days later, the Sky City, impregnable under any assault by Indians, fell, its defenders unable to withstand the devastating destruction inflicted upon them by Spanish guns. Zaldivar led soldiers up the narrow path to the pueblo. Dead and dying lay in the streets and on the parapets. Hundreds of living cowered in the houses. Many of them were dragged out one by one and hacked to pieces, limbs, heads, and bloody bodies being thrown over a sheer cliff.

Some eight hundred Keres died at Acoma. Five hundred men, women, and children were taken to Santo Domingo. On February 12, Oñaté, sitting as a one-man supreme court of New Mexico, announced the punishment to be suffered by the prisoners.

One foot was cut off of all males over the age of twenty-five, and they were sentenced to twenty years of slavery. Males between the ages of twelve and twenty-five were not maimed but received a sentence of similar length in personal servitude. The right hands of two Hopi Indians who happened to be in Acoma at the time of the battle were amputated, and they were sent to their people as living examples of what Indians who defied Spaniards might expect to suffer. Boys and girls under the age of twelve were taken from their families and placed under the supervision of the priests, who were ordered to place them in monasteries where they could be converted to Christianity and their souls salvaged. Old men and old women were given as slaves to the Plains Apaches, traditional enemies of the Keres. Acoma was burned.

The *just wars* as decreed by the New Mexico clergy could be little as well as big, perhaps involving nothing more than the execution of a few recalcitrant Indians. Indeed, under the interpretations rendered by the priests of all laws, religious, martial, and natural, blasphemy by a medicine man or by an entire tribe could be declared justifiable reason for the infliction of severe punishment. As for civil laws, it was not difficult to relegate violations to the category of self-defense necessarily performed by political and military officials. Challenges to the supremacy of God could be tolerated no more than infractions of established social behavior. It was reaction and reasoning that had little if any relation to justice, and it would be instrumental in opening gates to chaotic situations, but it would prevail as long as the Province of New Mexico existed under the banner of Spain.

In the summer of the last year of the sixteenth century, Vincente de Zaldivar, with thirty soldiers, set out on another exploration. Just where they went is not certain. Fragmentary information indicates that they may have wandered for three months through the deserts of New Mexico and Arizona before returning to San Gabriel. It is known, however, that on the first part of their journey they traveled southward, east of the Manzano Mountains, to the Piro pueblos in the vicinity of Abo and probably visited some settlements of the Tompiros. They found these people rude and inhospitable, and Zaldivar's demands for provisions were bluntly refused. Apparently because the Indians greatly outnumbered his small force, he did not attack, but he did send a message to Uncle Oñate about the insulting treatment he had received. Then he went on west.

Oñate was soon on his way with a company of cavalry to the pueblo—it cannot be definitely identified—to punish its occupants for the insolence toward his nephew. He demanded a tribute of blankets. He received only a dozen, and the Indians told him they had no more to give him. Whereupon, acting on his orders, his soldiers killed six men, wounded several others, and fired the houses. Then, believing he had taught the Indians to be more respectful of Spaniards, he returned to San Gabriel. A small war.

Shortly afterward, five soldiers deserted and set out for Mexico. Two of them were slain by Indians in the vicinity of Abo; the other three were able to get back to San Gabriel, where they pleaded for forgiveness. What punishment they suffered is not known, but because of the killing of the two deserters, Onate declared war on the Piros. No documentary evidence showing that any priest objected has survived. When Zaldivar returned from his wanderings he was commissioned to command the offensive. He took with him a hundred men.

In a six day battle the Piros courageously defended their homes, but at last succumbed to the power of Spanish guns. Zaldivar enhanced the reputation he had gained by his butchery at Acoma. He slaughtered six hundred Piro men, women, and children. Four hundred were taken captive and awarded as slaves to his soldiers. However, the survivors would soon be set free, as the poorly paid soldiers could not afford to feed and clothe them, and besides San Gabriel was overrun by a great surplus of slaves.

The Christmas season and the advent of the new year 1600 were celebrated with impressive and prolonged religious services, gay festivals, plays, and drunken orgies.

CHAPTER FIVE

New Mexico:
State Versus Church

At least twenty-two governors—who also had the title of Captain-General—held office in New Mexico between 1598 and 1680. If a few of them deserve to be described as capable administrators, it also must be noted that each of them employed his talents to his personal advantage, and some were charlatans, unscrupulous adventurers, and plain thieves.

How many missionaries served in the colony in this eighty-two year period is a question for which no reliable answer is available. It may be safely asserted, however, that there were no less than five times as many of them as there were governors.

No great mineral treasures were recovered, and, as one historian succinctly states, not many years had passed after the founding of the colony before the "kingdom was regarded essentially as a missionary field. The civil authority, and the armed garrison, were to exist primarily to protect the friars at their hazardous work, whose object was the peaceful conversion of the Indians. But the position of the Indians under the guardianship of the *encomienda* was poison at the heart of the province."[1]

There were two majesties—the Church and the State—and neither of their representative forces would submit to the other.

The seeds of the controversy began to sprout in the first decade of the colony's existence, thereafter rapidly becoming prodigious growths, seemingly immune to all potions employed to eradicate them.

In these early days the priests accused civil and military officials of blaspheming the word of God before Indians, while stealing from them everything they owned, including their food and the clothes on the bodies. For this and other reasons many Indians ran away, joining the wild tribes, such as the Navajo and Apache. Stores of maize were hidden from agents of governors, and to find them it was necessary to torture Indian leaders. Natives in some areas were virtually naked and reduced to eating leaves and bark and single grains of corn left in the fields. A desperate Indian warrior was hanged for crying out: "If you who are Christians cause so much harm and violence, why should we become Christians?" Indian women dared not appear alone, for they were raped by soldiers, even in the open along the roads.

Denials of these accusations were made by military officers, governors, and aides loyal to them, who were profiting from Indian labor and the tributes the Indians were forced to pay. Communications went to Mexico City charging the friars with perpetrating falsehoods and claiming that not one of them had ventured two leagues into the country to preach the holy gospel. The natives were plentifully supplied. There was no danger of famine. Before the arrival of the Spaniards, the Indians had constantly fought each other. Now they were at peace, Spanish guns providing them with protection they had never known. According to provincial authorities, the Indians continually implored the priests to enlighten them regarding God in Heaven, and if the friars would take the trouble to teach them, all would soon be Christians. As for the clashes that had occurred, all had been the fault of the Indians, who were always the aggressors.

Proposals that New Mexico be abandoned came regularly before the Viceroy and his cabinet in Mexico City and before the court in Seville, but each was rejected. The colony was publicly described as a great missionary field. It was that, to be sure, but there was another reason besides the desire to convert Indians from paganism to Christianity that influenced the sovereign's decision in the problem. It was power politics. Other European nations, notably France and England, were challenging Spain's New World territorial claims. No attempt had been made by Spain to define the boundaries of New Mexico. Yet already established by Spanish explorations was the fact that north of it lay an enormous land mass. Actually only the fringes of this great region had been entered, and no one could be certain as to its extent. Under accepted international policies, however, as long as Spain maintained an armed force, even though small, and settlements and missions in the colony, it was justified in claiming possession of the vast uncharted northern realm.

Neither the governors nor the Franciscans were victims of the internecine conflict for which they were equally responsible. The victims were the Indians. Virtually every phase of their lives was dominated by one faction or the other, and not infrequently by both. Almost the only liberties granted them were sexual intercourse, childbearing, and bodily excretions. All other activities were subject to regulatory decrees that were rigidly enforced. They had no civil rights, no religious freedom, no political prerogatives.

The segments of the native population, over which the priests claimed suzerainty, worked long hours in the fields, vineyards, gardens, and workshops of the missions. The fruits of their labors were euphemistically called contributions to God. Their only rewards were enough food to keep them alive, which they themselves produced, and the few garments and blankets they were permitted to keep out of the large quantities they were forced to manufacture. They could expect to receive greater rewards, of course, when they went to heaven.

Only one difference existed between the *encomiendas* of the missions and those under the jurisdiction of the governors. Profits from a chief executive's farms, ranches, and sweatshops went into his own pocket. God got no part of them.

Thus the two main causes of the controversy were commercial greed and religious zeal, two forces that appear at first glance to be irreconcilable. Closer scrutiny, however, reveals links that prevent them from being defined as completely unrelated elements.

The priests dressed their greed in ecclesiastical garments, but the disguise in no sense weakened its virulence. Civil officials defended their actions on the ground that they were upholding the colonial laws, maintaining the security of the colony, fulfilling their sworn duty to make possible the conversion of savages while building a sound economic structure. Few, if any, of their contributions were allowed to seep through the pores of this superficial facade.

The priests were saving souls, and the more snatched from the hands of the devil the more their church and their king would benefit, the more favors they would receive when their earthly work was completed. The governors were making money, and the more put away the more they would enjoy life when they returned to Mexico or Spain.

So the battle was joined.

In one important respect, the church had an advantage. It controlled the only established transport service linking New Mexico with the outside world. Naturally, under such a monopoly, cargos for and from the missions received top priority. Normally, a caravan—thirty to forty wagons, each carrying two tons of merchandise and drawn by eight to ten mules—took from a year and a half to two years to complete the journey of three thousand miles, but accidents, and not infrequently attacks by Apaches and Navajos, disrupted operations for long periods.[2]

Besides such commonplace items as pots, dishes, tools, agricultural implements, and munitions, manifests of the northbound wagons included paintings of saints, heavy bronze church bells, altar supplies, and wall hangings depicting angels, the crucifixion, and other events. And there were silver and gold ornaments, life-size statues of Christ and the Virgin, and kegs of wines and other spirits. Returning to Mexico City, the wagons were loaded first with products from the missions, such as tanned buffalo and deer hides, piñon nuts, blankets, leather goods and other salable items produced by Indians. If there was any room left, the governor was permitted to utilize it—paying freight rates—for articles he wished to send to his own marketing agents.

Trudging along beside the lumbering vehicles of the southbound trains were files of captives, unregenerate and uncontrollable Navajo, Apache, and Pueblo men and women, most of them young and healthy, taken prisoner in raids by the governors and their soldiers. The men would be sold to Mexican mine owners. The women would be sold as household servants, and if attractive enough might be purchased by operators of brothels.

Spanish law decreed that only Indians captured in warfare could be held as slaves. The statute could hardly be termed a handicap for anyone wishing to engage in the vicious trade. For one thing, raids by Navajos and Apaches on missions and ranches occurred with the regularity of the moons. Therefore, as confirmed enemies of both church and state, they were fair game for slavers. But in times of quiet, it was easy to stir up trouble. All a governor had to do was to send out a band of men for the purpose of taking Navajo and Apache prisoners, and any defense attempted by the quarry could be termed an act of war. Dealing with recalcitrant Pueblos involved even less effort. As they were already captives, they could be removed simply by branding them enemies of the Two Majesties. Priests, of course, always baptized captives before they were executed or sent south to the flesh markets.

No official mail service moving with regularity existed between Mexico City and Santa Fe, which became the provincial capital in 1610. There was almost no chance that a lone dispatch rider could complete the journey. They were forced to travel with armed guards, a heavy expense. Except for occasions of great urgency, mail, as well as incoming and outgoing friars, civil servants, and colonists, traveled with mission supply trains, which were accompanied by guards. If one arrived in the course of a year, the people of Santa Fe considered themselves fortunate. Quite appropriately, new governors were invariably accompanied by military escorts.

Indians were the only source of revenue for both governors and missionaries. All of them wanted to get rich, the governors for themselves, the priests in the interest of the church, if not for themselves. Colonial statutes and royal cedulas designed to protect natives were meaningless, for the remoteness of the colony made it impossible for either high church or civil authorities to enforce them. In New Mexico the clergy and the governors could ignore them with impunity.

The schism steadily widened, conditions steadily deteriorated, until violence, plotting, slander, treachery, and debased emotions, engendered and exhibited by both factions, had destroyed any possibility of peace or compromise.

At one time the church hierarchy in Mexico City descended to a scheme that might have been expected of an outlaw junta but hardly of persons proclaiming their devotion to the principles of Christ. An arrogant, crude, intolerant man garbed in a Franciscan habit and giving the name of Fray Isidro Ordonez arrived in Santa Fe and displayed personal credentials and other documents that immediately augmented the existing turmoil.

He handed Governor Pedro de Peralta (1609-1618) a paper purporting to be a royal cedula granting all soldiers and colonists permission to return to Mexico of their own volition, if they so desired. Most of them did so desire, but Peralta refused to acknowledge the document, charging that it was a forgery. Nevertheless, the results were catastrophic. In a short time, only forty-seven lay Spaniards were left in Santa Fe.

Ordonez blustered about from mission to mission, but some of the priests rejected his authority and denounced him as an imposter. If he was an ordained priest, he was also a first rate scalawag. No reliable record of either his background or his true purpose has come to light, but both his attitude and his actions suggest that he was an unscrupulous soldier of fortune employed by the Church to engineer a coup d'etat by which the New Mexico clergy would gain control of the colonial government.

The clash between Peralta and Ordonez reached a crisis in Taos. Several soldiers arrived there to collect tribute for the governor, and the Indians were preparing to pay it when Ordonez emerged from the pueblo and ordered them to ignore the demand. The soldiers returned to Santa Fe empty-handed. Ordonez followed them. In a stormy scene, an outraged Peralta shouted that he would not be intimidated. Thereupon, Ordonez called him a heretic, a Lutheran, a Jew, and excommunicated him. The governor picked up a pistol and fired. The bullet missed Ordonez but wounded two other men, one a friar. Ordonez went before the Santa Fe Council—or what was left of it— and demanded that Peralta be removed from office, but the council refused to act.

Ordonez's next moves were to throw the governor's chair out of the Santa Fe church and issue a warning that anyone who dared to carry Peralta's reports to Mexico City also would be excommunicated and charged with treason. Peralta decided to go to Mexico himself and make a personal appeal to the Viceroy for relief. He started with a small escort, but had gone only a few miles when agents of the Inquisition, obviously taking orders from Ordonez, arrested him. He escaped, returned to Santa Fe, and sought asylum among loyal friends. Ordonez imprisoned him again, this time on short rations.

If his purpose was to gain control of the civil government, Ordonez succeeded, but his triumph was short-lived. Perhaps his employers in Mexico City began to fear their own boldness, or the Viceroy got wind of their plot. In any case, both Peralta and Ordonez were recalled.[3]

However, the fighting did not abate with their departure. Indeed as a succession of new governors and friars continued in the ensuing years the violence and intensity of the struggle increased. Events occurring were repetitious, and only a few need be recounted as illustrations of prevailing conditions.

Governor Juan de Eulate (1618-1624), a former army officer who had won honors on the fields of Flanders, considered priests nuisances. He expropriated *encomiendas* and increased the amount of tribute each pueblo was required to pay to him. Having brought soldiers and sycophantic civil servants with him, he sent them about the country to force Indians to labor for him under gunpoint.

In Eulate's view, New Mexico was not a missionary field. It was his private domain. He issued an official edict granting permission to Indians to engage in their traditional religious practices to hold the ceremonials and dances which the priests had striven to suppress. By a new statute, governors were prohibited from engaging in trading enterprises, but Eulate acted as if he had never heard of the law. He accumulated cattle and sheep, not always by legitimate means, and held them in well-guarded pastures, intending to build large herds to be driven to Mexico. He sent traders with trinkets to acquire buffalo hides and other goods from Plains Indians, but barter was not the only means employed to obtain them. The Plains Apache had no monopoly on banditry.

Although he did not neglect opportunities to augment his own fortunes the next governor, Francisco Manuel de Silva Nieto, did make some effort to perform his sworn duty to aid missionaries in their work to win converts. He elected to accompany priests being sent to stations among the western pueblos. With him as he set out on the journey were thirty soldiers, eight missionaries, and a supply train tended by a score of Indian servants. The company was apprehensive as Acoma came into view, for not long before the priest stationed there had narrowly escaped martyrdom. Fray Juan Ramirez, being informed that the people of Acoma were extremely hostile, had asked and had received permission to attempt to reduce them to Christianity. He had set out from Santa Fe alone and on foot. As he approached the penol on which the reconstructed pueblo stood, he had been greeted with a shower of arrows but had not been struck. It chanced just then that a small girl had fallen over a cliff, and had landed badly shaken but not seriously injured near Ramirez. He took her up, carried her to the summit, and restored her to her family, who thought she had been killed. After this apparent miracle, Ramirez had been favorably received. He had remained at Acoma, had built a church, taught the inhabitants Spanish, and induced them to construct a trail to the summit over which horses could pass.

Fray Estevan Perea, Father Custodian of New Mexico, reported that Governor Nieto and his party were cordially received. He might have added that the Acoma were not fools. Confronted by thirty heavily armed soldiers, and holding a vivid memory of the tragedy they had suffered in Onaté's time, they obviously decided that diplomacy was the best course for them at the moment. Another priest was welcome to stay with them, if he desired, they told the governor. They would not bother him. The identity of the priest who remained is not certain.

The company went on to Zuni, where they were accorded a hospitable reception. Fray Francisco Letrado and Fray Martin de Arvide remained there. Fray Estevan de Perea would report that the Zunis, "having tendered their good will and their arms, received the party with festive applause—a thing never before heard of in those regions, that so intractable and various nations with equal spirit and semblance should receive the Frailes of St. Francis as if a great while ago they had communicated with them."[4] The people of Zuni appeared to be impressed by a sermon delivered by Perea, but it would soon be learned that the priest, if not all the other Spaniards, had been gullible, and the expressions of the congregation had been deceptive.

Governor Nieto was too timid to travel farther west, and, with a military escort, he turned back to Santa Fe. However, he ordered twelve soldiers to accompany Fray Francisco de Porras, Fray Andres Gutierrez, and Fray Francisco de San Buenaventura to posts assigned to them among the Hopis.

Left alone at the Hopi pueblo of Awatobi, Fray Porras wasted no time in condemning Hopi idols. The medicine men were profoundly angered and branded Porras as a liar who had come to harm them. This was an accusation the fiery Porras felt he could not overlook. Purportedly he fell to his knees in the pueblo plaza, crossed himself, and said a prayer. Then he arose, spat on his hands, picked up some mud and daubed it on the face of a blind boy, whose sight was immediately restored.

Whether or not the incident occured is irrelevant, for, whatever they may have been, Porras's actions did nothing to endear him to the medicine men. A short time later he died from eating food that had been poisoned.

At the Zuni pueblo of Halona, Fray Letrado transformed an old crumbling house into a chapel. One Sunday, the Indians refused to respond when he summoned them to Mass. An impatient man who often showed his temper, he went into the street to gather his flock. Meeting a group of idolators, he excoriated them. Suddenly, he seemed to sense that his end had come, for he knelt down, holding in his hands a small crucifix. Arrows tore into his body, instantly killing him.

A day or two earlier, hearing that pagan tribes lived to the west of Zuni, Fray Arvide had set out to carry the word of God to them. He had journeyed only a short distance when Zuni warriors murdered him.

CHAPTER SIX

New Mexico:
Propaganda and Failures

Although they railed continually at governors, the Franciscans serving in New Mexico in the first three-quarters of the seventeenth century comprised a propaganda organization that may be likened only to an unrestrained chamber of commerce. Letters extolling the wonders of the province, portraying the opportunities to spread the word of God as being without limit, and exaggerating their own accomplishments, poured forth from most members of the clergy. Two missionaries, however, appear in the historical record as extraordinary public relations practitioners. They were Fray Geronimo de Zarate Salmeron and Fray Alonso de Benavides. Their purpose, of course, was to attract more priests to the region, and to obtain larger appropriations from both the royal and church treasuries, yet this hardly seems a justifiable excuse for the deceptions and untruths they knowingly set down with their pens.

Zarate, who spent several years among various Pueblo tribes, repeatedly exaggerated the number of Indians to be saved, the number converted, and the value of the natural resources. As if he were trying to revive the great dream, shattered so many times since the days of Coronado, he would write in a *Relaciones* of vast mineral treasures awaiting recovery in every part of the colony. He complained: "The Spaniards that are there are too poor in capital to work the deposits, and are of less spirit; enemies to work of any sort. Well, in that country we have seen silver, copper, lead, loadstone coperas, alum, sulphur, and mines of turquoise which the Indians work in their paganism, since to them (the turquoise) is as diamonds and precious stones.

"At all this the Spaniards who are there laugh . . . if they have a good crop of tobacco to smoke they are very content and wish no more riches. It seems as if they had taken the vow of poverty— which is much for Spaniards, who out of greed for silver and gold would enter Hell itself to get them."

Tales of great metallic wealth in New Mexico were the purest myths and fables, but no more reliable was Zarate's statement that the blood of martyred priests "hath so fructified the land that there have been baptized 34,650 souls, as I have counted on the baptismal records, not counting the many that at present continue to be converted. In the which mystery are working, with the greatest spirit, the laborers in the vineyard of the Lord; who have erected forty-three churches in all, large and small, at their own cost . . . thus relieving His Majesty of these expenses. And as ministers continue to come in with each expedition, these conversions are always extended."

Priests continued to come in, but they also continued to go out. At the time Zarate wrote, perhaps in 1629, many of the pueblos were without priests and were *visitas*. He claimed that he alone had baptized seven thousand Indians at Jemez, but it is doubtful there were half that number at the pueblo.[1]

As a propagandist, Benavides put Zarate—indeed, all other missionaries who served in New Mexico before and after his time—in the shade. In many cases his Indian population estimates were ridiculous, and his report of the eagerness of the Indians, especially the Pueblos, to be converted and of their devotion and

loyalty to Christianity were figments of his own fancy. He possessed the faculty of seeing things only as he wished to see them,
and he did not hesitate to use it, yet the journal he wrote—he
called it a *Memorial*—left to posterity an incomparably valuable
picture of Indian life in colonial New Mexico. He must be credited
with another noteworthy accomplishment. During his tenure as
custodio of the colony, which included the term of Governor
Felipe de Zotylo (1621-1628), the church-state controversy sub-
sided to some extent. Neither ambition nor a determination to
augment his personal wealth were lacking in Zotylo, but in the
Father Custodian the governor was forced to contend with a man
who was his equal in influence and shrewdness, and his superior
in intelligence.

Benavides brought with him to New Mexico, in 1621 or 1622,
twenty-six priests. He was a missionary as practical as he was
dedicated and enthusiastic. He saw before him great work to be
done, and he applied himself relentlessly to the task. He had no
time for petty squabbles and made every effort to avoid administrative conflicts. He traveled extensively and was soon fully informed of the problems of each mission. A man of indomitable
courage, he journeyed through the wilderness, often with no more
than two or three companions, until he had visited every pueblo of
his vast *custodia*. He sat in council with the Apache, who had let it
be known that priests entering their lands would be slain.

Benavide's *Memorial,* completed in 1630, made him famous.
His readers, who included not only high church officials but King
Philip IV and ministers of state, were thrilled by his dramatic
accounts of his own experiences and of the miracles which had
occurred in the far-off land of the heathen Indians.

He wrote of the "temporal good which God our Lord hath been
pleased to manifest in this Province, wherewith your Majesty may
recoup the great costs which you are making . . . For all this land
is full of very great treasures of mines, very rich and prosperous in

silver and gold." He told of one series of mines "very prosperous minerals, which run from north to south more than fifty leagues,[2] and for want of someone who might spend money working on them, the greatest riches in the world are not enjoyed . . . The ease with which the silver can be taken out is the greatest and best within all the Indies."

With regard to the Indians working in these great mines, he thought that in the beginning they "might be scared off by the labor, but everything considered, I feel that if the mines were administered by persons of moderate greed, who would treat the Indians well and pay them for their work, they would win them by this path, and they would submit themselves to treating and communications with us. With this it would be easier for us ministers to reduce them to peace."

Benavides was well aware of the thousands of Indian slaves working to their deaths in the mines of Mexico, well aware that neither by statute nor by political force could mine owners be induced to pay them for their labors.

He drew for the King an idyllic picture of relations between the missionaries and the Indians, stating: "Today, to the honor and glory of God, with the affable care which we Religious have used with them, they are so well doctrinated and good Christians that when we ring the bell for Mass and the teaching of the Doctrine, they all come with the greatest cleanliness and neatness that they can, and enter the church to pray, as if they were Christians of very long standing; and the boys and girls who always come morning and evening to the Doctrine, attend with very great care and without fail; and the choristers in the chapels change week by week, and sing every day in the church, at their hours, the Morning Mass; the High Mass, and Vespers, with great punctuality. And all make confession in their own tongue, and prepare themselves for the confession, studying out their sins and bringing them marked on knotted threads."[3]

This was wishful thinking on the part of Benavides. The eminent historian, Hodge, states: "none of the Pueblos were ever so thoroughly converted to the teachings of the missionaries as Benavides states, for there has never been a time from the period of Coronado to the present day (1916), that they have not held tenaciously to their primitive beliefs and practiced their ancient rites. To be sure some of the Pueblos have assumed an outward form of Christianity, but this in no wise has influenced their purely aboriginal religious ceremonies."[4]

Blythely Benavides continued: "If the missionaries go passing along the roads, and the Indians see us from their pueblos or fields, they all come forth to meet us with very great joy, saying: 'Praised be our Lord Jesus Christ! Praised be the most holy Sacrament!' "

These pleasant assertions are not reflective of recorded facts. The struggle between the administrative executives and the clergy had, since the founding of the colony, kept all pueblos in a state of turmoil. Their inhabitants lived in constant fear of being cruelly punished for failing to attend church services. They were no less slaves in the vineyards of the Lord than in the *encomiendas* of the governors. The missionaries did not halt, much less destroy, Pueblo ritual; they never succeeded in making true converts out of them. As the authority, Eggan states: "The Pueblos have managed to retain their cultural independence in the face of almost overwhelming political and religious pressures . . . They became nominal Catholics, but they took their own religion underground and have maintained it to the present day (1950), guarding their ceremonies and their inner life against the outside world."[5]

As Benavides described New Mexico it was a natural paradise: "The land is most fertile, yielding with very great abundance all that is planted, corn, wheat, beans, lentils, peas, vetches, pumpkins, watermelons, muskmelons, cucumbers, cabbages, lettuce, carrots, artichokes, peppers, onions, prickly pears, pitahayas, plums, apricots, peaches, nuts, acorns, mulberries, trees of piñon nuts." So fertile was the land "that it has been seen to harvest a hundred and thirty fanegas to each fanega sown of wheat."[6] Rivers were full of many kinds of fish, and the abundance of game appeared to be "infinite." He asserted that so highly esteemed were piñon nuts in Mexico City that a fanega of them brought twenty-four dollars at wholesale. Deerskins, so excellently tanned by Indians, brought six dollars from Mexican dealers. He does not say, however, that the Indian producers saw none of this money. It flowed back into the coffers of governors and missions. He listed several species of deer as being extremely abundant, (some as large as mules) also foxes, wolves, mountain lions, wildcats, bears, wild sheep—the ewes ordinarily gave birth to three lambs each year—and millions of buffalo. A hunter's heaven, if he could be believed, but in reality there was almost no big game in the deserts of western and southern New Mexico, and no buffalo at all. Deer inhabited the high forested country, as did mountain sheep, and the realm of the buffalo was the High Plains bordering the colony on the east. There were a great many trout in the cold mountain streams, but in the larger part of New Mexico the few rivers existing were not suitable habitats for fish, being either excessively muddy, alkaline, or subject to great flooding and depletion by droughts.

Failure to achieve any progress among the Apache and their relatives, the Navajo, never ceased to be an extreme aggravation to the missionaries. Indeed, that situation still exists to a certain extent as these words are written. If most causes which brought about the defeat of the Franciscans in the seventeenth and eighteenth centuries have been removed, an explanation for the existence in those years is easily ascertainable.

After their migration from the far north to Dinetah, their southwestern homeland, banditry was the foundation of the Navajo economy. Through five or six centuries before the Spanish came, upon it they slowly built their independent agricultural and industrial wealth. Yet guardianship of their prosperity and maintenance of their security were no more intense than devotion to their own gods and their determination to prevent the intrusion of alien spiritual forces. As last they would be overwhelmed and nearly destroyed by American military power, but it was not until the last quarter of the nineteenth century that a religious would find it possible to remain in relative safety among them.

The western Apache of northern Mexico and the southern parts of New Mexico and Arizona had been deadly and implacable enemies of the Spanish since the last decade of the sixteenth century. However, the Plains Apache of eastern New Mexico, southeastern Colorado, western Kansas, and the Panhandles of Oklahoma and Texas had striven, despite repeated provocations, to maintain a peaceable relationship with the white invaders.

Disruptions of their commerce with other tribes by governors, swindling by Spanish traders, and even confiscation of their goods by officials, were acts which the Plains Apache had felt they could endure, injustices they could learn to prevent without resorting to extreme violence, but wanton murders and slavery could be neither forgiven nor forgotten.

There would never be a Spanish mission in the country of the Plains Apache homeland. Logistics, great distances, an enormous uncharted wilderness, lack of funds, the refusal of the New Spain more than belligerency and more than an indestructible determination to repel a people who so grievously injured them was responsible for preventing priests from establishing stations in the Plains Apache homeland. Logistics, great distances, an enormous uncharted wilderness, lack of funds, the refusal of the New Spain government to authorize the assignment of soldiers necessary for protection, and the southward advance of powerful wild tribes from the north and east—Comanches, Utes, Caddoans, others—

comprised odds that could not be overcome. In the end the Plains Apache would be driven out, scattered to the winds, many of their divisions annihilated.

Two missionaries, Fray Bartolome Romero and Fray Francisco Munoz, who had recklessly attempted in 1629 to establish a mission in Navajo territory (western New Mexico), narrowly escaped with their lives. Many years passed before any others ventured among these people, except with strong military forces engaged in punitive expeditions.

Writing of the Navajo—he called them Apaches de Navajo, for he was well aware of their relationship to the Apache tribes—Benavides stated that they were so numerous "that in two days there come together more than thirty thousand armed with bow and arrow. And this is very little exaggeration; for sundry times that the Spaniards have gone there to fight, although they assaulted them at daybreak and caught them off the guard, they always found the fields curdled with Navajos beyond number."[7]

It is most unlikely that in Benavides' time the Navajo population exceeded four thousand men, women, and children.[8] But Navajo warriors were without peers as fighters and raiders, and they constantly terrorized both the Pueblos and the Spanish colonists.

Benavides roamed into the realm of absurdity with his statements that more than five hundred thousand Indians dwelt in New Mexico, that the Franciscans had baptized some eighty thousand "in one stretch of one hundred leagues," and that the Apache Nation alone numbered "More than two hundred thousand souls . . . more than all the nations of New Spain put together."

The Indian population of Mexico was at least fifty times greater than that of New Mexico and Arizona. As for the Apaches, if he had estimated their numbers at five thousand he would have been approximately correct.

The event which destroyed the last hope of peaceful relations between the Spanish and the Apaches of the High Plains region east of the Rio Pecos occurred in 1627. A large band of Apache Lipans had come to Santa Fe on a trading mission. Much to the delight of the priests, some of them admired a statue of the Virgin they saw in the chapel and expressed an interest in learning something about its meaning. Then, as Benavides would sadly relate, "the demon had recourse to one of the wiles he is accustomed to employ, choosing as his instrument the greed of our Spanish governor."

The governor, Felipe de Zotylo, conspired with a Pueblo headman whom he knew held a grudge against the Apache to organize and lead an attack on their camp. The scheme was successful. More than a score of the friendly visitors, among them a young chieftain, were killed, and perhaps twice that number were taken prisoner. The governor intended to sell them as slaves in Mexico, but Benavides and other priests registered such furious protests that he was obliged to free the captives. Benavides publicly condemned Zotylo for his treachery, and wrote that the attack provoked a revolt throughout the entire province. It did more than that.

For the first time the Plains Apache sent word through New Mexico that they would henceforth wage unrelenting, all-out warfare against the Spanish conquerors. And it was soon raging along the entire eastern front of the colony. Although in ensuing years the conflict would be marked with periods of quiet during which the Plains Apache, for reasons best known to themselves, would curtail their aggressions, the peaceful intervals would be deceptive in their appearance. If the fire of revenge burning in Plains Apache blood was occasionally reduced to smouldering, it would never be extinguished.

In 1629 Benavides was visiting at Santa Clara, a Tewa pueblo on the upper Rio Grande and close to the country of the Jicarilla Apache. The schisms created by the brutality and blunders of the

governors between the Spanish and the Navajo and Plains
Apache gave every indication of being irreparable, arousing in
him both profound sadness and extreme anger. He recognized the
futility of attempting to approach Plains Apache leaders and plead
for their forgiveness, and he abandoned the thought. For some
time, however, he had entertained the hope of meeting with a
Navajo chieftain "to regale him and send him again to his land to
tell his captains that I wished to treat for peace." It would have
been a feather in his own miter if he could succeed, even to a small
extent, where his colleagues had consistently failed, and at Santa
Clara, according to his own claims, he undertook the venture.

"I determined to send to the Navajos twelve Indians of my
Christians. I called the captains and old men of the (Santa Clara)
pueblo together, and communicated to them the desire I had . . .
and that we might by this road attain the conversion of the (the
Navajo), which was my principal end."

The twelve emissaries departed, ostensibly to carry his message to the Navajo, "with very great spirit . . . God knoweth the
constriction in which my heart was, seeing the manifest risk in
which I was putting those Indians." He need not have been
worried, for his messengers were not in danger.

Although the Spanish sovereign, for whom he was writing, in all
likelihood would not have noticed the matter, Benavides does not
state the direction taken by the Tewas on their mission, nor does
he intimate how far they went, but he does say that the Navajos
lived only a day's journey from Santa Clara. This was certainly
untrue for persons traveling on foot, and most probably erroneous
even if the Tewas were mounted, which is doubtful, for Pueblo
Indians were prohibited by the Spanish from owning horses. To
reach the Navajos the Tewas would have had to cross the rugged
Jemez Mountains to the west. Moreover, Santa Clara had suffered often from Navajo raiders, and it seems irresponsible to
think that the dozen messengers would have gone willingly into

the country of people who had inflicted serious losses on them and had carried away Tewa women and children as captives.

Benavides knew too much about New Mexico and its Indians to believe that such a procedure would be undertaken. But, for the record, at least, he wanted a Navajo, and he claimed that the Tewas returned with not one but four.

They were undoubtedly Jicarilla Apaches, whom the Tewas could easily have reached by going up the Rio Grande to the vicinity of Taos. If Benavides were disappointed, he did not admit it. After all, Navajos and Jicarilla Apaches, even though they were different tribes, belonged to the same Indian family and spoke the same basic language, with only dialectal differences, and Benavides admitted his awareness of the variances of the Navajo and Apache tongues at one place in his *Memorial*. Why be fussy about a small matter of identity and spoil a good story that would certainly please the King and enhance his own reputation as a zealous and daring servant of God? As he recounted the tale, the Tewas moved cautiously into the country of "that untamed and ferocious nation," which Benavides often had identified as Apaches de Navajo, and when in sight of a ranchería signalled that they came in peace. Told that they might safely proceed, ". . . they went drawing nearer, although slowly and with mistrust."

A young chieftain came forward to meet the delegation. As he was unquestionably a Jicarilla, he will be designated here as an Apache. The Tewas delivered Benavides's message and gave him a packet of tobacco and a rosary. Having never seen a rosary, the Apache "asked what it signified that the thread had so many beads." It meant, explained the Tewas, that Benavides was sending "word that he would be his friend." Putting the rosary around his neck, the Apache declared that he welcomed peace, but it was apparent to the Tewas that "he was suspicious that they might have some double dealing." Allegedly to be certain that no trickery was involved, the Apache announced that he "would come and see us in our pueblo."

Here is a dramatic illustration of the haughtiness and boldness of the Apache. Despite the perilous situation, a young leader—Benavides did not supply his name—dared to go with only three companions to a pueblo that had been subdued and was controlled by the Spanish. One wonders why they took the chance, for they had no assurance that they would not be slain or sold into slavery, except the verbal promise of a padre that they would not be harmed—not to be depended upon under the prevailing conditions.

Excited and overjoyed by the way things had worked out, Benavides gathered "one thousand five hundred souls" to welcome the important guests. In order to assemble a throng of that size he would have been obliged to draw Indians from several pueblos, perhaps half a dozen. The population of Santa Clara was no more than three hundred.

The little Santa Clara church was suitably decorated, and "next to the altar I ordered a chair set upon a rug." Seated there, he received the young chieftain. Solemn and impressive ceremonies followed. A Pueblo presented his bow and arrows to the Apache, declaring that "before God, who was on that altar, he gave those weapons in earnest of his word that he would never break the peace." Not to be outdone, the Apache proffered one of his own arrows with the pledge "to that God, whoever he might be, I likewise give my word and faith, in the name of all my people, and that for my part and that of my people the peace and friendship shall never fail." Bells were rung and trumpets were sounded and hymns were sung, to the delight of everyone.

The Apache was quoted by Benavides as saying that he wished to establish "the same peace with the Spaniards" that his people had with the Taos. If he made it, the statement is revealing. The Jicarilla Apache lived in close proximity to the pueblos of Taos, and from time immemorial had maintained amicable relations with the Taos people. Each tribe had aided the other in times of war, and under intolerable Spanish oppression the Taos had fled to the Jicarilla and other tribes of Plains Apache, from whom they received protections. That could not be said of relations between the Navajo and the Taos.

However, not everything went smoothly between Benavides and the Apache chieftain. Try as he did, the Apache was not able to see the God which he had been told was on the altar. The explanation by Benavides that God would not be visible to him until after he had been baptized was not satisfactory. The argument ended with Benavides ordering the Apache out of the church. He left in high dudgeon, but after a good meal and perhaps a few drinks with his Tewa friends his temper cooled a bit, although he continued to remain "very vexed, because he wished to have seen God."

When the Apache found out the Benavides's given name was Alonso he demanded permission to use the same name for himself. Benavides refused, telling him he would be named when he became a Christian and was baptized. The Apache would not wait, and took the name, "and from that moment the Tewas all called him Don Alonso."

Despite his disappointment at not being able to see God, the Apache promised that he would return in a few weeks with a large number of his people, "to make a big fair," and that "peace between the Apache and the Spaniards would exist. And so it was."

So it was not. Fighting between Spanish colonists and both the Navajo and the Apache grew more bloody with the passage of almost each year—for more than another one and one-half centuries.

CHAPTER SEVEN

New Mexico:
The Road to Disaster

The church-state conflict descended to a level of unprecedented savagery during the tenures of Governor Luis de Rosas (1637-1641), who made it clear that he had come to Santa Fe for only one purpose, to get rich without undue delay, and warned that if the clergy got in his way he would obliterate every missionary in the colony. This was not an unusual attitude, but Rosas's methods of achieving his goal were extraordinarily stupid and unnecessarily cruel.

He had not been in office long before he laid the groundwork for his operations by openly accusing the priests of attempting to gain a monopoly of all Indian labor, the slave trade, and all wealth in the province. On the basis of these charges, he clapped several padres into jail. One of his next moves was to visit a number of pueblos and order their inhabitants to disobey the fathers. As a result the pueblos of Jemez and Taos staged celebrations that got out of control, and two priests and several colonists were slain.

Missionaries protested that Rosas was encouraging the Pueblos to perform dances that were an invocation of the devil, but they got no satisfaction from him. In reply Rosas scoffed that the Indian dances consisted of nothing more than "something that sounded like hu-hu-hu, and these thieving friars say it is superstitious.'' He laughed uproariously when he heard the story of a priest at Isleta who attempted to stop a native ceremony by parading naked through the pueblo plaza with a cross on his shoulder and a crown of thorns on his head. Not so amusing to him was the scene at Quarai. He sent soldiers to give Indian choristers there fifty lashes each for singing the High Mass. Next he sent a warning to all pueblos that any Indian who assisted in reaping the harvests of mission fields would suffer severe punishment.

The Franciscans charged that Rosas was encouraging the Navajos and the Apaches to steal horses belonging to the missions. This, of course, was ridiculous. Navajos and Apaches needed no encouragement to steal horses from whomever possessed them—horses were horses. The truth was that the Pueblos themselves were aiding the Navajos and Apaches in stealing livestock of all kinds, and warriors from both of these unconquered tribes were conducting raids on Spanish herds quite of their own volition. And Rosas knew these things. He didn't send out troops against the raiders, although he made some slave raids and caught a few of them in his net. He sent aides to confiscate the possessions of Pueblos thought to be guilty, and carried off a number of Pueblo women and children to be sold into slavery, sparing most of the Pueblo conspirators from this fate because he wanted them as workers in his *encomiendas*.

Rosas blamed the priests for all the colony's troubles, and dispatched military contingents to drive them away from the missions at Jemez, Nambe, San Ildefonso, Santa Clara, and other pueblos. Fearing for their lives, the displaced missionaries gathered at Santo Domingo, where they fortified themselves. The churches were dark and deserted, the bells silent. Rosas reigned supreme, virtually controlling the colony's economy.

Reinforced by some soldiers and settlers who were opposed to Rosas's brutality and irreverence, the priests in Santo Domingo adopted Navajo tactics. They became raiders, stealing stock from the herds of the governor and the colonists loyal to him. Two missionaries murdered a strong supporter of Rosas when they caught him off his guard.

The turmoil provided the Pueblos with opportunities to escape, and hundreds of them fled to the Navajo and both the Western and Eastern Apaches. The Taos abandoned their towns and found refuge among their friends, the Apache bands in the El Cuartelejo region of southeastern Colorado and western Kansas. In each place they were welcomed, not so much because they were enemies of the Spanish but because they brought with them stolen horses, cattle, sheep, and guns.

For more than three years the war of attrition continued. Then Juan Flores de Sierra y Valdez arrived in Santa Fe to replace Rosas but died shortly after taking office. Although Rosas was officially out, he had not yet left for Mexico. The colony was without a governor. Taking advantage of this situation, the missionaries stormed into the capital, forcefully took control of the government, clapped Rosas into jail, and plotted his death.

Arrangements were made with an attractive young woman to be discovered by her spouse committing adultery with Rosas in his cell. Although Rosas purportedly was under guard, the allegedly outraged husband found no difficulty in avoiding detection. He murdered Rosas and escaped.

Alonso Pacheco de Heredia (1643-1646) replaced the dead Sierra. He had secret orders to punish the persons responsible for the untimely death of Rosas. Feigning friendliness for all factions, he quietly gathered evidence, then struck. After stripping the priests of all civil authority, he hanged eight Spaniards who had supported their revolutionary cabildo. The Franciscans sought to discredit Pacheco by injecting a racial issue into the controversy, charging that his support came from a Portuguese and mestizos and sambahigos, some Indian men, Negroes and mulattos. The accusation had no appreciable effect.

As the seventeenth century passed its half-way mark, the colony of New Mexico stood on the brink of collapse. Many of the pueblos were deserted. The missionaries saw themselves facing utter failure. They could only hope to survive if two conditions they sought were met: they must gain greater authority in directing the social and economic policies of the province, and they must receive more support in the form of military manpower over which they held jurisdiction. Some two score churches had been built, but the great number of conversions they reported had been made is without reliable substantiation in historical annals. However, there is no question regarding the steadily deteriorating relations between civil officials, the military, the friars, and the Indians. Many of the Pueblos still obeyed the ringing of the bells calling them to Mass, but the extent of their reverence was as undeterminable as their thoughts. Looking into their faces one saw nothing. Yet the sound of the drums, the shuffling of dancers' feet, and the chanting of acappella choruses, gave some indication of what was in their hearts. It was just as well, many of them believed, to submit to the demands of the padres and the governors and thereby escape the infliction of brutalities. But, as it would soon be demonstrated, the vaccine of Christianity so forcefully injected into them had created a fever steadily growing in its intensity, a fever that would soon be beyond the control of either God or man.

Even a brief chronology of events taking place in the years 1650 to 1680, when the end came, portrays with all possible vividness the chaotic conditions in the colony. When Pacheco left Santa Fe, of the one hundred and fifty pueblos occupied at the time of the founding of the province by Onaté, only forty-three contained any inhabitants. On the other hand, the population, prosperity, and power of the surrounding wild tribes were steadily increasing. The church-state controversy was comparatively quiet during the regimes of the two governors briefly in office after Pacheco, for they had all they could do to keep the Apache, Navajo, Ute, and Comanche from wiping out the colony.

The first sign that an organized Indian revolt was brewing came during the tenure of Governor Hernando de Ugarte y la Concha (1650-1654). His chief intelligence officer informed him that leaders of at least six pueblos were conspiring with the Navajo to strike in force against Spanish communities, Santa Fe among them, on the night of Holy Thursday, when it was believed all Spaniards would be assembled at worship.

Ugarte took quick action. Contingents of cavalry swept into Isleta, Alameda, San Felipe, Cochiti, and Jemez. Nine leaders of these pueblos were hanged without trial, and a number of others were sentenced to ten years slavery in Santa Fe. Ugarte placed most of the blame for the aborted uprising on Navajo medicine men. This was reason enough for him to launch a campaign to take Navajo slaves. He sent a force into the Navajo country, but nothing was accomplished. Navajo had to be found before they could be captured.

Juan de Samandiego (1655-1656) succeeded Ugarte. He instituted no new policies and made no effort to close the breach between his office and the clergy. But even if he had desired to halt the feuding, he would have had little time to devote to the problem. His troops were kept busy chasing Apache and Navajo raiders.

The Father Custodian of the province, Tomas Manso, a brilliant scholar of noble birth, demonstrated his talents as a politician. He bluntly wrote both government and church officials in Mexico City that unless drastic measures were taken to halt the state-church conflict in Santa Fe, the colony was doomed and would soon have to be abandoned. When he was asked what measures he thought would be most effective, he was ready with an answer. He made only one recommendation. It was that his brother, Joaquin, a highly reputable man well known in commercial and political circles, and a leading Catholic, be appointed governor. The authorities, weary of reading the venomous reports that flowed in a steady stream out of Santa Fe, endorsed the proposal.

Governor Manso found the assignment and the isolation disagreeable. How long he remained is not certain. However, he proved himself to be an extraordinary mediator. If his private feelings favored the clergy, he was able to conceal them. He was a wealthy man and probably made no attempt to augment his own fortunes. His policies, decisions, and actions, whatever they may have been, had a calming effect on the troubled waters. The only violence known to have occured during his brief tenure was the fighting between the military and Navajo and Apache.

The peaceful period came to an abrupt end in 1659 when Bernard Lopez de Mendizabel became governor, and Fray Juan Ramirez succeeded Fray Manso as head of the New Mexico missions. Both were hotheaded, sensitive, and stubborn. Mendizabel was a successful businessman and openly anti-clerical. Ramirez was a scholar and had no patience with anyone dedicated to making profits in commerce. They quickly became avowed enemies. Ten priests who had traveled north with them, disgusted and discouraged and seeing themselves as helpless pawns in the factional conflict, turned about and went back to Mexico.

Passion soon flared with new fury in New Mexico. Mendizabel proclaimed his right to control all trade and receive all rewards from goods produced or obtained from Indians. He was a slaver and sent out squadrons of men to capture wild Indians to be sold in Mexico. Ramirez thundered that Mendizabel was endangering the safety of the colonists by keeping all the soldiers on slaving expeditions, most of which turned out to be wild goose chases.

When Ramirez launched a strong new campaign to halt all Indian religious rites, Mendizabel issued an order permitting all natives to conduct their ceremonies and dances whenever they wished. When the friars attempted to rebuild a church burned in a riot at Taos, Mendizabel named as governor of the pueblo a Taos Indian who had stabbed and killed a priest. Fray Luis Martinez had been assigned by Ramirez to serve at Taos, but Mendizabel told the Taos people who had been persuaded, or forced, to return from the country of the High Plains Apaches, not to obey or work for Martinez, and charged that Martinez after raping an Indian woman had cut her throat and buried her under his house.

The torrent of protests sent to Mexico City by Ramirez and other missionaries resulted in the sending of agents of the Inquisition to Santa Fe to make an investigation of Mendizabel's irreverence and illegal activities. The investigation had not been long underway when Mendizabel escaped possible punishment by dropping dead.

The depths to which the clergy were willing to descend to injure an adversary — even a dead one — was amply demonstrated by charges filed with the Inquisition against Dona Teresa, Mendizabel's widow. Among the accusations, all declared to be crimes against the church, were: (1) she bathed and changed linen on Fridays, a Jewish custom; (2) she primped on Saturdays in violation of the law of Moses, which demanded that the day be observed with religious service; (3) she and her husband had preferred to sleep in different bedrooms; (4) she read exotic books in foreign tongues and had been heard to laugh at jokes in them. Only one book was identified. It was Ariosto's *Orlando Furioso*. The complaint failed to mention that Dona Teresa had been reared in Italy, spoke fluent Italian, and found delight in books published in that language.

The fathers made a mistake in taking on Dona Teresa. She sent to her persecutors a lengthy and spirited written defense, and did not neglect to enumerate the transgressions of numerous persons, some of whom held high rank and were thought to be of commendable virtue. She ruined reputations on the record, describing in detail, and noting time and place, the immoral conduct, the drunken orgies, the sacrilegious activities, the marital infidelities, and other crimes of the men and women she named. A good many residents of the colony wished that the priests had minded their own business.

Surrounded by soldiers and aides, Diego Dionysio de Penalosa Bricena y Bertugo made a grand entrance into Santa Fe as Mendizabel's successor. He was wanted in Peru, his native land, for the commission of a series of felonies, but influential friends in Mexico City had prevented his extradition. He was a charlatan, an adventurer without scruples of any sort, a corrupt politician, and an *embustero*. Governor and Captain-General were not enough titles to satisfy his ego, so he created another for himself. He became the Conde de Santa Fe and insisted on being addressed as such. Indians interested him only for what he could get out of them. The work of converting them to Christianity interested him not at all, for there was no monetary profit in it. Every evil and illegal practice of all his predessors was not only adopted by him but was augmented and brought greater returns than any previous chief executive had enjoyed. For three years (1661-1664) he held absolute control of the colony's economy, conducted large-scale slaving raids, collected heavy tributes, and forced all captive Indians to work for him.

He countered the protests of the missionaries by charging them with debased cruelties. They lashed Indians for failing to attend Mass on time. They cut off the hair of Indian women for minor infractions. Most of the priests, he declared, were ex-sailors, ex-artillerymen, ex-criminals, who had taken holy orders to escape punishment for their crimes or to avoid work and to live in luxury off contributions paid by taxpayers. The padres burned the homes of farmers to keep Indians from working for them. Posted on the doors of churches, he maintained, were more excommunications than bulls. Worst of all the friars usually aimed their critical arrows against governors and justices. Thus the royal jurisdiction was much humbled and violated, and the few colonists who dared to uphold their governor, besides suffering poverty, were afflicted and snubbed by the religious with ugly and insulting words.

Governor Penalosa was riding high, but in his third year in office he made a fatal mistake and gave the clergy the opportunity to strike back for which they had been waiting. Two Pueblo prisoners slipped away from their guards and ran into the church at Santo Domingo. Penalosa sent soldiers to recapture the men and drag them from under the church altar, if necessary. The church door had been locked by the pastor, but the soldiers took the keys from him, opened it, and took their prisoners, who were hiding under a bench.

When Fray Alonso de Posada, the president of the colony's missions, demanded the release of the two men, Penalosa imprisoned him in Santa Fe. Next Penalosa sought witnesses to justify his actions, but could find no one to stand behind him. As Horgan recounts the situation: "Santa Fe and the missions stirred with excitement. It was unheard of, to throw a prelate and a commissioner of the Inquisition into jail. Penalosa searched for a diplomatic formula that would allow him to climb down with dignity. Surely the friars would petition to free their president, whereupon he would do so with clemency. But the clergy kept an offended silence. Finally desperate, he wrote to the pastor of Isleta (Pueblo), asking him to call. With a show of diplomatic mediation, the incarcerated commissioner was released, and promptly made charges to the Holy Office in Mexico."[1]

Penalosa decided that it might be wise for him to get out of New Mexico, and he resigned.[2]

CHAPTER EIGHT

New Mexico:
Days of Terror and Death

Four governors held office in Santa Fe between 1664 and 1680. Governor Fernando de Villanueva inherited from Penalosa a land not only aflame with warfare but stricken by famine. The drought, which continued for more than two years, was not simply the enemy of priests and officials but of all living things, plants, animals, and humans. The colony had been torn asunder by factional forces, and now it was being destroyed by an elemental power that only nature, in its own decision, could overcome.

In the first year, snows were light, and after April no rain fell. The cloudbursts that usually swept in summer across the mesas like great purple brooms did not come. Grass that had started with the spring thaw was soon burned to powder, and the ranges lay parched and bare. The little creeks were consumed by the thirsty earth, and even the Rio Grande was hardly more than a thin sheet of wetness. Leaves curled and fell, and empty tree limbs, gray with blowing dust, were like naked arms of ghosts uplifted in appeal to the sweep of azure sky and the ball of merciless fire traveling across it. There were no piñon nuts, no wild herbs or roots or berries. Needles of pine trees were red and fell like showers of dust at the slightest movement of air; the dying trees were shaggy and cracked like disreputable old men and women. The wild creatures were gone—no one knew where. Buffalo had vanished from the parched High Plains. The wilderness was empty, silent, not even a bird song being heard.

And the second year and part of the third year were the same.

It was only with great effort that enough water was obtained to keep mankind and a few miserable cattle and sheep alive. Little reservoirs were built to catch trickles and holes were dug to recover seepage water with pans and cups. There were no crops, and a friar wrote that there was not a fanega of corn or wheat in the entire province. People ate not only the meat of the domestic animals they killed but the hides as well, rolling them in corn flour, if they had any, and cooking them with whatever herbs or roots remained unrotted in earth cellars.

Snow and rain came at last, but another year or two had to pass before the land would be restored and the bounties of corn and beans, game, wheat and grass, nuts, berries, and tubers would be plentiful once more.

Hundreds of Indians had died of starvation, four hundred and fifty of them in a single pueblo. Around almost every town and along the road lay the bones of men, women, and children stripped of flesh to gleaming white.

Strangely, the deaths and the devastation seemed to fertilize the seeds of rebellion, and when the drought diminished the young plants of revolt grew faster, some bearing fat buds, signifying the fruit to come. Governor Villanueva, desperately seeking to halt the growth, employed the only methods he understood. He cooperated with the priests by prohibiting Indian religious ceremonials, and sent soldiers to arrest medicine men. Most of them escaped, but forty-seven were captured, charged with witchcraft and sorcery—felonies under Spanish law— and sentenced to terms in prison. All were lashed until they collapsed under the torture. Three who openly defied the court were hanged.

Then Villanueva learned something that he had failed to realize—a unity was developing among the Pueblos, under which their traditional tribal independence was being suppressed. He awakened one morning to find seventy Pueblo leaders waiting at the gate to the governor's palace. After eating a leisurely breakfast, he granted them an audience. What did they want? They wanted several things. First, they wanted him to understand that they did not intend to abandon their own forms of worship. Second, they wanted to make it clear to him that without their doctors to lead them in their ceremonies, they would be without the power to overcome evil spirits, and that would be bad for the Spanish as well as for themselves. Third, they wanted him to release the imprisoned spiritual leaders at once.

It was not the custom of Spanish officials to be intimidated by Indians, said Villanueva. He could throw them all in jail by snapping his fingers. What if he refused to grant their requests?

In that case, the Pueblos answered, they and all their people would abandon their homes and join the Navajo and Apache. There were not enough soldiers to halt such a mass exodus.

Villanueva could count without taking pebbles out of one box and dropping them into another, and he could keep records without tying knots in a string. All the statistics he needed were in his head. They were some twenty-five hundred colonists of both sexes and of all sizes. There were no less than sixteen thousand Pueblos. How many Apache and Navajo there were he had no way of knowing but, whatever their number, there were too many. Moreover, his munitions were in short supply, and it might be months before more arrived.

The medicine men were released. One of them, Popé, was destined to know fame in a very brief time. A native of San Juan, Popé possessed extraordinary talents as a leader, was revered as a man with great magical powers that permitted him to communicate with supernaturals, and was recognized as an outstanding military strategist.

Now free, Pope announced that he was looking into the future, and in his vision he beheld a great fire burning red with the blood of Spaniards.

Governor Villanueva was not displeased when he was notified that Juan de Miranda was being sent to replace him. The future of the colony was anything but promising. His greatest troubles at the moment were caused by the Apache and Navajo, and it would be impossible to defeat them without a great many more troops than he had available. But recommendations that garrisons be increased had been rejected by the King, on the ground that they involved needless expenditures.

Governor Miranda learned something of the dire situation even before he reached Santa Fe. The supply train with which he was traveling was attacked by a large band of Navajo. Four of his aides were killed, and all the wagon mules were stolen before the raiders could be driven off. Enough horses were saved to get him and the remainder of his staff to the capital, but he arrived there a badly shaken man.

Word came that Pope was holding great dances and making threats. Soldiers watched, but he was not arrested. To avoid being harassed, he slipped out of San Juan and went to Taos, where he kept the fires of his great vision flaming. Miranda soon asked permission to return to Mexico, and Juan Francisco Trevino was sent to succeed him.

Reports of an unprecendented situation awaited Trevino. The Pueblos were not only plotting rebellion but openly calling for it. Missionaries were being "bewitched"—probably a way of saying that they were being scared out of their wits—and half a dozen had dropped dead. Pope was claiming that he was in communication with the ancient war god Montezuma through three underworld spirits. The spirits came each night to talk with him in the shadows of his Taos sanctuary and to urge him to lead the Pueblos in revolt.

Trevino hanged three Tewas suspected of defying the faith, but he remained away from Taos. Indeed, in his brief stay in Santa Fe he seldom strayed beyond his patio. As soon as he could he scurried back to Mexico City, hardly waiting for the arrival of his replacement, Antonio de Otermin.

If he lacked experience in frontier warfare, Governor Otermin did not lack courage. Fury burned in him as he listened to accounts of the situation he faced, and he swore that it would no longer be tolerated.

In a raid on Abo Pueblo, the Apache had torn Fray Pedro de Ayala's garments from him, flogged him until his body was crisscrossed by bloody slashes, and ended his suffering by smashing his skull with a stone hammer. During another Apache attack at Senecu, Fray Alonso Gil de Avila, standing at a window and holding aloft a crucifix, had been riddled with arrows. No Spanish colonist dared venture away from a settlement. Bands of murderers wandered through the country. The King had reversed his penny-pinching policy and had permitted the military strength of the colony to be increased by fifty men. Although he feared the number of soldiers available to him would still be inadequate, Otermin announced his intention to chastise all enemies, Apache, Navajo, and rebellious Pueblos. All colonists were ordered to serve in the campaign, and columns would be sent out to sweep their antagonists from the province.

It was too late. On August 9, 1680, the fuse Pope had lighted reached the bomb he had magically constructed.

Some historians attribute the uprising chiefly to religious oppression, a conclusion with which this author disagrees. The causes were many. The Spanish did not succeed in supplanting Pueblo beliefs with the doctrines of Christianity. Indeed, they fell far short of achieving this goal. The forceful methods employed by the missionaries to stamp out every vestige of Indian rites, every element of Indian faith, of course generated resentment and defiance, but they were not in themselves responsible for the ultimate catastrophe.

The causes stemmed as much from hunger of the belly as from spiritual craving; as much from emotional trauma as from injuries caused by the suppression of ritual; as much from Spanish demands for complete obedience and undeviating submission to social and economic systems that held Indians in bondage and perpetual poverty as from the burning of ceremonial paraphernalia and the profanation of Indian gods.

The fire had smouldered for more than three-quarters of a century before becoming an unquenchable conflagration. Small spurts of flame had risen periodically during this time, but the Spanish had been able to extinguish them quickly because the Pueblos had no leader with the ability to unite the tribes, to induce the people to suppress, even temporarily, the jealousies and superstitions and petty grievances that created discord and enmity.

Fate filled that void with Pope'.

"Spaniards," wrote a wise Spanish historian, "always end by devouring their institutions with the acid of their corrosive individualities."[1] That was an essential ingredient of the Spanish character, and it nurtured the debacle in New Mexico. But, although it weakened the beams it was not alone responsible for the collapse of the entire colonial structure. What finally brought the whole house down was the conflict between equally destructive forces, the shattering collisions between two ways of life, two civilizations; between social, judicial, and economic systems with nothing in common, and between deeply ingrained faiths impossible to reconcile. It was not that the Indians were unwilling to compromise. It was the Spanish, not only in their insistence that the Indians submit to totalitarian rule but in the factionalism existing within their own ranks. Neither of the two majesties would give ground, and the struggle could have ended in no other way but a draw ruinous to both of them.

Following Popé's signal, hordes of Pueblos swept through New Mexico. In the first few days of the fighting more than four hundred Spanish men, women, and children were killed, and twenty-one priests achieved martyrdom. A few of the most attractive young Spanish women were taken alive and delivered to Popé and other leaders for their pleasure. Scores of persons were missing, but their fate would never be known. Churches and homes were ransacked, their contents burned.

Most of the colonists, by extraordinary bravery and desperate fighting, escaped, and in September, destitute, ragged, and starved, they reached safety in the presidio at El Paso.[2]

The vast Province of New Mexico had been abandoned to the Indians, eighty-two years after it had been founded. But it had not been irretrievably lost. Twelve years later the powerful army commanded by Governor and Captain-General Diego de Vargas Lujan Ponce de Leon would retake it, and for another hundred and twenty years Santa Fe would be a Spanish colonial captial.

CHAPTER NINE

Kino:
Builder for God and Man

It was a land no living white man had seen. Indeed, when Father Eusebio Francisco Kino rode into it on a bright March morning in 1687 no one but the Indians who dwelt along its few streams and about its widely scattered water holes had traversed any of its mountain and desert trails for nearly one hundred and fifty years.

The international border between northwestern Mexico and the American Southwest intersects the region now in an angular delineation. North of the boundary is Arizona, and south of it is the northwestern part of the Mexican state of Sonora. In Kino's time, however—and long before and long after that—all of it belonged to one country, Spain, and it bore the name, loosely applied, of Pimeria Alta. If the designation was appropriate for perhaps half of Pimeria Alta's sixty-some thousand square miles, it was not suitable for the remaining territory. The eastern part was the homeland of Indians the Spanish called Upper Pimas, including under this erroneous appellation the Sobaipuris and the Papagos, but to the west of the Upper Pimas were peoples who spoke various dialects of an entirely different language, the numerous Yuman tribes.

There is an old tale, and it probably is true, that the first missionaries pushing northward through the wilderness from central Mexico heard the word *pim* so often from one tribe they encountered that they though it was their name. Actually these Indians identified themselves as the A-a'tam, which means simply *the people*. In their language, the Nevome dialect of the A-a'tam tongue, *pim* signified *no*. Adding the letter *a*, perhaps to alleviate linguistic strain on Spanish ears, the name of Pima was mistakenly applied to them.

After the passage of some years, the padres of the Mexican frontier had learned that far to the north, in country no missionary had reached, were many more Indians who spoke the same language as the Pimas they knew. Thus, the terms Upper Pimas and Pimeria Alta, and Lower Pimas and Pimeria Bayo came into usage. It was, if nothing else, a means of differentiating the unknown heathens of the north from those of the same nation farther south who already had been exposed to Christianity.

The first man of the Old World to pass through any part of the realm of the Upper Pimas was Estevanico the Black.[1] Following the Rio San Pedro, he touched it only on its extreme eastern edge, entering Arizona in May 1539. Several days behind him was Fray Marcos de Niza, but how far into present American territory he traveled is uncertain, for the report he made to Coronado and Antonio de Mendoza, Viceroy of Mexico, contained numerous falsehoods.

In the fall of the same year, Mendoza, a shrewd and cautious man, sent Melchior Diaz, a veteran frontier official of Culiacan, to verify the fabulous claims of Fray Marcos. Diaz and his company of forty-five mounted soldiers were forced to halt their journey by blizzards and intense cold in the vicinity of the confluence of the Rio San Pedro and the Rio Gila, but they went far enough north to obtain evidence exposing Fray Marcos as a prevaricator. Diaz's expedition is historically important because he and his men took the first horses into territory that eventually would comprise the western United States. Coronado and his army in 1540 traveled over the trail Estevanico had opened.

Also in 1539, Francisco de Ulloa had touched the western border of Pimeria Alta. Sailing up the Sea of Cortez (Gulf of California), he turned back after encountering shoals he thought to be impassable that spread across the delta of a large river not known to exist. The river was the Colorado. In the next summer three supply ships of the Coronado Expedition, under the command of Hernando de Alarcon, were stopped by the same shoals. But, taking to small boats, Alarcon and his sailors fought their way through the perilous reefs and ascended the Rio Colorado until they had passed the site of the present town of Yuma, Arizona. Alarcon had turned homeward after learning from Indians that he and Coronado were separated by several hundred miles of desert.

In 1540, therefore, only the eastern and western perimeters of Pimeria Alta had been skirted, and between them lay a vast territory about which cartographers had no reliable information. But some pinpoints of light would be thrown into the darkness before the year had ended. Coronado, desperately in need of supplies, would send Diaz to search for Alarcon's ships.

With twenty-five Spaniards and a number of Indian guides, Diaz left the Valle de Sonora in September. The little company not only crossed a land never before entered by white men but a land that in its larger part was one of the most terrible deserts of the North American continent. The trail they followed passed from the Rio Sonora through Magdalena to Sasabe (in Arizona), then ran close to the international border to the Rio Colorado, which was reached near the mouth of the Rio Gila.[2]

Diaz found letters left in a hollow tree by Alarcon. Although profoundly disappointed, for an unknown reason he did not turn back at once but chose to explore more of the country, and he crossed the Rio Colorado and rode some distance westward. He and his Spanish companions were the first white men to traverse any part of the land that would one day be part of the state of California. A short distance south of the California-Mexico boundary he was gravely injured when he accidentally fell on a lance, the point of which ruptured his bladder. For three weeks his loyal men carried him on a litter, but somewhere along the desert trail in Arizona he died. His grave has never been found.

For the next sixty-three years only noises made by Indians, animals, and the elements broke the silence of Pimeria Alta. In all that time no more bearded white men appeared, no horses' hooves beat their rhythms on the earth, no guns spit fire and deadly lead and acrid fumes. Undoubtedly most of the few people who had seen the first invaders were in their graves. But stories survived. They told of how strangers came in large canoes on the Rio Colorado, and how others came on great snorting beasts, and of how some of the men had black bodies, and of how many wore iron that no arrow could penetrate, and how all were adorned with plumes and garments and decorations of extraordinary beauty.

Suddenly these tales were no longer folklore related by wrinkled grandfathers about the campfires. They had counterparts in real life. In 1604, Juan de Onate, governor of the Province of New Mexico, and thirty soldiers, left the upper Rio Grande, rode across western New Mexico and Arizona, descended Bill Williams Fork to the Colorado River and went down its left bank to the Gulf of California. But they soon vanished as quickly as they had come, and for another two generations no more intruders appeared, and the stories once more were like fables or legends.

Then, again suddenly, new tales were carried over the trade trails to the villages of the Upper Pimas, the Papagos, the Quahatikas, the Sobaipuris, the Halyikwamais, the Halchidhomas, the Cocopas, the Kohuanas, the Maricopas, the Yavapais, the Yumas. In 1687 the desert communications network in its mysterious methods of operations carried startling news;

men in black robes were coming.

At this time, except for the thin thread of Melchior Diaz's trail from Magdalena to the Colorado River, for one hundred and forty-seven years the interior of Pimeria Alta had remained a blank on Spanish maps. Even its boundaries were hardly more than speculations and often wandered off into the wild blue yonder of cartographic dreams. Not much time would pass after Kino came, however, before the blank space would be filled with geographical facts, and Pimeria Alta's limits would be clearly defined on charts he drew in great detail and with remarkable accuracy.

Kino was forty-two years of age when he was assigned as the first missionary in Pimeria Alta. He was born of simple people near the Italian village of Segno, in the shadow of the Tyrolese Alps, on August 10, 1645. The family name was Chinuas, but he never explained why, as a young man, he sometimes spelled it Chinus or Chino. Not until some years later, when he was in Spain, did he change it permanently to Kino. Purportedly he adopted this form to avoid the nickname of *Chinaman*, for all his friends, classmates, and colleagues were well aware that since his early youth he had harbored a dream of serving as a missionary in the Far East. It was widely known, as well, that during his years in the Jesuit colleges in Hala and Ingolstadt, and as a young priest, he had written numerous letters to the Father General in Rome begging to be assigned to a post in China.

Kino's proficiency as a mathematician, an astronomer, and a cartographer caused his mentors to give him unusual attention. They sought to induce him to remain in Austria as a teacher of these sciences, but he rejected offers of high academic posts, doggedly determined to cross the seas to heathen worlds. He would never see the Orient, but at last, in 1678, he was ordered to proceed to Cadiz, from which he was to embark for Mexico. He was stranded in Spain for more than two and one-half years. The filthy vessel on which he and several other missionaries at last obtained passage sailed in January 1681, arriving in Vera Cruz on May 2. The crossing had taken nearly a hundred days.

The old dream of going to China still lingered in his mind, but soon after his arrival in Mexico City it was forever shattered. A new attempt was to be made to reestablish missions in Baja California. All previous efforts, conducted over a period of a century and a half, had ended in failure, not only because of the extreme aridity of the country but also because pearl fishermen and soldiers had treated the Indians with such cruelty that they fled to the interior at the sight of a white man and could not be persuaded to return. The proposed new undertaking was to be different. Missionaires, not the military, would be in command, and all money to support it would come from the provincial treasury. No private investors would be permitted to participate. The wealth to be gained would be in the form of souls that were saved.

If he lacked experience in the wilderness, Kino possessed all the other qualifications the Father Provincial, Benardo Pardo, demanded of the man he was obligated to appoint to direct the missionary work in Baja California. With the sanction of the Viceroy, Kino was named to lead the expedition.

The story of Kino's long struggle to reopen and maintain the Baja California missions is a dramatic account of extreme hardship, logistical chaos, violence and religious defeat deserving of detailed treatment that is beyond the scope of this narrative. Supply ships were not sent on schedule, and some that were sent were lost at sea. Missions that were established had to be abandoned, either because neither crops nor animals could survive through long droughts or because of troubles with resentful natives. Yet, Kino did not give up. He explored the country, rebuilding where he found dependable water and cultivatable land. He was the first white man to break a trail from the Sea of Cortez across the peninsula to the Pacific. Funds were curtailed, and he was forced to take his colonists back to the mainland to avoid starvation. Sickness and diseases took a heavy toll of the company.

Yet Kino must be credited with winning the battle. Only for a short time after he left Baja California was the region without a mission. Others would be sent to build on the foundation he had erected. He returned to Mexico in 1685 and was sent with a ship to explore the Baja California coast for a better location for a mission than those previously selected. Before the year ended the search was called off temporarily, and he was ordered to remain with the ship as chaplain while a hunt was made for pirates believed to be lurking off Mexican ports. No pirates were found. In the spring of 1686 he was in Acapulco when he was informed that a new assignment would be given to him. It came in November. He was to found a mission among the Seri Indians who dwelt along the mainland coast of the northern Sea of Cortez.

A few weeks later, bearing instructions to the Father Visitor of Sonora, Manuel Gonzales, who resided in Oposura, he left Guadalajara. But he would not reach his new station among the Seri. Gonzales changed the plan, appointing him to be the first missionary to the Upper Pimas.

Kino entered Pimeria Alta in the valley of the Rio San Miguel.[3] With him were two colleagues, three Indian vaqueros, and five heavily loaded pack-mules. The mission at Cucurpe, where they had spent the previous night, was soon lost to sight behind them. It was the last outpost of Christendom in northwestern Mexico. Immediately ahead stretched the vast desert and mountain wilderness about which they knew almost nothing. The few brief reports that had been written—those of Ulloa, Alarcon, Diaz's men, Onate—had long gathered dust in official depositories, forgotten. If Kino knew of their existence, which is doubtful, he knew nothing of their contents. The extent of his ignorance of the geography of Pimeria Alta is demonstrated by several facts: before he began the explorations that would make him famous he did not know that Baja California was not an island but was a peninsula; he was not certain where the Rio Gila had its delta; and as for the great Rio Colorado he believed it to be a tributary of the Gila.

Kino's companions on the March morning of 1687 were Father Gonzales from Oposura and Father Aguilar from Cucurpe. They had elected to travel with him a short way on his *entrada* into the enormous and mysterious domain over which he would have jurisdiction. It was a small procession for such a significant event, but it would rapidly increase in size as Indians joined it during the next few days, Indians who had never seen a Black Robe.

Descriptions of Kino's arrival in Pimeria Alta, as well as of his appearance and physique, are woefully inadequate, but scattered references in some contemporary documents, when put together, provide valuable, if vague illustrations. He rode with the ease of a veteran horseman, his outward calmness concealing the excitement within him. As he would relate, he might have rested a few days at Cucurpe after his long and circuitous saddle journey all the way from Guadalajara, but he had been too eager to meet the Indians to whom he was to minister, too eager to see the wild land in which they dwelt, to waste precious moments in leisure.

He was not tall, perhaps standing in his scuffed boots no more than two inches under six feet. An associate who would serve under him would employ the adjectives lean, hard, and agile in describing him, and others would mention his sharp, darting, dark eyes, and his thin, handsome face that was deeply burned by years of exposure to the suns and winds of the Sea of Cortez and Baja California. Kino himself would recall that the magnificent vistas surrounding the Rio San Miguel—the countless twistings of the little stream through cottonwood and oak groves and the flowering meadowlands squeezed between canyon walls and immense tilted mesas that swept away on every side under a brilliant blue sky—not only fascinated him but stirred in him an almost youthful vigor that a man of forty-two hardly could expect to experience.

He was journeying into darkness, and he could do no more than ask himself what was to be discovered between the indefinite boundaries of Pimeria Alta. The question fired his blood, and he understood that he should not rest as long as he had the strength to seek an answer.

He would find the answer gradually in ensuing years. He would come to know Pimeria Alta's peaks and its hot sands burning with the fires of a hell. He would come to know its waterholes and its barrancas, its gorges and canyons and mesas. He would come to know its many hues and its contrasts and its changeableness and the variability of its climate. He would come to know the strangeness and the extraordinary diverseness of its vegetation, its gnarled forests and its seas of sage and yucca and mesquite, the weird forms of its cacti, and its lovely flowers splotching the hillsides. He would come to know its terrors and its beauty, its peacefulness, the ferocity of its winds and the stillness of its starry nights.

But when he first saw it, a very small part of it, in the spring of 1687, he could be certain of only one thing: it contained people, people who had never seen the Cross, who had never heard a mission bell, who had not emerged from the Stone Age, who knew nothing of Christianity and the blessings of civilization. That was all he needed to take him into it, and to hold him there.

Kino had brought with him to Pimeria Alta a copy of a royal document that would influence the course of history in northern New Spain. It reflected upon his humaneness and his determination to achieve reforms in the unconscionable injustices inflicted on the native people of the New World.

He had been horrified by the enslavement of Indians by the owners of estancias, mines, and commercial enterprises throughout Mexico. Before leaving Guadalajara for the north he had submitted a petition to the Royal Audencia requesting that the slave traffic be prohibited in areas in which he would serve. Being practical, however, and recognizing the political strength of the slaveholders, many of whom were extremely wealthy, he had entertained no hope that he could eliminate slavery entirely, but he did believe that he might be able to achieve some type of beneficial compromise.

In part his petition said: ". . . alcaldes mayores and other officials . . . under the color of *repartimientos de sellos*, cause the Indians to be taken involuntarily, even before they are baptized . . . by which violence they are terrorized and caused to flee from conversion to the Holy Gospel, and to refuse to accept the gentle rule of our Holy Faith, thereby imperiling not only the welfare of their souls but also the royal hacienda."[4]

In order that the "Holy Gospel may be propagated in remote lands," Kino pleaded for a decree directing that no one "shall take or cause any Indian to be taken . . . until five years have passed after their conversion." He also asked that converted Indians who volunteered to work in the mines or at any other labor be paid a fair daily wage, and that heavy penalties should be imposed for violations of the decree.

King Carlos II beat him to the goal, sending to Mexico about the same time an even more stringent order pertaining to the same issue. The royal cedula commanded that all Indian converts must be promised in His Majesty's name that they would not be required to serve in mines or on estates during the first twenty years after their conversion.

Kino had hoped to save baptized Indians from involuntary servitude for five years, and, purportedly, under the king's order they would be protected from enslavement for twenty years. He had set out for Pimeria Alta with "this royal cedula, which by its admirable Catholic zeal might well and should astonish and edify the world," in a pocket over his heart. On the journey he presented it to officials he met. Some of them viewed it with a noticeable lack of enthusiasm. Most mine and ranch owners to whom he showed it were openly angry. The alcalde of San Juan, the military and political capital of Sonora, however, kissed the document and declared: "I obey it. I place it about my head." Kino would not let him forget his promise.

It was not only an inherent characteristic that provided Kino with the power to keep himself from harboring unpleasant memories or from succumbing to moods of deep depression. He had disciplined himself to avoid dwelling on the vicissitudes of his personal life or on misfortunes he had experienced. His optimism was indestructible. He saw the rosy glow of assured success when others about him saw only the creeping shadows of prospective defeat. This attitude would lead him into dangerous situations, but Fate—if not the Lord—seemed to have ordained that he was to emerge from his ordeals with no loss of determination to defy others that awaited him. He went to Pimeria Alta with a profound conviction that his mission would be a resounding success.

His belief was bolstered initially only a short distance from Cucurpe at the little Pima settlement of Cosari (Bamotze). Having received word by an Indian courier sent ahead by Aguilar that Kino was approaching, the villagers and their chief, Coxi, had prepared a gala welcome for him. Kino had heard of Coxi and had looked forward to meeting him. Some time earlier Coxi had appeared in San Juan and had requested that Black Robes be stationed among his people. The chief was known to military authorities as a strong Piman leader, whose intelligence was not to be discounted.

While Coxi's appeal was encouraging to all officials interested in enlarging the realm of the Catholic Church, they gave careful consideration to the probability that it was not inspired alone by a sincere desire for religious instruction. Indeed, they favored the opinion that Coxi was motivated by the knowledge that in the normal course of affairs a presidio was established in close proximity to, if not within, a wilderness mission. As it was known that Apache raiders periodically attacked Piman settlements along the Rio San Pedro and the Rio Santa Cruz—both of these rivers flowed northward to the Rio Gila in Arizona—the presence of a garrison in the area would have afforded protection most advantageous to them.

Coxi's request had been deferred, and he had concluded that it would not be granted. The arrival of Kino, however, revived his hope that the military also would appear. He pledged full cooperation in building a permanent mission, and asked that he and his wife and children be the first to be baptized. Kino was not to be hurried, explaining that there was much more to conversion than the rite of baptism. Coxi proclaimed his willingness to be patient.

At Cosari, Gonzales turned back, and Kino and Aguilar went on over the mountain ridge to the west and down into the valley of the Rio San Ignacio. In every village they visited the inhabitants manifested their delight with wild dancing and singing and feasts.

As he rode on over more mountains and through deep canyons Kino took special note of water supplies and cultivatable lands. He and Aguilar camped where night overtook them, and each day paused numerous times to converse as best they could and the vaqueros could do in signs with Indians waiting along their trail to greet them. At the tiny village of Imuris they turned up the Rio Cocospura, and the rich bottomlands and groves rapidly vanished as rocky gorges with high sheer walls dominated the country.

Passing through a network of defiles, they reached the town of Coagibubig, which lay nestled among small fields where the canyon walls withdrew. There, inspired by the beauty of the scene, Kino made his first selection of a church site. He had a name for it: Nuestra Senora de los Remedios. The name Coagibubig would soon be forgotten, and Remedios would become the name of both the village and the clear little stream that curved through the pleasant valley.

Leaving the Rio Remedios, they returned over high ridges to the valley of the Rio San Miguel, riding leisurely through the live oaks and poplars, the tiny maize and melon patches, to Cosari. There Kino made a decision of great importance to him and to Pimeria Alta.

He made his way to a promontory that was approachable only from the west. Standing upon this lofty place he gazed over the valley that spread out from the mouth of a canyon with walls that stood several hundred feet in height. He had seen no place he thought more magnificent, but moved as he was by this vista, practicality was more influential in bringing him to the determination to make the high mesa his home.

Below were fields and meadows and running water. On three sides were impregnable slopes. Only one side would require defense against Apache raiders, whose homelands were not a great distance to the east. Trees marched majestically over the surrounding hills and fringed the bottomlands. Food, security, building materials were at hand, and, most important of all, manpower. Not omitted from his deliberations was the fact that Cosari was the home of Chief Coxi. Kino never ignored political ramifications of an enterprise.

On the mesa he would construct buildings, a church and mission houses, with beauty he deemed comparable to their setting. Again he was ready with a name: "On account of the noble picture of Nuestra Senora de los Dolores, which some months previously was given me by the excellent painter, Juan Correa, we named this place Nuestra Senora de los Dolores."

He rode only a hundred miles on his first journey among the Pimas, and as he enlisted workers and began to assemble materials he had difficulty in restraining himself from taking again to the saddle—there were so many more people to meet,

so much more to be discovered. Aguilar departed for his station
at Cucurpe, leaving Kino hard at work with his Pima helpers
constructing the first chapel in Pimeria Alta.

Kino took time off from the work to ride with a hundred Indians
to Tuape to celebrate Holy Week. When he returned to Dolores
he was astonished and delighted to find that, in response to letters
sent out by Aguilar by special couriers, provisions, livestock,
silverware, pictures, statuettes, decorations, and no end of messages of advice, had begun to arrive there. Of inestimable value to
him were an interpreter and a teacher sent by Father Roxes from
Urea. The interpreter, a Christian Indian named Francisco
Cantor, spoke Spanish and the Pima tongue with equal fluency.
The teacher was Cantor's brother, and he was blind.

Hundreds of Pimas came from the surrounding countryside to
live at Dolores and assist in the building and other work.
Throughout the summer the valley and the promontory rang with
the pounding and the tree cutting, and scores of Indian men and
women were busy with farming, planting fruit trees, herding
animals, and making adobes, doors, window frames, and laying
stone foundations. The walls rose, graceful in their proportions.
In the fall, two bells arrived, carried in carts over a torturous road
all the way from the Pacific coast in the vicinity of Mazatlan. They
were soon in place in the square tower, and "the natives were
very fond of listening to their peals, never before heard in these
lands . . . they are pleased also by the pictures and ornaments of
the Church."

Great excitement reigned on the day Chief Coxi and his wife,
having prepared themselves to Kino's satisfaction, were baptized. Indians came from far and near for the event, and Spanish
soldiers, officials, and colonists rode in from mining towns and
settlements, some far to the south and east. Aguilar brought his
entire choir from Cucurpe. In writing of the celebration, Kino did
not forget to note that five important chiefs from the distant

interior were present and each had requested that missionaries be sent to instruct the people over whom they ruled.

Their pleas would have been excuse enough for him to leave at once to visit their respective homelands—a most enticing prospect—and give him a chance to explore, but he overcame the temptation. Yet he admitted that his thoughts were not always on the work of completing the mission, his gaze often was held by distance, and that he was not infrequently absorbed by a vision of himself riding where no man of the cloth had ever gone. God willing, he scribbled in his notebook, the time would soon come when he would feel himself completely free to set out in good conscience, with no feeling that he was neglecting his duties.

His pen was busy, not only recording events of the day and recounting past experiences but writing a stream of begging letters. They were clever letters, for he was a genius at getting things out of people. There were so many things he needed to carry out the plans he had in mind—more tools, animals, clothing, seeds, fowls—the list was endless. He offered to make one father with whom he corresponded a co-founder of Dolores "if you should be pleased to send a little wax, a little sayal, some little chomites, some glass beads, a little Ruan de China, some little blankets, or any of those trifles . . ." The recipient of the letter thought the word "little" a bit overworked, but his irritation did not prevent him from promptly sending the requested articles by mule packs from Metape.

Kino succeeded in controlling his restlessness through the winter, but by the spring of 1688 he found himself unable to resist longer his craving to look into the most remote parts of Pimeria Alta, and he began the series of desert journeys that would not only bring him renown as an explorer and cartographer but as a wilderness missionary.

The following years, numbering more than two score, would be a pattern in themselves, standing apart as a complete whole from those preceding them, each welded inseparably to the others. They would be years in which he was cruelly beset upon, not only by renegade Indians, but by colleagues who charged him with neglecting his religious duties and by mine and ranch operators who accused him of inhibiting the economic growth of Mexico by defeating their attempts to exploit Indians. They would be years in which his courage would undergo gruelling tests, adventurous, violent, bloody, sweet and joyous years. Every quality and talent he possessed would be permitted its fullest expression, and some of the plans and programs dearest to him would be throttled and prohibited, leaving him dejected and on the verge of abandoning Pimeria Alta. Few missionaries would be sent to assist him, and most of those who came soon departed, unwilling or unable to endure the isolation, the loneliness, the rigors of life among wild tribes in an uncompromising wilderness. Yet he would stay, and the years would end much as they had begun, with a symmetry and conformity that left few undisciplined fragments.

Kino was the founder of at least thirty missions in Pimeria Alta, one of the most notable being San Xavier del Bac, near Tucson, Arizona, annually visited by thousands of persons of all faiths, who go there to see the magnificent cathedral that stands today where he built a small chapel.

Yet it would be an insufficient tribute if he were portrayed only as a builder of religious shrines. He established an equal number of ranches, with herds of livestock, with fields and orchards and vineyards, and he constructed irrigation systems to water them. He was the founder of the great cattle business that still thrives today on the immense ranges of Arizona and northern Mexico.

His missions and his projects were not penal institutions, not *encomiendas*. No Indians were held in bondage, or forced to labor, or thrown into dungeons, or lashed, or starved, all in the name of God, by Kino. He placed no restrictions on the freedom of the Indian workers, and he did not seek to destroy their culture.

He sought to win the Indians to Christianity through patient teaching and gentle training, by awakening in them a sense of responsibility, by demonstrating that only through their own toil and reasonable behavior could they progress and enjoy the fruits and comforts of civilization.

As a desert explorer, both for his intrepidity and his achievements, Kino has no equal. He penetrated virtually every part of Pimeria Alta, opening trails hundreds of miles in length and charting them on superbly executed maps. He crossed the Rio Colorado near its delta, establishing beyond question that Baja California was an unbroken peninsula. He discovered thousands of Indians who had never seen a white man. The geographical and geological knowledge he recorded brought acclaim from the greatest scholars and scientists of both the Old and New Worlds.

Kino in time saw no alternative to the use of martial methods in defending the prosperous ranches he had established among the Pimas and Sobaipuris. As an apostle of peace, the realization came as one of the most profound disappointments he had known. He had clung as long as possible to the hope that an amnesty might be negotiated with the Apaches, but at last understood that he had been guilty of wishful thinking. The implacability of the Apaches obviously was impervious to all academic means usually employed in seeking an accord; for them warfare was a way of life; banditry was the cornerstone of their economy. Condemnation of them as demonic savages and unreconcilable infidels was nothing more than rhetoric which, if it served to relieve the intensity of his emotions, contributed nothing toward a solution of the problem. That could be accomplished only by strong defensive measures and violent retaliation.

He set out to bring them into operation, dispelling with the strength of his conviction that he was right all doubts that God would choose to forgive him for the cruelties and bloodshed he prepared to condone. Spanish colonial statutes prohibited trading in fire arms and ammunition with all Indians, and penalties for violations were severe. Kino made no attempt to circumvent the laws, but he did propose a plan which the military officials of Sonora, who held jurisdiction in Pimeria Alta, found acceptable.

Kino's proposal involved training Pima and Sobaipuri warriors—to be selected by him—as soldiers. These trustworthy Indian fighters would not be supplied with guns, but would be taught to use them. The Apaches were a known quantity, their intensions were unmistakable, their incursions could be expected, and, moreover, there was no doubt of their guilt. The number of soldiers available to halt, or even to curtail, their raiding was insufficient. Therefore, in times of emergency, the military would have available strong contingents of Pimas and Sobaipuris. Retaliatory campaigns could be quickly plotted and executed. When the offensives were completed the weapons could be taken from Kino's reinforcements and withheld until use of them was needed again. No law would be violated, for the Pimas and Sobaipuris selected would be duly sworn in a reserve troops.

Kino wrote of his plan to his superiors, and it was rejected on the grounds that it might be construed as improper interference by the Church in military and civil affairs. Having the support of the commanding general of Sonora, however, he proceeded to implement it. The results were gratifying. On several occasions Apache invaders were routed with heavy losses. About all Kino wrote of the bloody Indian war he had started, however, was: "Through some good victories of our Pimas the hostile Apaches were greatly restrained, and now molest us somewhat less frequently."

In every report he submitted, probably in every communication he sent to church officials in Mexico City, Kino included a fervent plea for more missionaries. But during his twenty-four years in Pimeria Alta only twenty-nine appeared at Dolores, and most of their number, as will be seen by the following accounting, were on trips or held only brief tenure.

Augustin de Campos served the longest, eighteen years, and Geronimo Minuteli served for eight years. Four were there for three years. Two served two years, and one for one year, before departing. Sixteen left after serving less than a year. Francisco Gonzalvo died after three years' service. Death took Juan Bautista Barli and Ignacio Yturmendi less than a year after they arrived. Francisco Xavier Saeta was murdered by outlaw Indians only five months after he had taken his post.

The projects, tasks, and obligations Kino designed and specified for Pimeria Alta were formidable. He was neither so impractical nor so optimistic, however, as to believe it possible to accomplish more than a small part of them during his lifetime, but he did believe that others would carry on after he was gone. He could be elated and encouraged, but never was he blind to realities.

If the Pimas were no more than a step out of the Stone Age, they were not stupid. If they were simple, they were not unwilling to improve themselves. If they were ignorant, they were not unwilling to learn. He was cheered by their eagerness for knowledge, to progress, to obtain the miraculous resources of the white man. Yet, he recognized the limits of their capacity to absorb, to utilize, to comprehend; progress would come slowly; no drastic changes would be quickly achieved. For he knew that they must be made to understand that new ways of life meant a loss of much of the freedom they had known, meant acceptance of responsibilities unfamiliar to them, meant restrictions on passions and urges to which they had always given free rein, meant adherence to customs and mores and beliefs that were totally foreign to them.

In Kino's philosophy faith was a two-way street. If he wanted the Indians to have faith in his God, he must first convince them that his God had faith in them.

He saw himself as an uncommon middleman, a teacher as well

as a purveyor, and upon his own shoulders must rest the burden of the results of his efforts, be they good or bad.

And he understood that people to whom a small ironware utensil, a horsehoe nail, a glittering trinket, brought forth cries of pleasure could not be expected to accept without qualms or objections, rules and decrees which were beyond their comprehension.

In Indian minds all forces governing them emanated from the sun and stars and moon; regulations were born of winds; rules were promulgated by thunder and lightning and rain. Their gods, any number of them, dwelt in both animate and inanimate objects, in the unreachable beyond.

He knew that Indians were not dumb animals, as so many persons, even some of his colleagues, held them to be. God had created them in the image of all mankind, and to him that meant that they were like all other people on earth. It meant that among them were dull minds and brilliant intellects, bullies and cowards and degenerates, wastrels and profligates, thieves and false prophets. Indians were flesh and blood and brain, sensitive to physical and mental pain, to deception, to hunger, to illness, capable of joy, of remorse, of humor, of grief, of savage anger—of every human reaction.

The hope of transforming them from heathens to devout Christians had brought him to them. That was the supreme objective of his life, but it could not be permitted to stand as his only objective. His holy work must of necessity be performed in conjunction with secular endeavors which he believed, by virtue of every law propounded either in heaven or on earth, he was morally and legally obligated to execute to the fullest extent of his ability. He waged two crusades in Pimeria Alta: to conquer for God and to conquer for man.

Plentiful and assured food supplies, comforts and security, held Indians in their villages. He adhered to a formula of extraordinary simplicity: people could not be instructed, could not be catechized, could not be converted, if they could not be held together, if they could not be found.

Every attribute Kino exhibited stirred admiration in the Indians and won their trust. He was a physical man they could understand, and he was an intellectual man that awakened them to curiosity and wonder. His endurance seemed to be inexhaustible. When he was more than fifty years of age, still lythe and bony, he could swing a saddle onto a mount, rope a cow, and tie a packload hitch with the efficiency of a vaquero. He could butcher and reap, labor in the fields, dig in an irrigation ditch, herd stock, lay bricks.

The Indians thought that he could hear the talking of the stars, because he knew so much about them. He could tell why the sun and the moon rose and the winds blew and the grasses grew, and he could put mysterious words and lines on pieces of paper, showing the ways of the rivers and the contours of hills and mesas and mountains.

The Indians knew and sometimes feared a man whose eyes could grow cold and burn with hot fire in quick changes, a man who could be hard and stern and thunder at them for their mistakes and their infractions, and in the next moment laugh with them and be patient and applaud their songs and dancing. They also knew a man who brought soldiers to guard them against invaders, and who would, if necessary, fight himself to protect them.

It was not a single attribute, however, any more than it was a single achievement, that set Kino apart from, and above, the colleagues and others with whom he was associated in his adventurous life. It was a unique and complex mixture of intellectual gifts, moral and spiritual beliefs, and physical qualities which, even though each was pronounced and well defined in itself, united in motivating and guiding him and functioned in smooth accord.

Kino was not only a shepherd of souls, but a hard riding

herdsman of cattle. Leather chaparejos were as much a part of his dress as the black robe of his office. His earthly flocks were comprised not only of converts, but of sheep and chickens and ducks, geese, and turkeys. He sowed not only the seeds of gospel but the seeds of wheat, maize, oats, cotton. He fashioned adobe bricks not only for naves and altars but for houses and barns.

To Kino religion meant more than piety and devotion, more than instructing neophytes, more than saying Mass, more than prayer. It also meant building, creating, opening unknown lands, and leading the Indians in them to peace and progress through social enlightenment and the development of a stable economy.

Kino understood—as so many missionaries did not—that without the harmonious blending of the material with the spiritual into a force beneficial to all, the walls and bell towers of his missions could not long stand and his flourishing fields could not long survive.

He was right. Within a few years after his life came to an end, the slavers, the exploiters, the money-mad mine owners and cattlemen, spurred by their insatiable greed, had swept through Pimeria Alta. Starving, hunted down, slaughtered, the Indians, although they fought bravely to save themselves, were destroyed. And Kino's churches and ranches fell into dust, and soon there were only small piles of rubble to tell the world that they had existed.

Early on a bright March morning in 1711, Kino strapped on stained buckskin pants under his black woolen habit, and went to the corral behind his residence at Dolores. He had not felt well for several days, knowing a weakness in his legs, and it was with some strain and unsteadiness that he gained the saddle on the fine large mule a vaquero held for him.

Alone he set out for Magdalena, taking the trail through the hills that stood to the west of the Rio San Miguel. It was the same trail over which he had ridden in 1687, also on a bright March morning, on his first journey into Pimeria Alta. And as it had been on that day twenty-four years before the country was brilliant in the dress of spring, new leaves rolling emerald billows against a clear blue sky, and flowers covering the slopes in ragged yellow and red blankets, and the perfumes of the awakened earth filling the soft airs.

He was on his way to Magdalena to dedicate a new chapel at the request of his old and dear friend, Father Campos. Sitting in the sun, gazing down from the mission on the fields and orchards of Dolores would have been a more agreeable way to spend the day, but he had mustered his strength, determined not to disappoint Campos and the Indians he knew would be awaiting him.

On March 15, 1711, Campos wrote in his church record:

"A little after midnight, Father Eusebio Francisco Kino died with great peace and edification in this house and pueblo of Santa Magdalena. He is buried in a coffin in this chapel of San Francisco Xavier on the Gospel side."

CHAPTER TEN

California:
The Northern Threat

The conversion of Indian infidels and the establishment of the Catholic faith in new lands were not the chief purposes underlying Spain's occupation of Alta California. Some efforts, however, were made to affix upon the military action the outward appearance of a spiritual crusade.

In reality, the conquest, launched in 1769, was seen as politically expedient. Territorial protection was the primary objective, but economic factors relative to international commerce also were given due consideration by government officials. Religious elements were injected into the costly and complex undertaking with impious practicality. The coffers of the Church were a source of revenue, and affluent old missions of Mexico and Baja California could be forced to contribute food staples, livestock, clothing, blankets, vehicles, leather products, utensils, church furnishings, and a variety of other articles, all to the relief of the royal treasury.

Yet, despite the low priority accorded ecclesiastical programs in plans for the northern expansion, it would be the missions of Alta California that, before many years had passed, would wield the greatest influence on the affairs of the colony. Established at convenient intervals northward from San Diego to San Francisco

Bay, their agricultural and industrial prosperity would surpass by far successes of this type by any civilian endeavors. If the missionaries would hold no political or judicial offices, they would be suzerains whose social, commercial and religious powers would be, for more than half a century, virtually unassailable.

Colonization of Alta California was by no means a new idea in 1769. Indeed, it was a very old proposal, having been under consideration by the Spanish Court and the Council of the Indies for more than one hundred and sixty years. In May 1602, the three ships of the expedition of Sebastian Vizcaino, a wealthy Basque merchant and adventurer, had sailed from Acapulco for the purpose of exploring Alta California, determining its suitability for settlement, reporting on its natural resources, mapping its geographical features, and examining and noting the landmarks of protected harbors. Some of this information was already recorded, for a number of voyages had been made earlier along the California coast and landings, although brief, had been made.[1]

However, after Vizcaino's voyage of 1602 no other exploring vessel had passed along the northern Pacific shores. Galleons in the Spanish Oriental trade, returning with prevailing winds from Manila, sometimes sighted the snow-capped peaks of California ranges. Battered by the vicious north Pacific storms, badly in need of refitting and relief, their crews ravaged by scurvy, these ships carrying heavy cargoes of Far East treasures, dared not stop in ports that were not protected by Spanish guns or equipped to fulfill their needs.

If not forgotten, California was neglected land, and all efforts of Vizcaino and Fray Antonio de la Ascension, who was with him, to persuade the government to possess and utilize the fine California harbors and establish presidios and missions were futile.

The expedition of Vizcaino merits consideration in this work because it marked the beginning of the long struggle by various ecclesiastical orders to carry Christianity to the Indians of the immense region that would become American California.

Another important reason for its inclusion is that the great bulk of the findings, reports, accounts, studies, and maps resulting from it were either written by or prepared under the direction of the missionary, Fray Ascension.

A learned man of many talents and achievements, Ascension was a noted cosmographer, a student of natural history, an expert navigator, and a distinguished religious of the Barefoot Order of Nuestra Senora del Carmel. He left to posterity invaluable descriptions of Indians, animals, fish, and birds, and he drew remarkably accurate charts and scientifically recorded the topography of the Pacific Coast from Cabo de San Lucas, at the southern tip of Baja California, to Point Reyes, north of the waterway that would become known as the Golden Gate. He fell in love with Alta California, ecstatically praised its beauty, repeatedly expressed the conviction that the land contained great treasures of gold and other precious metals, and extolled its natural resources of fertile soils, forests, and grasslands.[2]

Vizcaino's flagship, on which Ascension was a passenger, was the two-hundred-ton *San Diego*. It was accompanied by the *San Tomas,* about half its size, and the *Tres Reyes,* an open *fragata,* probably no more than forty tons burden. Crowded aboard the vessels were more than two hundred men. Progress was slow as they worked their way northward in the Pacific for they encountered adverse winds and thick fogs, and they stopped frequently to chart the coast and make observations. It was not until the beginning of November 1602, six months after they had started from Acapulco, that they passed to the north of the future borderline between Mexico and American California. "Little by little," wrote Ascension, "they made their voyage, coasting along the land, on all of which many fires and smokes were seen by day and by night. These the Indians made, as if calling to the ships to come close to their country, which showed indications of being good, fertile and level and was of pleasing aspect."

On November 10 they entered a bay which they named Puerto

de San Diego, "a port very capacious, good, large and safe, as it was protected from all winds."[3] With warm fall weather prevailing, Vizcaino decided to rest for a time in the pleasant harbor, clean and repair the ships, and take on wood and fresh water. He "ordered a spacious tent set up on shore to serve as a church where the friars could say mass every day they were there." Undoubtedly these were the first full Christian services before a properly adorned altar to be conducted in Alta California.

The Indians were extremely friendly and hospitable, bringing the Spaniards "fine skins of martens, cats, seals and other animals, net bags and little nets with which they fished." The waters gave up a rich harvest of "white fish called smelts, skates, oysters, mussels, sardines, lobsters . . . and there were many white and brown geese, ducks, quails, hares, and rabbits." On one beach "there was a great quantity of sparkling golden pyrites," which Ascension took as "a sure sign that there must be gold mines in the mountains." On a sandbar "there were some great large pieces like cow dung, very light in weight . . . some said they were pieces of amber."

On December 16, the three ships entered a large bay which Vizcaino christened Monterey in honor of the Viceroy of New Spain.

The beauty of the harbor and the surrounding country deeply stirred Ascension. He thought it an ideal place to establish a colony, a mission, and a haven for the homebound galleons from the Orient. "Those who come from China," he said, "could very well resort to this port. It is in the same region and parallel of latitude as Seville, and is almost of the same climate . . . It is a very good port and well protected from all winds. There is much wood and water in it and an immense number of great pine trees, smooth and straight, suitable for the masts and yards of ships; many very large live-oaks with which to build ships . . . There are rock-roses, broom, roses of Castile . . . beautiful large lakes, which were covered with ducks and many other birds; most fertile pastures; good meadows for cattle, and fertile fields for growing crops. There are many different kinds of animals . . . large bears, lions, elk, deer, stags, rabbits, geese, doves, quail, partridges . . . many good fish . . . oysters, lobsters, crabs . . . many large seals and whales."

He expressed the belief that all the great kingdom of Alta California could be "pacified very peaceably in a very short time. Not only would large numbers of heathen be brought into Christianity's fold, but great economic progress would be achieved. From Monterey expeditions could be sent to occupy kingdoms farther north, "and from there to Great China, the Great Tartary . . . Thus His Majesty could come with great ease to be king and supreme emperor of all the world with a good and quiet conscience . . ."

Interwoven into Ascension's glowing account of Alta California is a tragic tale of terrible sickness and death. Even before the ships had departed from San Diego many men of the company had begun to succumb to the great scourge of the sea, scurvy, caused by a deficiency of ascorbic acid, obtainable in fresh fruits and leafy vegetables, and so vital to good health.

By the time Monterey had been reached, sixteen men had been buried at sea, and "there was not scarcely one who could say he was entirely sound and perfectly well . . . there were deaths each day . . . The sensitiveness of the bodies of these sick people is so great that the very clothing put on them is felt like sharp darts or cruel lances . . . they emit cries so pitiful that they reach the heavens . . . this sickness and pestilential humour brings on other results more insufferable and loathsome . . . the upper and lower gums become swollen . . . the teeth become so loose and without support that they move." Victims "spat out unexpectedly a couple of teeth at a time." The disease "attacks the back and the kidneys so that one cannot move . . . there is no consolation except to ask God to help one or to take one away from this life."

In a council on the desperate situation it was decided to send the

Santo Tomas back to Acapulco with the seriously afflicted. The *San Diego* and the little *Tres Reyes* would go on with the "rest of the men who were with some strength," and attempt to carry out the Viceroy's order to explore the coast at least as far north as Cape Mendocino. Reports for the Count of Monterey were quickly prepared, and on December 29 the *Santo Tomas* sailed southward with its pitiful cargo.

More than forty soldiers, sailors, and officers had died as the year ended, and others would perish, but Ascension believed that "our Lord, Jesus Christ, was pleased that all passed away after having been confessed and received extreme unction, and having made their wills, arranged for the welfare of their souls and discharged their consciences."

On January 3, 1603, the *San Diego* and the *Tres Reyes* sailed on a disastrous voyage to the north. The ships became separated. The *San Diego* touched at Puerto de San Francisco (Drake's Bay) and then went on until, on January 13, Cape Mendocino came in sight. There it was struck by a fierce storm and was forced to turn back. Ascension recorded that "there were not six men on board all told who were well and up." Ascension and the other two friars were among the afflicted. A course was set for Mexico.

A ship of death, the *San Diego* reached Mazatlan with only five men possessing enough strength to handle the sails and steer. Miraculously within three weeks the health of all survivors was restored. The cure came, as Ascension recounted, "not by doctors or surgeons, medicines or other drugs from the pharmacies, not by any human remedy....." It came from "papayas, bananas, oranges, lemons, pumpkins, and *quiletes* (a vegetable eaten as greens).

Manned by healthy sailors, the *San Diego* sailed into Acapulco on March 19. The *Tres Reyes* arrived a few day later, its surviving crew and passengers also restored to good health by fruits and vegetables which had been obtained at Navidad.

The proposals of Vizcaino and Ascension for economic and

religious projects in Alta California were submitted to the Spanish Government at the beginning of an era of decadence in Mexico. Officials in both Spain and New Spain found them feasible, but withheld endorsements and advocated postponement with the vague excuse that the time for such expansion and developments was not propitious. The apathy was, in reality, reflective of several conditions, each of which steadily continued to deteriorate as the years passed.

The adventurous spirit of the conquerors was rapidly fading away. The dreams that great cities and fabulous treasures existed somewhere in the mysterious north no longer inspired royal advisers to advocate organizing expensive fleets and armies for new conquests. By virtue of discovery and landings, Spain could legitimately assert its sovereignty in Alta California, and that, at least for the time being, was all that was required. Should the claim be rejected by some other power—admittedly a possibility, for it was still believed that somewhere in the far north there was a water passage between the Atlantic and Pacific—counter measures could be taken as the situation demanded. The seventeenth century passed with every province of Mexico wallowing in commercial and spiritual stagnation. The northeastern frontier was continually aflame with Indian warfare, and New Mexico was lost in the Pueblo revolt for twelve years before being retaken.

The first half of the eighteenth century brought no improvement in some areas and none at all in most sections of New Spain. Poorly equipped soldiers carried on their routine duties, fighting frontier savages "in a listless mechanical way that but feebly reflected old-time glories. Presidios were a kind of public works for the support of officials, and the drawing of money from the royal coffers . . . The most famous mineral districts had yielded their richest superficial treasures and were now, by reason of savage raids, inefficient working, and the quicksilver monopoly, comparatively abandoned. Commercial, agricultural, and manufacturing industries were now at a low ebb. The native population had lost more than nine-tenths of its original numbers, the survivors living quietly, toiling in the mines or on the haciendas practically as slaves."[4]

If the missionary zeal of the Franciscans, Jesuits, and other Orders had not abated, the missions of Mexico had passed the era of their greatest prosperity. A number in the south had been reduced by secularization, their lands taken by vicious politicians and settlers. Pestilence, Indian warfare, and the desertions of neophytes had decimated the population of missions in Texas, New Mexico, and other areas of the northeastern frontier, forcing consolidation or abandonment. Appeals of the Church and of the missionaries for assistance and protection were largely unheeded by Spanish officials.

Partial awakening from the lethargy occurred in the middle of the century, when it became known to Spanish authorities that Russia was conducting explorations along the northern Pacific Coast. Obvious questions held the attention of the Spanish court: What were the Czar's intentions? How far south from Alaska did he intend to send his ships? Was it only the fur trade that prompted the advance? The answers proffered were no more than mere speculations, and they gave way to a growing fear that a real threat to Spanish claims had at last arisen. King Carlos III, acting in accordance with the opinions of his advisers, took urgent action.

In the early summer of 1768, the Marquis De Croix, Viceroy of Mexico, received a royal order to occupy Alta California and fortify the ports of San Diego and Monterey. He promptly sent it on to Inspector-General Jose Galvez, at the time on the west coast, with instructions to see that it was fulfilled with the greatest possible speed. The Viceroy also received a letter from the Spanish Minister of Foreign Affairs, the Marquis de Grimaldi, which said: "The Russians have at different times made various efforts to open communication with America, and they have at last succeeded by entering the South Sea from the north. The king has commanded me to inform Your Excellency so that you may instruct the governor appointed for California, and give him your orders concerning the vigilance and care which he must exercise in order to observe the attempts which the Russians might make, frustrating them as much as possible, and giving to your Excellency prompt notice of everything for the information of his Majesty.''[5] This document was also sent at once to Galvez, who replied that organization of the expedition was underway.

Galvez, a member of the Council of the Indies, had been sent to Mexico in 1765 to effect badly needed administrative reforms, particularly with regard to financial affairs. By royal command, he was invested with almost absolute powers. He had authority to operate independently under the provisions of his assignment; therefore, except in title, he was the ranking official in New Spain. Viceroy Croix, a dutiful and complaisant man, did not attempt to interfere in his activities or overrule his decisions.

Thus, it came to pass that a man who would never set foot on Alta California soil was alone responsible for organizing and giving orders to the expeditions that would occupy the north country on the Pacific. Moreover, it was Galvez who made possible the founding of the famous California mission system, but, as will be seen, the methods he employed in this accomplishment were not within the confines of traditional practices.

Galvez crossed the Sea of Cortez to Baja California in July 1768. He had already formed his plans for the conquest. To lessen the possibility of failure, he would send two forces by sea and two by land. The assembling of equipment and supplies, the fitting-out of ships, the enlisting of personnel, including craftsmen, the issuance of orders to presidios to assign troops to both land and sea divisions, proceeded with dispatch. Now he gave his attention to the religious aspects of the great enterprise.

Determined to save the royal treasury all possible expense, Galvez announced that missions in western Mexico and in Baja California would be called upon to contribute generously to the task of founding new missions in Alta California. These contributions were to be in the form of livestock, seeds, implements, household and church furnishings, food supplies, and all manner of products and equipment. Galvez did not permit any of the old missions to submit a list of the donations it would make. He sent military aides through the country to determine how much each mission could spare. The result was that some missions were almost stripped of material possessions. This arbitrary action marked the beginning of the policy under which, in the years ahead, the missions of Alta California were heavily taxed for the support of presidios and the civil government. This practice would be strenuously opposed by California missionaries and high church officials for more than half a century, to no avail. In view of the prosperity of the California missions and the fact that all labor was performed by imprisoned Indians who were rewarded with nothing but food and poor clothing, the hardship on the missions was not as severe as the objectors made it out to be.

Next Galvez, without legal right and most significantly without opposition from any high official, seized control of the account called the Pious Fund. It contained money, voluntarily donated by religious persons, that was to be expended only for missionary purposes, and the Spanish treasury had no authority to order disbursements from it. Galvez used Pious Fund money, amounting to more than $136,000, to help defray the costs of the land and sea companies.

Intelligence regarding Galvez's large-scale preparations was soon widely disseminated and no doubt reached the ears of foreign emissaries in the West Indies who, of course, would send urgent dispatches to Europe. Probably as a diplomatic cover and to weaken anticipated complaints by the clergy, he publicly asserted that the objective of the expeditions was to extend the Catholic faith. Hence no efforts could be spared without offending God.

Superior of the Franciscans in Baja California at the time was Junipero Serra, a highly educated and enterprising Majorcan Fray who had been a theologian and professor of philosophy at the University of Palma before being transferred to Mexico in 1749.

He had been a New World missionary twenty years when he was requested by Galvez to undertake the conversion to Christianity of all Indians residing in the northern regions which were to be secured for the Crown.

Although he was fifty-six years of age and suffering from a badly ulcerated leg, for which he had found no cure, he readily accepted the commission as spiritual leader of the venture. Before conferring with him he was well aware of what Galvez had done, well apprised of his boldness in levying heavy tributes on the missions and his usurpation of the Pious Fund. However, Serra's unquenchable zeal, rising to new heights with the unprecedented opportunity to carry the word of God to untamed lands, blinded him to all other considerations. If he had any misgivings, about either the Inspector-General's motives or his confiscatory actions, he chose not to reveal them. He announced that he would join one of the land divisions, and would at once make a tour to obtain priests whom he thought qualified for the conquest.

Galvez was not only persuasive, but uncommonly thorough, even to the point of issuing edicts regarding religious procedures. "It is but just," he wrote Serra, "that each missionary should invoke the protection of his own patron saints, and particularly the numerous and great saints of the seraphic family of our holy Father San Francisco. We see to this day that the ancient discoverers for that reason, as though in happy prophesy, applied the names of some of them to the principal places on the coast below and above Monterey. They called San Diego the port where now one of the new missions is to be located. This appellation must not be changed. To another famous port, situated in thirty-eight and one-half degrees, they assigned the name of the glorious Patriarch San Francisco. Nor must we alter this appropriate title; for, after having secured a foothold at Monterey, the first mission beyond shall belong to him; and our great Father, so beloved of God, will facilitate its founding by means of his power of intercession."

There was to be an "intermediate mission" between San Diego and Monterey, and, declared Galvez, it "shall be called San

Buenaventura in order that he defend it. Those missions that shall be established thereafter shall take the names of other saints of the same Order.''

No detail in the execution of the conquest was too small to be ignored by Galvez. He was a master logistician, and, with one significant exception, he was as well informed about the personalities, characters, and abilities of the commanders he selected as he was about the manifests of the cargoes to be transported to the north. The exception was Junipero Serra, the frail, quiet, outwardly gentle Franciscan who would be *presidente* of the Alta California missions.

Both Serra's physical appearance and his mild manner were deceptive in that they might cause an observer who did not know him well to misjudge his inherent qualities. He was excruciatingly thin, his shoulder bones creasing the well-worn if not frayed habit he customarily wore, his bare feet, bound in stained rope sandals, hardly larger than those of a youth. He stood no more than an inch or two over five feet. Nothing is known of his facial features, except that his eyes were dark and quickly, but normally only briefly, reflective of his emotions.[6]

The nature encased in this unprepossessing body was extraordinary in its composition. Indomitable courage, indestructible optimism, extreme stubbornness, stern discipline, unusual practicality, and religious fanaticism—only some of the elements—seemed to live in him without engendering harmful conflicts. Indeed, all seemed to contribute in some mysterious way toward moving him along the course to the supreme objective of his life, unqualified devotion to his faith.

Fray Palou, who was Serra's closest friend and his confessor for more than thirty years, wrote more than any of his contemporaries about Serra's asceticism and self-mortification. He recorded that often Serra prayed throughout the night, denying himself sleep until he was near to collapsing from exhaustion. Serra ate hardly enough to sustain himself, disdaining flesh, and partaking hurriedly of fruit, nuts, vegetables, and seafood, as if he thought eating a wasteful exercise to be dispensed with as quickly as possible.

Serra frequently resorted to violent dramatization in his preaching. He would drop his habit to the waist and cruelly lash his bare body with a chain. After delivering a sermon on sin and repentence, he would take up a large stone in one hand, a crucifix in the other, and beat his chest with such force that persons in his audience would sob and rise in terror, fearing that he would kill himself. On other occasions he burned his hands and arms with lighted tapers. Alone in some mission room, he would flog himself until he was bleeding from numerous lacerations. Palou states that this bodily chastisement, "inflicted as an act of Penitence and to bring his body into subjugation to the Divine Will, was stealthily observed by some friars, who were edified by the sight."[7]

Galvez was aware of Serra's extreme devoutness and his record as a capable missionary, but I have found no evidence to suggest that in selecting him as president of the missions to be founded Galvez entertained the slightest suspicion that he might also be sanctioning the creation and development of a religious autonomy. It appears doubtful that Galvez ever thought of Serra in the role of an uncompromising spiritual dictator.

Seemingly more realistic is the assumption that Galvez didn't care how well he understood Serra, or perhaps didn't care whether he understood him at all. In any case, I think it most unlikely that Galvez would have changed his mind after a *fraille* of Serra's prominence and experience had so willingly and agreeably endorsed his plans. For Galvez, the occupation of Alta California was the important goal; preservation of Spain's position as a dominant New World power must be accorded priority over all other considerations.[8]

On April 11, 1769, the deep-sea packet *San Antonio* twenty-four days out of Cabo San Lucas, dropped anchor in San Diego Bay. The captain was Juan Perez, a veteran of the Royal Navy who had seen service in both the Atlantic and the trans-Pacific trade. Aboard were two friars, Juan Vizcaino and Francisco

Gomez. No soldiers were on the vessel, the only other passengers being a number of carpenters and blacksmiths. Every inch of cargo space was filled with supplies and equipment. Several members of the crew were afflicted with the first stages of scurvy.

The conquest of Alta California had begun, but not quite in accord with the hopes of Galvez. More than a month before the *San Antonio* had put out from Cabo San Lucas, the *San Carlos,* flagship of the expedition, had sailed from La Paz. Commanded by Vincent Villa, a sailing master of the Spanish Navy, the *San Carlos* was to meet the *San Antonio* at San Diego, and the two ships, after landing padres and a small garrison, were to proceed northward to Monterey.

Captain Perez stared from the bridge of the *San Antonio* over a bay empty except for a few Indians in crude canoes who made gestures of friendship and proffered gifts of seafood. The *San Carlos* had not arrived. Nor had the advance guard of the first overland division which had started from Velicata, Baja California, in March, reached the San Diego rendezvous. As if he might have feared that such a situation would occur, Galvez had provided Perez with instructions dealing with it. Perez was to wait at San Diego twenty days for the *San Carlos* before sailing on to Monterey. As no soldiers were on the *San Antonio,* no landing was to be made. Perez obeyed.

Eighteen of the twenty-day period had passed, and Perez was making preparations to depart, when the *San Carlos* appeared and dropped anchor, but gave no signal nor lowered a boat. Perez sent crewmen in a launch to ascertain the reason for the silence. They found almost everyone on board stricken with scurvy. Hospital tents made of sailcloth were quickly erected on shore, and the sick were removed to them by the *San Antonio's* sailors.

The *San Carlos* had been one hundred and ten days at sea. Storms had driven her more than two hundred leagues—nearly six hundred miles—southwestward from the Baja California coast. After weeks of fighting gales, with very little potable water remaining in broken casks, a landing was made at Cedros Island, but only water of bad quality was obtained. Repairs were made with great difficulty, for there were by this time few men aboard who were not seriously weakened or totally incapacitated by scurvy.

The *San Carlos* had started with a complement of three officers, twenty-three seamen, two cabin boys, and four cooks. Passengers were a surgeon, Pedro Prat; a friar, Hernando Parron; two blacksmiths; and twenty-five soldiers commanded by Lieutenant Pedro Fages. Two sailors had been buried at sea. Of the remaining sixty men, twenty-seven crewmen and soldiers would die of the dreadful scourge in the pest house on the beach. At least nine crewmen of the *San Antonio* also had died of the same cause while that ship was waiting in the harbor for the *San Carlos*. By a strange twist of fate, none of the officers of either ship, nor the three friars, nor Dr. Prat, suffered seriously from the disease.

The land divisions fared better. The first came in sight of San Diego Bay about noon on May 14. It was comprised of twenty-five soldiers under Captain Fernando Rivera; a diarist and geographer, Jose Canizares; three muleteers; and a group of Christianized Indians from the northern missions of Baja California. The latter were to assist the muleteers as packers and *vacqueros* in handling the supply train and livestock, clear passages through dense desert thickets, and perform all menial tasks. Probably from a combination of excessive toil and terror—they were being taken into strange lands inhabited by traditional enemies— several sickened and died, and a number—nine on one night— deserted and were not recaptured. Forty-two of these miserable natives started from Velicata but only fourteen completed the journey. At all times during the last three weeks of the march, which took fifty-one days, at least one and often two seriously ill soldiers had to be carried on litters. Only one friar was with the company. He was Juan Crespi, a close friend of Serra, and he, too, kept a diary.

The second land division arrrived in several parties. First to appear in the last week of June were Sergeant Jose Ortega and one soldier, who announced that the others were a few days behind them.

Next, with a small retinue, came Governor Gaspar de Portola, who besides having been chief executive of Baja California also held the rank of Captain and had been commander of troops stationed on the peninsula. Now he would begin his tenure as the first governor of Alta California. Bancroft describes him as "an easy-going, popular man, but brave and honest withal."

On July 1, Serra, a platoon of soldiers, four muleteers, two personal servants, and twelve Indian neophytes, trailed by a packtrain and a herd of cattle, were welcomed by shouts and gunfire. As they had followed Rivera's trail, no serious difficulties had been encountered, and all were in relatively good health. No deaths had occurred, but the fate of thirty Indian laborers who deserted and vanished into the Baja California mountains was not known.

During part of the journey Serra had endured great pain from the ulcers on his foot and leg, at one time being so badly crippled that he was unable to ride a mule and scarcely able to walk. Portola had wanted him to return to Mexico for treatment, but Serra refused. The governor ordered a litter made for him. Serra seemed to be deeply troubled by his situation, declaring that he would not impose on the Indians the extra hardship of carrying him. He spent several hours alone in prayer, pleading for the courage and strength to go on, but expressing his willingness to die beside the trail if that were God's will.

Relief came quickly and in an unexpected manner. Juan Coronel, a muleteer, prepared a hot ointment of herbs and tallow with which he had had some success in healing galls on the backs of pack animals. He applied the potion liberally to Serra's foot and leg. The pain soon vanished, and Serra slept well. The next day he walked with comparative ease, suffering not at all, and the company moved on. From San Diego he would write Fray Palou: "Now the foot is all sound like the other, while from the ankle half way up the leg it is as the foot was before, an ulcer; but without swelling or pain except the occasional itching." His colleagues believed to a man that they had been privileged to witness a most unusual case, in which the Lord had chosen to answer Serra's prayers in a most extraordinary manner—through the medium of grease used on beasts of burden. It was a matter to be reflected upon with reverent thought.[9]

On July 14, taking with him most of the men strong enough to travel, Portola started north by land on his famous trail-breaking expedition to Monterey Bay. He and his men would look upon it but would not recognize it from the descriptions in their possession. Continuing the search, some of the company would go on north and would be the first Europeans to gaze upon what they mistook for a great inland sea. They had discovered the southern reaches of San Francisco Bay. In January 1701, Portola was back in San Diego, profoundly discouraged by his failure. But Monterey would be found and properly identified by a second expedition, also led by Portola, the following May.

Meanwhile, the first California mission, christened San Diego de Alcala, had been founded by Serra near an arm of San Diego Bay. It comprised a cluster of huts, one of which had been dedicated as a Church, and a corral. The Indians, who would come to be known in history as Dieguenos, were ugly, clearly manifesting their resentfulness at the intrusion. They would be described by Serra, Crespi, and Palou, as proud, rancorous, boastful, covetous, given to jests and quarrels, passionately devoted to the customs of their fathers, and resolute. Not especially formidable as warriors, they did not shrink from warlike actions. Within a month they raided the scrubby little camp for plunder. In the fighting several attackers and two Spaniards were killed. A brush and pole stockade was erected. To the great sorrow of the padres, no missionary work could be undertaken. Only one Indian boy would be induced to live in the mission. He would become a competent interpreter, but not even with his assistance could any other Dieguenos be lured into the fold. For more than a year, and probably for a longer period—the original register would be destroyed—no one but the youthful interpreter would be baptized. The mission subsequently would be moved to its present location, but in the first five years the missionaries would succeed in enrolling less than a hundred neophytes. Thereafter progress was more rapid, but, as Kroeber suggests "the very success of the priests appears to have been the stimulus that drove the unconverted into open hostility."[10] In the seventh year of its existence, the Indians would make a strong assault. They would be driven off, but a number of Indians, two soldiers, and a priest would be slain in the fighting, and some buildings would be burned.

The stubborn defiance of the Dieguenos, who belonged to the Yuman division of the large Hokan Linguistic Family, was the only instance when Serra and his lieutenants were for so long frustrated. They would doggedly persevere under dangerous conditions, but their ultimate victory would be attributable chiefly to protection provided by military forces, always stationed in the area. In the end, San Diego de Alcala would boast of an enrollment larger than any other mission.

Two small missions on the lower Colorado River would be lost and never rebuilt, but their destruction resulted from a situation that did not exist in any other sector. They were located in pueblos in which missionaries were subject to the jurisdiction of political and military officials and had no voice in governmental affairs. When the establishment of these towns was proposed, the Franciscans had sternly warned Teodora de Croix, Captain-General of New Spain's internal provinces, that soldiers, settlers, civil officials, and the unruly Yumans of the vicinity could not long dwell together in harmony. The Franciscans, of course, always opposed any project involving Indians in which priests were denied temporal control, but in this case their advice would prove to have been well grounded.

Ignoring the counsel of the friars, and even similar admonitions from experienced frontiersmen, Croix proceeded with his plan to establish pueblos with garrisons on the dangerous land route between Sonora and California. If his main purpose, which was to provide some protection for travelers, was sound, his timing and his choice of locations were, under existing circumstances, wholly irrational. Indeed, several historians have charged that he was guilty of a criminally stupid blunder.

In the fall of 1780, the pueblos of La Purisima Concepcion and San Pedro y San Pablo de Bicuner were founded on the west bank of the Rio Colorado, not far from the present town of Yuma. Quarters for soldiers and houses for settlers—probably numbering altogether no more than sixty men, women, and children—were hastily erected adjacent to two small churches. Lands thought suitable for cultivation were distributed, but neither officials nor colonists gave consideration to the rights of Indian residents. The livestock of the Spaniards trampled the little fields of the natives and destroyed natural vegetal plants from which they customarily obtained a large part of their food. Soldiers abused them, and in response to their protestations they were lashed and confined in stocks.

The Yumans endured the cruelties and injustices for only a few months. In July 1781, several hundred desert warriors suddenly attacked both pueblos. All buildings were ransacked and burned. All fields, livestock, and newly planted orchards and vineyards were destroyed. The number of Spanish casualties is uncertain, for records are conflicting, but it is known that four padres, all adult male colonists, and the entire garrison were systematically butchered, and their bodies left to rot in the fierce desert sun. Spanish women and children were taken away as captives, later to be ransomed by a force sent to search for survivors. One of the victims was the noted missionary-explorer, Fray Francisco Garces. Another was Captain Fernando de Rivera, who had led the first land division of the conquest to San Diego. Rivera, now Lieutenant-Governor of Baja California, unfortunately happened to be passing through the pueblos, on his way to Los Angeles, at the time of the Yuma uprising.

CHAPTER ELEVEN

California:

The Mission Chain and the Chained

The twenty-one missions built along the coastal trail of California, the Camino Real, comprised a penal system both extraordinary and unique. It was extraordinary in that it was virtually self-supporting, deriving its revenues from agricultural and industrial enterprises that were, according to allegations advanced by its highest officials, the common property of its inmates. It was unique in that all prisoners were automatically sentenced to life terms, yet the only crime any of them had committed was not being born of Christian parents.

One man must be given credit for compounding the stringent basic regulations under which it would always be operated, and for developing the remarkable coordination with which the branches would always function. He was the redoubtable Junipero Serra, who personally founded and assigned names to the first nine missions of the syndicate, and was planning to establish several more when he died in 1784 at the age of seventy-one.

No delay occurred, however, in advancing the program Serra had inaugurated. Colleagues, similarly imbued with the asceticism and ambitions he had possessed, unrelentingly carried on the work of expanding and enlarging the project. Indeed, under their guidance it would be developed to a degree beyond that which Serra, even under the pressure of an incurable optimism or the influence of the inspiring dreams he was known to harbor, had thought possible.

THE MISSION CHAIN OF COASTAL CALIFORNIA

NAME	ESTABLISHED	FOUNDER
1. San Diego de Alcala	1769	Serra
2. San Carlos Borromeo de Carmelo	1770	Serra
3. San Antonio de Padua	1771	Serra
4. San Gabriel Arcangel	1771	Serra
5. San Luis Obispo de Tolosa	1772	Serra
6. San Francisco de Asis	1776	Serra
7. San Juan Capistrano	1776	Serra
8. Santa Clara de Asis	1777	Serra
9. San Buenaventura	1782	Serra
10. Santa Barbara	1786	Palou
11. La Purisima Concepcion	1787	Palou
12. Santa Cruz	1791	Palou
13. Nuestra Senora de la Soledad	1791	Palou
14. San Jose de Guadalupe	1797	Fermin de Lasuen
15. San Juan Bautista	1797	Lasuen
16. San Miguel Arcangel	1797	Lasuen
17. San Fernando Rey de Espana	1797	Lasuen
18. San Luis Rey de Francia	1798	Antonio Peyri
19. Santa Inez	1804	Estevan Tapis
20. San Rafael Arcangel	1817	Mariano Payeras
21. San Francisco Solano	1823	Jose Altimira

In comparison with the difficulties encountered at San Diego the problems that arose at the other missions were mild and easily resolved. In all but the southernmost region, the early missionaries were able to entice a considerable number of Indians into their religious traps with trinkets, food, clothing, and promises of material wealth and security. Once they were caught in the webs, there was little chance of escape, for traitorous Indian guards were always on duty, and in the event neophytes succeeded in slipping away soldiers, never very far off, could be sent to recapture them. Invariably runaways suffered cruel punishment.

As a means of explaining the successes of the padres, some writers ascribe to the California Indians inordinate tractability and peaceableness. This is an unacceptable generality. Blood feuds, clashes between villages belonging to different tribes, raids for plunder, and other forms of warfare were incessant and often costly in lives and property. It would be erroneous to assert, however, that banditry and warfare were honored ways of life among Indians in California, as they were in other regions of the American West, notably both the Northern and Southern Great Plains and the Rocky Mountains. In comparison with those of such tribes as the Sioux, the Navajo, the Comanche, the Blackfeet, and the Apache, the martial tendencies of California natives were insignificantly developed.

Nor may the so-called Mission Indians be classified, as some authors are wont to do, as generically stupid, childish, and culturally retarded. One prominent scholar, for example, goes even farther in his criticisms, describing them, as being "without native energy, and probably, in their original condition, lower in the scale of civilization and morality than any others within the limits of the United States."[1]

The damning appraisal seems tinged with prejudice in that it infers that the Mission Indians achieved new and higher mental and moral standards under the aegis of the Franciscans. Not only is that untrue but ethnological findings show that the ranking occupants of the base category were some tribes of the salt deserts of Utah and Nevada, the arid brush and cactus areas of southern Texas, and the Imperial Valley of eastern California. The highest degree of cultural progress among all western Indians was achieved by the Pueblos of New Mexico.

The missionaries, of course, made no effort to understand the Indians, making no attempt to identify, and least of all interpret, their motives, but condemning them forthwith as pawns of the devil. As Engelhardt very well states, they deviated little from a preordained course:

"The purpose in view was none other than the conversion of the savages to Christianity. The friars came as messengers of Christ. . . . They paid little or no attention to questions or things that could not aid them materially in gaining the good will of the people whose salvation they had at heart. Like the Apostles, the Franciscans came not as scientists, geographers, ethnographers, or schoolmasters, nor as philanthropists eager to uplift the people in a worldly sense to the exclusion or neglect of the religious duties pointed out by Christ.

" . . . we do not find that Christ directed His Apostles to teach reading, writing and arithmetic . . . . such knowledge is not absolutely necessary for admission into the kingdom of God, and therefore it is not the duty of the missionary to impart it. He will use it as a means to further his principal object whenever he finds it expedient; but he will carefully beware of creating the impression that such human knowledge or accomplishments or 'education' should precede or supersede the knowledge of divine truths."[2]

The Mission Indians stood on numerous social and economic plateaus. Therefore, any evaluation of them as a territorial people must of necessity contain wholly unwarranted conclusions. Their environments varied greatly, ranging from the sea coast to the inland valleys, from deserts to evergreen mountains. A variety of factors—geography, climate, natural resources, as well as traditions, spiritual beliefs, and human qualities—each in its own peculiar way, not only controlled social development in every

California Mission tribe but determined the economic level upon which every tribe was forced to exist.

Approximately sixty-eight thousand Indians dwelt in the region affected by the chain of missions that stretched for more than five hundred miles between San Diego and Sonoma. They comprised at least twenty-three identifiable tribes, speaking dialects of four linguistic families, many of which were as mutually unintelligible as Chinese and English.[3] The families were the Hokan, Ukian, Penutian, and Shoshonean.[4]

Considering them in the above order, the Indians with whom the missionaries came in contact, their tribal affiliations, and estimated numbers, were:

HOKAN: Pomo, 3,000; Esselen, 500; Salian; 3,000; Chumash, 10,000; and Diegueno, 3,000.

The word *Pomo* is a native ending sometimes placed after the name of a village or a group, but its significance is unknown. They dwelt in the drainage area of the Russian River. Prehistoric Pomo men went naked in summer, wrapping skins about their hips in cold weather. Women wore a double skirt, made usually of either shredded inner redwood bark, willow bark, or tule rush, varying in the locales in which these materials were most available. Where deer were plentiful the garments might be made of their skin. Both men and women wore moccasins with soft soles, and sandals and leggings made of tules. Because the Pomo were spread over a region of divergent altitudes and climates, their dwellings were of numerous types. On the coast the houses were built of slabs of redwood bark erected to form a cone ten to fifteen feet in diameter. Farther inland frameworks of poles were set up and covered with thatch.

The Pomo were famed for their basketry, some archaeologists considering it the finest made by any primitive people in the world. Basket-making was not a utilitarian routine to them; it was an art with unlimited possibilities. Describing some of the finest

Pomo baskets as "splendidly showy," Kroeber states: "Black, wavy quail plumes may be scattered over the surface . . . or fine bits of scarlet from the woodpecker's scalp worked into a soft brilliant down over the whole of a coiled receptacle . . . . . The height of display is reached in the basket whose entire exterior is a mass of feathers, perhaps with patterns in two or three lustrous colors. Some of the baskets had edges of beads and fringe of evenly cut haliotis shells."[5] To the Pomo these magnificent creations served as gifts and treasures, but no higher use could be made of one than to destroy it in honor of a beloved relative or friend.

The meaning of the word Esselen is unknown, but it may have been the name of one of their villages on the Carmel River, and upon hearing it the early Franciscans, following the usual custom, applied it to the entire tribe. It is believed that the Esselen were the first Mission Indians to become extinct. Almost nothing is known of their culture, and only a few words of their tongue were preserved long enough to give them a vague linguistic connection.Their homeland was in one of the most beautiful parts of California, on the Carmel and Sur Rivers and along the coast from Point Lopez almost to Point Sur. Carmel Mission still stands in their territory, a few miles from Monterey. The sites of five of their villages have been located.

The Salinan lived along the Salinas River, from which their name derives, and on the coast immediately south of the Esselen. How they identified themselves is uncertain. Forcefully brought under missionary control, their culture was destroyed, and they rapidly decreased in number. Only two peculiarities are known of their rude civilization. They used a kind of musical rasp made of notched sticks which were rhythmically rubbed against each other. According to the padres of Mission San Miguel, they lent each other shell money at an interest rate of one hundred per cent per day. The transactions were restricted to tribal members.

Usury is not known to have been practiced by any other California Indians.

The prehistoric civilization of the Chumash was seen by Juan Rodriguez Cabrillo in 1542. The first Spanish navigator to land on the southern California coast, he found a large population concentrated along the balmy shore between Malibu and Point Conception. The Chumash, who were more nearly maritime in their habits than any other California aborigines, also occupied three large northern islands of the Santa Barbara archipelago, and their villages extended northward from Point Conception to Estero Bay. The significance of *Chumash* is unknown, but the name was originally applied to the occupants of Santa Rosa Island.

The Chumash constructed canoes of various sizes, some being large enough to carry twenty sailors. The boats were made of planks laboriously split from logs, and caulked with asphalt, which was found on the beaches. Chumash dwellings were large, sometimes as much as fifty feet in diameter, and were made by planting poles in a circle and bending and tying them together at the top. The walls were laced with sticks over which mats and thatch were fastened. Some structures accommodated as many as fifty persons.

The mainland Chumash were one of the few people to construct true beds and to divide their dwellings into rooms with hanging curtains. This custom was not followed by those living on the islands, who slept crowded together on the ground. The Chumash were excellent weavers, their work being superior to that of the neighboring tribes. They did not make pottery, but used steatite utensils, some of which they obtained in trade. Their money was the clam shell disk bead, and they were the "bankers" dealing in this currency, probably furnishing the bulk of the supply for the southern half of California.

Five missions were established in Chumash territory, but none of the missionaries or other Spaniards took the trouble to record details of their culture. By the time American ethnologists began to study it, the old way of life of the Chumash had all but faded from memory. As many scientists have regretfully stated, there is no California tribe that once equaled the Chumash in importance about which so little is known. According to Kroeber, the Chumash surpassed the adjacent Shoshoneans in their industries, in the arts that accompany ease of life, and possibly in the organization of society. "Chumash culture presents the appearance of a higher development on the material, technological, and economic side than on the religious," he states, "but of that we cannot be certain."[6] The reason for the doubt, of course, is that very little knowledge about their spiritual beliefs and religious ceremonies has been preserved. The Spanish settlers, the owners of large land grants, and the Franciscans were far more interested in obliterating the Indian way of life than in preserving any aspect of it. In their endeavors they were eminently successful.

The Diegueno may have called themselves *Ipai,* meaning "people," but they have come down through history bearing the name of the first mission established in California, a name they hated and a religious institution they tried to destroy. As they belonged to the Yuman branch of the Hokan stock, they were related to tribes of the lower Colorado River. They dwelt both on the coasts and in the interior of the present San Diego County and held some territory in Baja California. They were encountered by the earliest Spanish explorers of the Pacific Coast.

Their way of life reflected traits of their cultural affinities, but it was strongly influenced by their environment and by tribes of other families that adjoined them. In some ways the Diegueno culture was unique. They were, for example, the only California tribe who possessed a color-direction symbolism. East was white, south was green-blue, west was black, and north was red. The Diegueno were divided into exogamous patrilineal clans. The system was vestigial. The totemic moieties of more northerly nations were lacking, as were the totemic names of the cognate Yuman tribes east of them.

Both men and women wore their hair long. The males bunched it on top of the head, but the women let it hang loose, and trimmed the front at the eyebrows. At times women wore coiled basketry caps. Diegueno houses were constructed of a framework of poles over which layers of mat brush were laid, then plastered with a layer of soil. They made pottery, but did not practice agriculture. They were fishermen, gatherers of wild foods, and hunters.

The opposition shown by the Dieguenos to the intrusion of their land by the Spaniards was reflective of the spirit of independence inherent in the characters of almost all Yuman peoples.

YUKIAN: Wappo, 1,000.

The Wappo were isolated from other groups that spoke the Yukian tongue, most of their relatives dwelling in northern California. Moreover, the Wappo were surrounded by half a dozen tribes speaking entirely different languages. They dwelt in small villages on the Napa and Russian Rivers, and along Pope, Putah, and Sonoma Creeks, in the jurisdictions of the Sonoma and San Francisco Missions.

Their name is an American corruption of the Spanish word *guapo,* signifying "brave." They earned the sobriquet in the mission period by their stubborn resistance to Spanish soldiers sent by the Franciscans to capture them. A small people, they were soon broken, some being absorbed by the mission melting pot, and others vanishing among neighbors.

But they were not only distinguished for their fighting against the Spanish invaders. They spoke a dialect of the Yukian language exceedingly different from that of their congeners, in fact, differing more than Spanish from Italian. The Northern Yukians had the longest heads of any Indians in California and were unusually short of stature. But the Wappo were tall and had broad heads, indicating that, although their speech had a Yukian base, they had intermarried with peoples of other families adjacent to them. The Franciscans learned little or nothing about the Wappo, except that they were fiercely proud and were dangerous adversaries in battle. Perhaps that was all the padres wished to know. The customs of the Wappo, according to later investigations by scientists, were similar in many respects to those of the Pomo. The few Wappo artifacts that have been preserved are practically indistinguishable from Pomo wares. Nothing about their religion may be offered as fact. They may have held the spiritual beliefs and performed the ceremonies of the Yukian groups from which they were so widely separated, but that is merely conjecture.

PENUTIAN: Miwok, 4,000; Maidu, 1,000; Wintun, 4,000; Yokuts, 13,000; Costanoan, 7,000.

The tribal names Miwok, Maidu, Wintun and Yokuts, despite their great lack of similarity, all signify "people" or "person." The name Costanoan derives from the Spanish *Costanos*, "Coast People," and was applied to them by the Franciscans. How the Costanoans identified themselves in the Penutian language is not known.

The Miwok were divided into three main branches. The Lake Miwok occupied territory in the basin of Clear Lake; the Interior Miwok, the largest group, dwelt along the western slope of the high Sierra, overlooking the southern end of the San Joaquin Valley. The Coastal Miwok, who were more affected than the others by the inroads of missionaries, made their homes in a triangular area of hills, forests, and marshlands extending northward along the Pacific from the Golden Gate almost to the mouth of Russian River and eastward to Sonoma Creek.

When the famous raider, Sir Francis Drake, stopped in 1579 to repair his ship, *Golden Hind,* presumably in the little bay near Point Reyes that would be named for him, he and his sailors were hospitably received by the Coast Miwok. This was nearly two centuries before the arrival of the Franciscans in the San Francisco Bay region.

The narrative of Drake's great voyage depicts the Coast Miwok as a physically strong people, some so powerful "that one of them could easily carry without pain what two or three Englishmen there could hardly bear . . . The men generally go naked, but the women make of rushes a loose garment, which tied around their middle hangs down about their hips. They wear likewise about their shoulders a deer skin with the hair thereon . . . Their long hair is tied up in a bunch behind, and stuck with plumes of feathers . . . Their king had on his head a knit cap, wrought somewhat like a crown, and on his shoulders a coat of rabbit skins reaching to his waist."[7]

The Drake account speaks of the strings of disk beads worn by many men. The links in a few chains were "almost innumerable," and as the wearers "exceed in chains are they accounted more honorable." It seemed to escape the English chroniclers that the strings, made from haliotis shells, were the money of the California region. The houses of the Coast Miwok were "dug round into the earth, and have from the surface of the ground poles of wood set up and joined together at the top like a spired steeple, which being covered with earth, no water can enter, and are very warm . . . Their beds are on the hard ground strewed with rushes, with a fire in the midst round which they lie, and the roof being low round and close gives a very great reflection of heat to their bodies." As the baskets were described they were typical of the ornate type made by the Pomo. The Coast Miwok were expert swimmers and were seen to take fish by diving for them in tidal pools.

Many Wintun and Maidu dwelt in areas more remote from the range of missionary activities than other Penutians, some of their settlements being located in extreme northern California. Comparatively few Maidu, who ranged along the Feather and American Rivers to the crest of the Sierra Nevada, were brought under mission control. The territory of the Wintun, however, was long and narrow, and the settlements in the southern part of it, from the Sacramento River to the Coast Range, were sadly familiar with the tricks used by Franciscans to draw them into the concentration camps.

The Yokuts, who occupied the San Joaquin Valley, were unique in that they were divided into at least forty, and perhaps fifty, true small tribes within the main tribe. Each of these tribes had a name, a dialect, and a territory. "Such an array of dialects is unparalleled," says Kroeber, "and gives to the Yokuts alone nearly one-third of all the different forms of speech talked in the State. The differences of language from tribe to tribe were often rather limited, but they are marked enough to be readily perceptible . . . Since the total length of the Yokuts' area does not much exceed 250 miles and the breadth nowhere near attains to 100, the individual geographical range of these little languages was exceedingly narrow."[8]

The Yokuts were not possessed of striking physical characteristics, most of them being of medium stature. They were not as skilled in craftsmanship as some of their neighbors, but their bows and arrows were well-made and were effective against such large game as elk, deer, antelope, and bear. In most years they enjoyed adequate supplies of wild plant foods, such as acorns, seeds, and tubers. Each spring and fall countless millions of migrating wild fowl paused to feed in the many lakes and marshlands of the San Joaquin Valley. The religious beliefs of the Yokuts were dramatically illustrated by long, colorful, and complex observances, notably the mourning, boys' initiation, and rattlesnake ceremonies, the latter a performance by shamans lasting several days and similar in some aspects to the famous snake dance of the Arizona Hopi.

The Costanoans lived in a long coastal corridor between San Francisco Bay and Point Sur, at its widest part extending inland to the Mount Diablo Range. Thus their territory was intersected by the *Camino Real,* making them easily accessible as the northern links of the mission chain were forged. Much in the manner of a rabbit drive, Spanish soldiers accompanied by Franciscan padres drove them into the Christian fold.

Seven missions were established in the Costanoan homeland. In these institutions no attempt was made to segregate Indians of different tribes or of sharply contrasting customs, whose languages were mutually unintelligible. Under this unintelligent practice, Costanoan, Coast Miwok, Pomo, Wappo, Wintun, Maidu, Yokuts and other nationalities were thrown together, creating a babble of tongues and dialects and perpetual social discord, as well as augmenting the anguish of all inmates.

The Costanoans held a low position on the roster of California Indian civilizations. They made an unfavorable impression on early voyagers, who described them as squalid, dark-skinned, and apathetic. One observer remarked that he had never seen a Costanoan laugh nor had any he had met looked him in the face. But these visitors saw them only as prisoners in the missions at San Francisco and Monterey. It may not be said that they were not human beings, were not without commonplace emotions, not so stupid as to be without comprehension of the direness of their situation. Indeed, no such allegation could be made against any Indians, regardless of their inherent qualities and cultural ranking, who were caught by the tentacles of religious fanatics.

SHOSHONEAN: Gabrieleno, Nicoleno and Fernandeno, 5,000; Juaneno, 1,000; Luiseno, 4,000; Alliklik, Kitanemuk and Vanyume, 3,500; Cahuilla, 2,500; Cupeno, 500; Kawaiisu, 500; Serrano, 1,500.

The native names of the Shoshonean tribes inhabiting southern California, with two or three possible exceptions, have not been preserved. Even the exceptions are subject to question, for the evidence supporting them is in itself slight.

The Gabrieleno, Juaneno, Luiseno and Fernandeno are known

in history by names derived from those of the missions in which they were incarcerated: San Gabriel Arcangel, San Juan Capistrano, San Luis Rey de Francia, and San Fernando Rey de Espana. Nicoleno came from San Nicolas Island, which they occupied. The significance of the names Alliklik, Cahuilla, Kawaiisu, Kitanemuk, and Vanyume is unknown or at best uncertain. Cupeno is thought to be a Spanish misspelling of *Kupa,* one of the villages of this people. Serrano is a Spanish word meaning "mountaineers," but this tribe's native name may have been *Cow-ang-a-chem.*

One of the most widely extended linguistic stocks in the region of the United States, the Shoshoneans reached the sea in only one area—southern California. It is believed that their migration began no earlier than the first century of the Christian Era, but they may not have established themselves on the coast until several hundred years later. All of them came out of the Great Basin, (Nevada and Southern Oregon), but most of the tribes chose to make their new California homes in various inland locations, only four groups occupying lands directly on the sea and inhabiting some of the Channel Islands.

There was no mass migration. They reached southern California in successive waves, over many years, band after band moving to reunite with their respective congeners in a region that was warmer in its entirety, and in its greater part far more fertile, than the barren and bleak valleys of extreme eastern California and Nevada.

They brought their ancient skills and customs with them, and for most of them the way of life they had always known was not greatly modified, except in the respects that they enjoyed more dependable and more plentiful supplies of plant foods and game, and that seafoods and by-products of them were obtainable in trade.

However, this was not the case for the Gabrieleno, the

Nicoleno, the Luiseno, and the Juaneno. Scattered along the coast for nearly a hundred miles, they were obliged to adjust to an economy entirely alien to them. How many generations this required cannot even be guessed. Undoubtedly they learned from other peoples who had preceded them, particularly the Hokan Chumash and the Yuman Dieguenos; and succeeding waves of Shoshoneans learned from the relatives with whom they were reunited. That all of these four tribes became expert fishermen, swimmers, and gatherers of marine foods and shells—especially the highly prized abalone—there can be no question. The sea was the main source of their subsistence. Two of the tribes, the Gabrieleno and Nicoleno, truly became sea-going Indians.

Besides living on the mainland—present-day Los Angeles County—the Gabrieleno also occupied the islands of Santa Catalina and San Clemente. With the possible exception of the Chumash, they were the most culturally advanced Indians of southern California. Certainly they were the wealthiest of all Shoshoneans in the area, but their civilization also influenced the life-style of alien peoples.

The Gabrielenos constructed remarkable boats of planks, there being no trees large enough to be made into dugouts capable of sailing open waters. Johnston, a student of these Indians, writes: "Hard work and great skill were used in the making of these fine craft, with their two prows, and sometimes wing-boards as well. Driftwood logs had to be split into planks with wedges made of bone or antler, and planed with stone scrapers. Drills of stone cut and reamed the holes through which strong cords of fiber were laced. It is said that the planks were buried in wet sand with fires built above them in order to make it possible to bend them into place . . . even with the most thorough caulking with asphalt it was necessary on all extended voyages to take along a youth or two whose duty it was to bail out the inevitable and sometimes formidable seepage. These boats ranged from twelve to sixteen feet in length. Having no skeleton, they depended on the keel for strength.''[9] The Shoshonean coastal dwellers also used rafts made of logs and rushes for fishing in sheltered waters.

A natural resource that greatly contributed to the wealth of the Gabrielenos was the extensive deposit of soapstone, or steatite, on Santa Catalina Island. From this material they manufactured utensils that were far superior to pottery and were in great demand by surrounding tribes. Archaeologists occasionally have recovered unusually fine steatite vessels that were used in religious ceremonies. They were untouched by fire, inlaid with shell, symmetrical, delicately walled, and polished.

In only the case of the Nicoleno, can the last survivor of a California tribe be identified with certainty. These people lived on storm-swept, foggy, and rocky San Nicolas Island. In a brief and sad story, Kroeber says of them: ''Wood was scarce and small on the island. There was enough brush for huts, but most dwellings were reared on a frame of whale ribs and jaws, either covered with sea lion hides, or wattled with brush or rushes. Bone implements were very numerous . . . dugouts may have been burned from drift logs. Steatite was imported from Santa Catalina, but it is represented by small ornaments or charms rather than heavy bowls. Whales must have been very abundant and frequently stranded . . . . Sea otters were to be had in comparative profusion, and, to judge from the habits of other tribes, their furs formed the most prized dress and the chief export in a trade on which the San Nicoleno must have depended for many necessities. Seals, waterbirds, fish, and mollusks were no doubt the principal food, but roots were dug industriously.''[10]

This small tribe had suffered fatalities at the hands of Russian fur hunters before the Spanish conquest, and most of those living on the island at the beginning of the Franciscan crusade were forcefully removed from their home to southern California missions. ''The last handful,'' continues Kroeber, ''were taken to the mainland in 1835, soon after secularization (of the California missions). A woman who at the last moment missed her child was left behind. Eighteen years later, when California was American, she was discovered. Her romantic case aroused the greatest interest, and she was given the best of treatment in her new home at Santa Barbara; but she died in a few months.'' Her death marked the complete extinction of the Nicolenos.

The Juaneno, whose speech was a variant of the Luiseno dialect, lived on the coast near San Juan Capistrano Mission and in the highlands of the Sierra Santa Ana. The territory of the Luiseno touched the coast but inland was wholly west of the divide extending south from Mount San Jacinto. Immediately south of them were the Diegueno. The Alliklik dwelt on the upper Santa Clara River. The villages of the Cahuilla were scattered between the San Bernardino Range and the present Palm Springs. The little Cupeno tribe occupied a small mountainous district on the headwaters of San Luis Rey River. In the upper Los Angeles River Valley were the Fernandeno. The Tehachapi Mountains were the home of the Kawaiisu, and the Kitanemuk lived in the same general vicinity, ranging to the westernmost end of the Mohave Desert. Serrano territory lay in both the San Bernardino and the San Gabriel Ranges, and in fertile lowlands reaching from Cucamonga to San Gorgonio Pass. The Vanyume lived on the Mohave River in the present San Bernardino County.[11]

According to Hodge (Handbook), there are no Indians today along the old *Camino Real.* Indeed, at the beginning of this century there were not more than fifty still living in coastal California between San Francisco Bay and Santa Barbara.

In the interior mountain valleys and the deserts of southern California still dwell a few score who can claim to be directly descended from Mission Indians. They are predominantly Hokans and Shoshoneans. Most of them are impoverished, still little islands of people without resources or hope in a sea of incalculable riches—the cities, orchards, resorts, farms, and oil fields of southern California.

Worthy of note, however, is one exception to the wretched aftermath of uncontrolled religious passion and unrestrained economic greed.

For an unknown number of centuries, perhaps for several millennia, the little tribe of Cahuilla Indians had dwelt about small oases in the desert that rolled in its dunes and rugged ridges against the great walls of mountains dominated by the sheer splendor of San Jacinto Peak. Many of them had been taken away to missions on the coast and had never returned, but a few score still occupied their traditional homeland when Mexico surrendered California to the United States.

Years passed before the American Government got around to awarding them title to parts of their tribal homeland for a reservation. Under a so-called treaty, signed by President Grant in 1876, they were given "alternate sections" in the prescribed area. The assignments were made necessary by the fact that intervening sections already had been allotted to the Southern Pacific Company, under a policy by which Congress encouraged railroad building with gifts of public lands contiguous to a surveyed right-of-way.

The Cahuillas did not own their reservation as other persons in the United States, who are protected by Constitutional guarantees, and own property in fee. It was held "in trust" by the Federal Government, and their title was "in name only." They continued to exist for years in abject poverty, having no income except pittances grudgingly given them by an unsympathetic Bureau of Indian Affairs, but unprecedented good fortune would favor them in time. The title restriction not only protected them from rapidly being victimized by land swindlers but ultimately brought them advantages that were in their enormity beyond the capability of anyone, least of all themselves, to envision.

The "alternate section" allottments created what the distinguished editor and writer, the late Edward M. Ainsworth, so appropriately called "a golden checkerboard." Today the little tribe, still numbering only a few score, are the most affluent Indians in the United States. Their tribal lands comprise part of the richest winter resort in the world. Many of the fine hotels, residences, country clubs, golf courses, and commercial emporiums of Palm Springs are built on lands leased from the Cahuilla.

CHAPTER TWELVE

California:

The Holy Concentration Camps

Failure to establish a mission for a single tribe, or even exclusively for cognate tribes, was the cause of bitter dissension between neophytes, not infrequently with resulting violence that necessitated military action to restore order. Hatred and intolerance were as deeply ingrained in Indians as in European nationals. Tribal boundaries were well delineated and rigorously defended against trespassers. If warfare was seldom conducted on a spectacular scale and came irregularly, it was for the most part rooted in traditions of ancient origin. Migrants from Siberia were moving down the Pacific coast from Alaska long before the end of the Ice Age in North America. It would be illogical to assume that the friars were not thoroughly aware of such problems and emotions, for proof of their existence came in repetitious demonstrations, and no mission escaped from the burdens of discord and torment spawned by them. Yet the robed and barefoot apostles of California took little cognizance of them, deeming them issues that could have no substantive adverse effect on the march to spiritual glory.

The controversies between political officials and missionaries over economic and fiscal policies were never ending, but at no time ascended to the levels of rancor, vituperation, and vengeance that wrecked the colony of New Mexico. With the regularity of the Pacific tides, complaints from both factions flowed south to Mexico, and new regulations and decrees flowed back to the seat of government at Monterey and to the superiors of the missions. Documents bearing viceregal and church seals often were conveniently displaced.

Governors charged that missionaries were insisting on exorbitant prices for food supplies they were obligated by law to sell to presidios. Mission authorities countered that provincial officers were sacrilegious, ignored ecclesiastical edicts pronounced by priests, and would not attend mass with Indians at mission churches. The priests refused to hold services in the presidios without increased compensation, maintaining that the government stipends they received did not obligate them to perform such extra duties.

One of the chief protests registered by the clergy was that civil and military officials were interfering in mission affairs, especially those having to do with industrial and agricultural projects. The wily Serra approached these issues in a manner that ultimately resolved them in favor of the missionaries. He journeyed to Mexico City in 1784 and presented to Viceroy Antonio Bucareli y Ursua a *Representacion* he had prepared which reflected his ability as a businessman and his shrewdness as a *religioso politico*. Most of the thirty some matters treated in the document were offered in the form of recommendations which indisputably would have augmented commercial progress and have strengthened Spain's sovereignty in California. But these were not Serra's major concerns. Interwoven among them were several appeals he considered more important than any of the others. In substance they were:

Serra thought it urgently necessary to retire Don Pedro Fages from the command of the presidio of Monterey in order to stop the desertion of soldiers and of other men who accused him of cruelty, violent temper, imposing excessive labor, and with not providing sufficient food."Of this," said Serra, "I am witness. . . not to speak of the damage his conduct has done to missions."

Serra suggested that the new commander be instructed, at the first request of a missionary, to remove a soldier who had set a bad example, especially with regard to chastity. A missionary should not be obliged to specify the crime or cause of complaint.

(Brutal sexual attacks on young Indian women, and even on immature girls, by soldiers and settlers, were frequent and a serious problem at all missions. If a missionary were not required to register specifications of such crimes, however, he automatically possessed extra-legal powers under which an innocent man he did not like or against whom he held a grudge could be falsely charged and dismissed from service or otherwise punished.)

Serra asked that the commander and soldiers should be made to understand that the control, management, punishment, and education of the baptized Indians, and of those under instruction for Baptism, pertained exclusively to the missionaries, except in matters requiring capital punishment, and, therefore, no punishment or ill-treatment should be inflicted upon any of the neophytes, either by the commander or by soldiers, without the consent of the missionary in charge.

Serra also pleaded that the military commander should be forbidden to interfere with the correspondence of the missionaries, was not to open or delay such letters, and should be ordered to notify the Fathers when the mail would leave. The letters of the missionaries should go free, since the missions had no funds for such expenses.[1]

With minor exceptions, Serra's recommendations were viewed as wise and timely by the Viceroy and other officials in Mexico City. Especially gratifying to the mission president was the ruling by the government council, with the approval of the Viceroy, that with regard to their neophytes the missionaries stood in *loco parentis*, that is, in the position of the father of a family, holding the parental right to instruct and correct his children and bearing the obligation of conducting the affairs of his household in a responsible manner.

The securing of neophytes involved two methods of operation: gifts and force. When a site for a new mission was selected, the first act of the missionaries and soldiers to be stationed in it was to erect a large cross on the ground where a church would be constructed and conduct appropriate religious ceremonies. This pageantry would attract numbers of curious Indians. They would be rewarded with trinkets and a little food, perhaps some atole (maize boiled in water) and a bit of ox or cow meat. They were given to understand that if they came to live at the mission and helped to build it they would never want for sustenance and would no longer have to engage in the arduous work of hunting and gathering seasonal foods. When structures strong enough to hold prisoners had been completed, soldiers began the taking of captives in the surrounding region, herding them into pens as they would sheep.

The daily routine to be followed was prescribed in detailed written regulations, scrupulously obeyed at each mission. Families lived in native brush huts which they constructed themselves. At some of the larger missions they would be quartered in individual adobe houses. Girls who had reached the age of eleven, single adult women, and wives whose husbands had not been captured or who had elected to vanish in the wilderness, were placed each night in a separate building or walled compound, the entrance secured with lock and chain. All keys were retained by a missionary. A soldier or civilian major-domo would unlock the gates in the morning, and "the inmates would be allowed to join the others in the exercises of the day."[2] This part of the mission was called the *manjerio*, or nunnery, and the inhabitants "remained under this gentle tutelage'' until they were married or their husbands were recovered for them.

When a young man wished to acquire a wife he made his desire known to a missionary. If his application was approved, he would be told to declare his choice. He would go to the pen of unattached females, make his selection, and the missionary would then introduce him to the girl. If she accepted, the espousal was duly recorded before witnesses, and a day for the nuptials was set. After the bands, in compliance with ecclesiastical law, had been "published" on three successive Sundays or feast days, the marriage was performed, blessed before the altar, and the young couple was assigned a bed in one of the native houses. If they didn't understand all the religious rigmarole, it is doubtful that either was sexually inexperienced, for most tribal standards of morality did not specifically condemn surreptitious affairs among young people. That was, after all, a practical, if not always judicious, way for a boy and girl to begin their education in the fundamental facts of life.

The first bell of the day tolled at sunrise, a signal that all Indians over nine were to proceed at once to divine service. Mass was celebrated by one of the padres. Another recited the prayers of the Doctrina, members of the audience joining in as best each could do. Next the Alabado was sung. The same melody was used in all missions. Lastly, on empty stomachs, the Indians were given a lesson in Spanish religious words, then dismissed for breakfast, but before being allowed to eat they were required to sing grace and ask God to bless their food. It was *atole,* prepared in large iron kettles. Each family was given its share in a wooden or clay vessel. Unattached men and women were not permitted to eat together, being obliged to carry their bowls to their respective quarters.[3]

The breakfast period lasted about thirty minutes, at the end of which married men and women and young men were sent to work in the fields and shops. Girls and single women were assigned various duties under the supervision of "matrons," usually the wives of soldiers. At noon the Angelus Bell summoned all to dinner, served in the same manner as breakfast. It consisted of *pozole,* a gruel to which small pieces of beef or lamb had been added, and, according to the season, perhaps beans, peas, lentils or some root vegetable. After the meal everyone was permitted a *siesta* until two o'clock, when work was resumed. A bell called everyone to church at five o'clock, the devotions lasting an hour. *Atole* was dished out again as supper. In the early evening the Indians were permitted to indulge in recreational activities—girls and single women being kept apart from the others—under the watchful eye of a friar, whose obligation was to ascertain that "Christian decency and modesty were not offended." The restriction excluded pagan dancing and heathen ceremonies, but not laughing and the telling of humorous stories. Quiet was mandatory soon after darkness, when gates were locked and guards took their stations.

Only infants under the age of five were allowed to while away daylight hours as they wished. One Serra *Regulacion* stated: "In the morning, as soon as the grown people shall have gone their way, and in the afternoon before sunset, the Fathers shall give instructions to the boys and girls who are five years old and more, *and they shall permit none to be absent.* The catechumens, those who are about to be married, and those who are preparing to comply with the precept of annual confession... shall likewise attend these exercises in the morning and in the evening..." Another *Regulacion* provided: "On Sundays and feast days the Fathers shall *exercise great vigilance lest anyone neglect the principal Mass or the sermon* ... When holy Mass is concluded, one of the missionaries shall call everyone by name from the *Padron* mission register. The neophytes shall then approach one after the other to kiss the priest's hand, *Thus it will be seen when anyone is missing.*" Succeeding passages treating of punitive measures explain why the author underscored the above lines.

As each mission was required to be self-supporting, agriculture was given precedence over all other occupations. The raw land, covered with deeply rooted plants and grasses, stubbornly resisted the crude wooden plows drawn by mules or oxen. Only shallow furrows could be cut, necessitating numerous criss-cross plowings. Harrows were unknown. Smoothing was done with logs. Irrigation ditches were dug with sharp sticks and bare hands. Sown seeds were covered with soil by feet or branches. Harvesting was done by both men and women, the crops loaded upon two-wheeled carts, the threshing completed either by beating or by spreading stalks on hard ground and driving horses and mules over them. Children were assigned to scare birds away from orchards and vineyards with plant brushes. Grazing lands were abundant, seemingly without end in some regions, and under the salubrious conditions the herds rapidly multiplied. Indian men vied with each other for duty as guards and herders, but not many were needed for this work, except when lambs and calves and colts had to be branded—each mission had its own brand—or in the fall when all animals were rounded up to be counted.

The larger the number of neophytes confined in a mission, the greater the diversification of its industries. As the wearing of clothing was mandatory, garment factories were established at all missions. Women and girls engaged in spinning, weaving and sewing, making of coarse material pantaloons and shirts for males, and chemises, loose dresses, and shawls for females. Blankets were woven of native wool, and moccasins and jackets were made of hides. Shops produced saddles, harnesses, wooden and clay utensils, candles, and furniture. Other routine labors included tanning, melting tallow, grinding corn and other grains into flour, making bricks and tiles, carpentry, masonry, blacksmithing, wood-gathering, cooking, and no end of other domestic chores.

The only reward for the endless toil was the privilege of being exposed to Christianity and the promise of eternal bliss in the heavenly hereafter. "All Indians and missionaries, shared alike in what was produced," says Engelhardt. "No one received wages, because the wants of all were supplied from the common property." In carrying this reasoning a bit farther, some cracks are seen in it. The producers were slaves. The missionaries sold tanned hides, tallow, grain, wine, blankets, olives, and dried fruits at good prices to presidios, merchants, and even directly to foreign ships stopping in California harbors. With the revenues from this lucrative commerce they bought metals (especially iron), cloth, tools, and other articles which would permit increases in production in the mission shops. But a large part of the profits was spent to embellish the churches; for religious goods, pictures, statues, crucifixes, and musical instruments. On rare occassions, a padre might succumb to impulsive generosity—if prices were low enough—and waste a little money on shiny buttons, handkerchiefs, and other gewgaws which would be distributed with ceremony among the Indians he thought most deserving of such honors.

In their writings, the California Franciscans consistently maintained that no Indian was forced to remain at a mission against his will. This was propaganda issued to conform with the hypocrisy that obtained in every Spanish colony. Royal decrees prohibited the enslavement of peaceful Indians, but these were either simply ignored or circumvented by the practice of paying monthly pittances to captive natives, or supplying them with a few ragged garments for which they were charged, and holding them, under threat of death, in abject poverty until they were no longer physically able to perform efficiently in mines and factories and on farms. In the case of the missions, they made no effort at all to comply with the laws, concealing their operations under the false contention that the Indians were working only for themselves and were giving their labors in the hope of lifting themselves above the status of animalistic savages and attaining eternal salvation. Such an assertion is not only without foundation but is refuted by a veritable mountain of documentary evidence, not a little of which is contained in the Serra regulations and the reports, diaries, and accounts of numerous missionaries.

The argument that they were saving souls was not the only one advanced by missionaries to justify the incarceration of Indians. There were political reasons as well. The friars believed that if an Indian neophyte would willfully reject the only true religion and rejoin his heathen tribesmen, he would not hesitate to turn against themselves, the colonists, and the Spanish government. Thus, the padres maintained that they had no alternative but to send soldiers after a runaway, bring him back, and punish him.

While penalties were specified for certain serious crimes, missionaries were granted considerable leeway in ordering the type of penalty to be carried out for the more commonplace infractions. As some padres were extremely strict disciplinarians, and others were possessed of little compassion, the latitude in the authority allowed them often resulted in excessively brutal punishments being inflicted for such minor misdeeds as failure to attend Mass, pilfering a bit of food or clothing, and neglecting to perform some small duty. Murderers, rapists, and those who exhibited tendencies of incorrigible felons were turned over to the military commander and sentences were imposed on them by the governor.

The missionaries had at their disposal a number of punitive methods that might be employed. Lashing was most widely utilized and was usually delivered before a group of Indian witnesses. Other forms included solitary confinement, chaining, the pillory, and extra labor. Women suffered similar punishments, and children were whipped for failing to pay attention to instructors, for disobedience, and smart-aleck antics.

Engelhardt expresses the belief that lashing was the only punishment "that convinced," and notes that "this manner of correcting the guilty in Lower California originated with the Rev. Juan Maria Salvatierra, S. J., and Fray Serra retained it for the Indians under his charge."[4]

In mid-September 1786, two vessels flying the French flag anchored in the Bay of Monterey. En route on a round-the-world voyage, financed by the French Government, they carried a scientific exploring expedition commanded by the noted oceanographer and navigator, J.F.G. de La Perouse. He and his company were the first subjects of a foreign power to land in Spanish California. They had been expected, the Spanish Foreign Minister having sent orders to Monterey authorities to accord them a gracious welcome and supply whatever needs or assistance they might require. This was done, and as La Perouse would report, not only with cordiality and extreme hospitality, "but vegetables, milk, poultry, all the garrison's labor in helping us to wood and water were free; and cattle, sheep, and grain were priced at so low a figure that it was evident an account was furnished only because we had rigorously insisted on it."[5]

Doubtless the fact that he represented a Catholic nation prompted the missionaries to join enthusiastically in the welcome to La Perouse. "The padres of San Carlos Mission (Carmel)," he wrote, "two leagues from Monterey soon came to the presidio . . . they insisted on our going to dine with them, and promised to acquaint us in detail with the management of their mission, the Indian manner of living, their arts and customs, in fact all that might interest travelers. We accepted with eagerness. After having crossed a little plain covered with herds of cattle, we ascended the hills and heard the sound of bells announcing our coming. We were received like lords of a parish visiting their estates for the first time. The president of the missions (at this time Fray Fermin Lasuen), clad in cope, his holy water sprinkler in hand, received us at the door of the church illuminated as the grandest festivals; led us to the foot of the altar; and chanted a *te deum* of thanksgiving for the happy issue of our voyage. Before entering the church we had crossed a plaza where Indians of both sexes were arranged in line; their faces showed no surprise and left room to doubt if we should be the subject of their conversation for the rest of the day.''

La Perouse showed keen interest in the mission system. He visited San Carlos several times, on each occasion asking penetrating questions about other missions of the chain and making extensive notes. The friars seemed to have held nothing back in responding to his interrogations. If they could have sensed the nature of the criticisms he would record—which obviously they failed to do—they undoubtedly would have been less generous in furnishing him with information.

While La Perouse unqualifiedly praised the dedication and zeal of the missionaries, he showed no hesitation in registering unfavorable opinions of a number of their policies and methods of operation:

(a) The mission regime was unfitted to dispel ignorance.

(b) Missionary efforts were directed exclusively to the recompenses of another life, the present being disregarded.

(c) The community system, based on extreme prejudices and impractical ambitions, created and supported a disadvantageous servility.

(d) The mission government was a veritable theocracy for the Indians, who were led to believe that the friars were in immediate and continual communication with God.

(e) In the *tout ensemble* of the Franciscan establishments there was an unpleasant resemblance to the slave plantations of Santo Domingo.

(f) Progress in instilling the faith in Indians would be more rapid if neophytes were not hunted by soldiers.

Describing himself as a "friend of the rights of man rather than theologian," La Perouse confessed to a profound desire "that to principles of Christianity there might be joined a legislation which would little by little have made citizens of men whose condition hardly differs now from that of the negroes of our most humanely governed colonies. To ardent zeal and extreme patience would it be impossible to make known to a few families the advantages of a society based on mutual rights, to establish among them a right of property so attractive to all men; and by this new order of things induce each one to cultivate his field with emulation, or to devote himself to some other class of work?

"I have only to desire a little more philosophy on the part of the men, austere, charitable, and religious, whom I have met in these missions."

In response to La Perouse's questions, Bancroft remarks that the distinguished French scientist "longed for the existence of qualities and views that have rarely been possessed by missionaries in California or elsewhere."

There is no reliable record as to how many thousand neophytes ran away from the missions in the sixty-five years of their existence. The reports of missionaries are understandably vague on the subject, but from the small amount of data preserved it may reasonably be concluded that more were recaptured than were successful in regaining permanent freedom. As there are among every people, there were men without honor or integrity among Indians, stool-pigeons who could be bribed to furnish information that would aid the military in tracking fugitives. Generally soldiers did not need such assistance, for runaways almost inevitably returned to their homelands, fearing to seek refuge among strange tribes.

Nor do mission records contain figures pertaining to abortions and the killing of newborn babies by their mothers. Yet references to these desperate practices are found in early histories and reports, and hundreds of fetuses and living infants must have been secretly destroyed. The statement of the noted ethnologist, James Mooney, that "infanticide prevailed to such a degree that even the most earnest efforts of the missionaries were unable to stamp it out" is undoubtedly accurate.[6]

Kroeber believed that the "influence of the missions was probably greater temporally than spiritually. The Indians were taught and compelled to work at agricultural pursuits and to some extent even at trades. Discipline, *while not severe,* was rigid; refusal to work was met by deprivation of food, and absence from church or tardiness there, by corporal punishments and confinement."

One may only wonder what punishments he would have considered *severe.* He continues: "Consequently the Indians, while often displaying much personal affection for the missionaries themselves, were always inclined to be recalcitrant toward the system, which amounted to little else than beneficent servitude."[7]

Property rights granted to the missions probably encompassed no less than two hundred square miles. Some, of course, were relatively small when compared with others, but all controlled enough grazing and cultivatable lands to produce livestock and crops adequate to meet their respective needs in most years. The American trader, Captain Shaler, an astute observer and highly educated man, who visited a number of missions in 1804, wrote that they "may be considered as so many valuable estates or plantations belonging to the king of Spain, and capable, in case of a conquest of this country, of furnishing abundant supplies of all kinds."[8] He recorded his pleasure at the readiness of the friars to engage in illegal trade with foreign vessels.

A graphic illustration of the prosperity of the missions is gained from contemporary reports, obtained from various sources, for the year 1820:

Livestock: Cattle 140,000; horses 18,000; mules 2,000; sheep 200,000. Value, according to price lists issued by the colonial governor, somewhat in excess of $2,500,000. No estimates of the number of hogs, goats, oxen, rabbits, and burros are available, but as the market value of each of these animals is given on the official price lists they obviously were raised in appreciable quantities by the missions.

Agricultural Products: Wheat 70,000 fanegas; barley 19,000; corn 25,000; beans 4,000; peas and miscellaneous vegetables 5,500. Market value approximately $300,000.[9]

Among other kinds of foodstuffs produced by the missions, both for their own consumption or to be sold to presidios, and their estimated values, were: cocks $.30; hens $.20; pigeons (pair) $.50; jerked beef (arroba) $1.30; wheat flour (arroba) $2.00 and eggs (three) $.08. Thousands of hides were tanned each year, surpluses being disposed of usually in exchange for merchandise offered by trading vessels. An arroba of lard had a value of $4.00. Tallow was produced in enormous quantities, and an arroba of melted tallow was priced at $2.30, while twenty-five pounds of candles brought $3.50.[10]

Between 1769 and 1834, the Franciscan missions of California recorded approximately 90,000 baptisms of Indian men, women, and children. This is the rounded figure proudly displayed in pamphlets one may purchase today in the souvenir stores of restored missions along the Camino Real. It is cited by religious writers as a kind of memorial to the missionaries who devoted their lives to saving the souls of the California savages. It is also used by less emotional historians, for it is a thoroughly reliable total obtained from mission records still preserved in archives and available to anyone who cares to examine them.

There are some other figures, however, that usually are seen only in unbiased and objective accounts, although they, too, are contained in old mission documents. They pertain to a gruesome aspect of mission history that many devout persons are readily willing to overlook and would like to forget.

About 66,000 Indians died in the California missions during the same sixty-five years.

Of this total of deaths, more than 25,000 were children. Deaths by infanticide were not enumerated.

In 1833 and 1834 the revolutionary government of Mexico passed decrees that provided for the secularization of the missions and the nullification of all previous prerogatives granted the Franciscan Order under Spanish colonial statutes. Mission lands, herds, buildings, and all other property were confiscated.

An indication of the intrinsic value of Franciscan assets, excluding structures and farm and grazing acreage, may be gained from official estimates that in 1834, when the missionaries were expelled, the twenty-one missions owned 424,000 cattle, 62,500 horses and mules, 322,000 sheep, and produced 123,000 bushels of wheat and corn.

There were in this fateful year, however, less than 30,000 Indians distributed among the twenty-one establishments. In spite of its great material wealth, the system was doomed. For the Indian death rate had become so enormous that it alone would have brought about the extinction of the missions, one by one, within a few more years.

Theoretically, all property of the missions belonged to the Indian inmates, held in trust for them by the Franciscans. If this noble principle had any legal force, which is questionable, it was in fact political pretense, and it was safely ignored by corrupt Mexican officials. Mission lands and all the herds upon them were soon deeded to white nationals avowing allegiance to the revolutionary regime. Vandals sacked the missions, even taking tiles from the roofs of churches, and vines and fruit trees from the gardens.

The Mission Indians, deprived of all rights and means of sustaining themselves, sank into a state of hopeless degradation at the end of their earthly road.

CHAPTER THIRTEEN

Oregon:
Strange Apostles

Doctrines of the Christian religion first reached Indians living in the valleys of the great Columbia River and its tributaries in an unusual way. No priest or minister was among their earliest disseminators. They came over the northern Rockies with two disparate groups—fur traders and trappers from Canada and Iroquois from New York and Ohio.

There were some Englishmen and Scots of Protestant persuasion with the trailbreakers, but if they spent any time at all in attempting to instruct Indians in their faith their efforts were too feeble to be recognized in contemporary accounts. By far the largest number of men comprising the fur brigades—*facteurs, voyageurs, couriers de bois, engagés*— were French-Canadians, and therefore Catholics. It cannot be said that they, any more than their Protestant associates, sought to convert natives, but they did manifest their religion, especially in times of peril and on Sundays, by signs, symbols, and verbal expressions, and some Indians they encountered thoughtfully observed this peculiar behavior and wondered about its significance.

Ironically, it was the Iroquois, nearly three thousand miles from their homeland, who awakened in tribes of the Northwest the curiosity from which evolved an unrelenting desire to know more about the white man's Great Spirit. How many Iroquois reached the Columbia Basin in the first three decades of the nineteenth century must remain unknown. If there had been very many, some record of their number probably would have survived. One old account mentions a group of twenty-nine. Perhaps one hundred would be a fair estimate. But generations would pass before their blood, carried in the veins of progeny born of unions with northwestern women, would diminsh to an immeasurable extent.

The Iroquois had come west with explorers, with both Canadian and American fur trappers, and with wagon and pack-trains that carried supplies to the annual rendezvous of the Mountain Men and brought back the valuable pelts that had been gathered in the previous winter and spring. Most, if not all, of them had grown to manhood under the influence of Christian missionaries and mission schools, both Catholic and Protestant. In the far west they earned their living as free trappers and employees of the companies engaged in the fur trade. On Sundays, adhering to their training, they refused to work, sang religious songs, and gave themselves to other devotions, some of which were spiritual hodgepodges that would have been unacceptable to ecclesiastics of any denomination. It did not matter to the Flatheads, the Nez Perce, the Walla Wallas, the Cayuse, the Spokans, or any other Indians who watched them. To all who displayed interest they related their experiences in the distant region of the Great Lakes, and told biblical stories, and expounded on the teachings and mysteries and the powers of the Christian Creator and Supreme Ruler. The seeds grew.

In 1831, General William Clark, co-leader of the famous Lewis and Clark Expedition, was Indian Agent at St. Louis. He was surprised by the appearance at his office of four Indian chiefs, two Flathead and two Nez Perce, who said they had come from beyond the Rocky Mountains. All were emaciated and obviously in need of medical attention. Clark supplied them with food and lodging, and asked the purpose of their visit. They had come to ask him, they declared, to send religious men to show them the way to the white man's heaven.[1]

Clark, of course, had no means of fulfilling their request, but he put them in touch with several men of the cloth. Two of the chiefs died. The other two, believing they had succeeded in their mission, started home. Later it would be known that a third had perished on the journey, and the lone survivor reported to his people that Black Robes would soon appear among them. This news spread rapidly throughout the northwest, but it would be realized by the Indians in the ensuing years that the bearer of it had not been able to distinguish between a promise and a possibility.

Stirring and emotional stories of the chieftains' appeal appeared in the general press, and in church publications. On the recommendation of Catholic officials in the eastern United States, Indians in the Northern Rocky Mountains and the Columbia River region were placed under the jurisdiction of the Jesuits. This did not mean that Jesuit missionaries would be sent at once to the remote country, for none adequately experienced in wilderness service was available. However, plans to recruit and train some young priests for the work were launched. Protestant groups were excited; sermons were preached on the subject; and numerous religious papers importuned mission boards to send apostles to carry the Word to the Canaan awaiting them on the broad river of the far Northwest and unite earthly empire with heavenly enlightenment.

The Methodist Board of Missions was the first to take action, but the project died aborning. According to one early history, two men, named Spalding and Wilson, were assigned as missionaries to the Indians of Oregon, but the fur trade supply train with which they expected to travel in 1832 was cancelled, and they were sent instead to Liberia.[2]

In the following year, Jason Lee and his nephew Daniel Lee, who had been engaged in missionary work in Canada, appeared before the Methodist board and offered themselves for service among the Flatheads.[3] They would be accepted, and their respective careers in Oregon would be illustrated by commercial enterprises, shady land deals, and denominational controversies of their own making, which left obscured in the annals of the Northwest whatever efforts they may have expended to guide Indians from the darkness of heathendom.

At the time of his appointment, Jason Lee was thirty years of age, tall, and powerfully built, slightly stooped, and rather slow and awkward in his movements. His complexion was fair, his lips thin, his nose prominent, his jaws heavy. One writer described him as having "somewhat long hair, pushed back, and giving to the not too stern but positively marked features a slightly puritanical aspect; and withal a stomach like that of an ostrich, which would digest anything. His eyes were of superlative spiritualistic blue. Some would have said that he lacked refinement; others that his brusque straightforwardness was but simple honesty, unalloyed with clerical cant, and stripped of university gown and sectarian straight-lace."[4] He seemed to delight in his physical prowess, and he would look upon his wilderness freedom as a great relief from the prison walls of the forms and customs prescribed for a minister in civilized environments.

Daniel Lee was a distorted shadow of his uncle, a man in stature, but a child in mind and manners. He was thin and bony, usually beaming in happy, good-natured unconsciousness of his lack of knowledge of things of the world. He was not an ordained minister, but he attempted to preach, and the results were sharply reflective of his ignorance and of his inability to comprehend Christian tenets. The impious wits of trading posts, and even

Indians, made jokes about his religious mouthings and his somewhat effeminate manners, but he saw their jibes as indicative of
their liking for him. Yet, he was in some ways a valuable adjunct
to Jason, for he was not a coward, and he was obedient and
conscientious.

The Methodist board appropriated three thousand dollars to
pay for the outfit of the Lees and authorized employment of two
workers to aid them. Jason Lee studied the enthusiastic communications of Hall J. Kelley, a promoter and religious fakir, who
had wandered in California and Oregon and was scheming to
found an American empire on the Columbia. He also journeyed to
Cambridge, Massachusetts, to obtain advice from Nathaniel J.
Wyeth, who had returned from a trading venture to Oregon.
Wyeth agreed to allow the Lees and their helpers to travel with his
expedition which was to leave for the annual trappers' rendezvous in the Rocky Mountains in the spring of 1834. Wyeth also
would send a supply ship around the Horn, planning to meet it on
the lower Columbia, and agreed to carry the supplies and equipment of the missionaries in the vessel. With these travel arrangements completed, Jason Lee spent the winter lecturing in the East
about the crusade he would undertake and raising funds from
members of both Methodist and Presbyterian missionary
societies.

In March he reached Independence, Missouri. With him, besides Daniel, were the two laymen he had hired, Cyrus Shepard
and Philip L. Edwards. His pocket funds permitted him to engage
a third assistant, and he chose Courtney M. Walker, a friend of
Edwards, who was a farmer and building craftsman. Shepard,
about thirty-three, was extremely devout and a missionary at
heart. He was tall and handsome and gave the appearance of being
robust, but was actually feeble in health. Edwards was only
twenty-three, and although he was of amiable disposition, he was
given to spells of extreme nervousness and, it would be revealed

in time, was handicapped by a delicate constitution. Walker, only a little older than Edwards, possessed extraordinary physical strength and stamina.

The expedition started from Independence near the end of April 1834. It was divided into three divisions, in all numbering some seventy men with more than two hundred and fifty horses. Wyeth's company led the way. With him were two scientists who would become celebrated for their work in the west. They were the British botanist, Thomas Nuttall, and John Kirk Townsend, an ornithologist and writer representing the Academy of Natural Science. Next in line were the traders and trappers commanded by Milton Sublette, also going to the trappers' rendezvous, which would be held on Green River. Last came the Lees and their retainers with a few horses and a small herd of cattle.

The first bonafide missionary, sent to save the souls of Indians beyond the Rocky Mountains, was on his way across the Great Plains of Nebraska, an event that heralded a dramatic and tragic period in the history of the American West.

It is difficult to determine when Jason Lee decided that he would not establish a mission for the Flatheads. By the time the Green River rendezvous had been reached, and certainly after he had been there a few days, he had learned much about the valley of the lower Columbia, about its salubrious climate, its vast resources of cultivatable land and timber and fine grass ranges and unlimited water. Veteran Mountain Men, notably Thomas McKay of the Hudson's Bay Company and Sir William Drummond Stuart, the Scot adventurer, told him that the Flatheads were a small tribe and that their country, besides being high, rough, and cold, was poorly situated for a mission. Lee noted this information in his own diary. He would also be advised that a mission among the Flatheads would be a dangerous undertaking, and that it would be best to locate in an area where there was more opportunity to attract and hold Indians around him.[5]

There were Flatheads and the Nez Perce at the rendezvous, and several of them appeared at Lee's tent, having been told that he and Daniel were en route to their country. These Indians offered their hands and expressed their pleasure at having missionaries among them, but when they asked to hold a conference with Jason he responded that he was too busy. He dismissed them with a request that they meet him later at Fort Hall.[6]

Each summer since 1831, Flathead leaders had attended the fur trade rendezvous, hoping that General Clark had kept his promise—which Clark, of course, had not made—to send missionaries to them. Now they had come, but the Flatheads and the Nez Perce were left to wonder about Jason Lee's true intentions. He gave them no answer. When he prepared to move on, they asked him if he would visit them in their homeland, and he replied only that he couldn't say positively just when. Perhaps he was telling the truth, that he hadn't yet made up is mind, for he would claim that he prayed to the Lord to advise him.[7]

In the light of subsequent events and the words he put to paper, however, it seems doubtful that when Jason Lee left the rendezvous early in July he needed advice from anyone. If he could not be sure of the locality in which he would attempt to carry out the godly duties of his commission, he was certain of other things; he had formed convictions that he would hold as long as he lived. He would not isolate himself in some gigantic, remote wilderness, like the Flathead country. Moreover, as De Voto analyzes his thinking and his attitude, it was altogether impossible for Jason Lee "to desire to do for Indians anything except what the prayers and sacrifices of many devoted people sent him out to do: to bring their souls to Christ. It was altogether impossible for him . . . to form a realization that the heathen souls were enclosed in an envelope of personality, which in turn had been born of a savage culture. When such a man met the Indians at last they might move him to compassion or even to despair. But also they moved him to overwhelming, overmastering disgust.''[8] Indians were not people to Jason Lee. Before they could be made into Christians, they had to be made into white men. He didn't trouble to hold any talks with the Flatheads, or with any other Indians. He went on as fast as he could across the Cascade Range and down the Columbia to Fort Vancouver.

Jason Lee would build a mission, but several hundred miles from the place selected for it by the board that had sent him west. Dr. John McLoughlin, the famed Hudson's Bay Company partner in command at Fort Vancouver, helped him with men and provisions, glad to keep the Americans from establishing a settlement in the mountains in which he maintained a profitable fur trade. McLoughlin was a physician who had found the life of a Northwest fur trader more interesting tha the practice of medicine. Physically a giant, he was cultured, a master of leadership and administration, a diplomat, just in dealings with Indians and trappers, a feudal lord who directed all operations in a fur trade empire that reached from western Montana to the Pacific coast, from northern British Columbia to California. It was not without good reason that he suggested the Willamette Valley to Jason Lee. He believed at the time that country north of the Columbia would be permanently British territory, not open to American settlement. Moreover, numerous French-Canadians who had been retired by the Hudson's Bay Company had built homes and farms along the Willamette. If they would not be enthusiastic about having a Protestant mission in their midst, at least they would be friendly, and the newcomers would have neighbors. McLoughlin demonstrated his own friendship by selling Lee seed and cattle and equipment.

The site chosen by Lee after some days of investigation was about sixty miles from the mouth of the Willamette, on a broad sweep of alluvial plain, land that could be cultivated with relative ease. On each side were grass meadows bordered by oak, fir, cottonwood, white maple, and ash trees. By November a rough log building had been completed.

The first American mission of the Northwest was opened, but the saving of Indian souls was far from being the paramount occupation of the members of the establishment. Lee promised that the holy work would be undertaken in good time. Meanwhile, there were more urgent matters to be considered. They comprised a dream, or perhaps it is better to use the word vision, a vision in which filthy, naked savages played no part, and in which the paths that led to sacred goals were obscured by the blinding glow of prospective commercial and agricultural prosperity.

Although the Methodists would not be certain of it for some time, Jason Lee had become a heavy liability, having deviated from the trail that led to the destination assigned to him. He would continue to expound every Sunday on the Holy Writ, but he was neither in the right place nor among the right people, and his progress in implanting Methodist dogma in the minds of those who heard him, largely French-Canadians and sad Indians, rapidly fell away until there was none at all. Yet, the inspiring cause for which he and his little party had been sent out beyond the mountains had not died—far from it. Other denominations gave it new vigor with injections of piety and sincerity that flowed from strong hearts.

If the American Board of Commissioners for Foreign Missions would have been hard put to explain the difference between a Flathead, a Nez Perce, and a Cayuse, its members knew that the souls of these peoples must be saved, for the good of their own consciences as well as for the benefit of the Indians themselves. The Presbyterian, Congregational, and Dutch Reformed Churches contributed funds for an investigation to determine the legitimacy of the Flatheads' request for religious instruction. Among the number of men who answered the call of the American

Board were two remarkable characters. They were the Reverend Samuel Parker, a Congregationalist of Ithaca, New York, and Dr. Marcus Whitman, a religious physician practicing in New York State's Yates County, two men of sharply contrasting natures.[9]

Parker was fifty-six, and the rugged men of the fur trade caravan with which he and Whitman would travel thought him too old · to face for the first time the ordeals they knew were ahead. He brushed aside their counsel with the blind confidence of a young greenhorn, acting as if he were setting out on an errand no more hazardous than going around an Ithaca corner for a loaf of bread. The Lord had called upon him, and he had prepared himself to make whatever sacrifices were necessary in responding.[10]

Fastidious, gentlemanly, scholarly, Parker was not a person who appealed to the crude French-Canadians, the half-breeds, and the American plainsmen. Obviously they didn't understand him or appreciate his qualities; they thought him snobbish and his dignity and reserve unattractive affectations; and they sometimes mimicked him unkindly in their horseplay. There were some justifiable grounds for their reactions. He refused to assist in managing the missionary party's animals; disengaged himself from such chores as making and breaking camp, gathering wood or buffalo chips, and cooking; appeared to have no stomach for hunting, although he seemed to enjoy with a certain voraciousness the conglomerations of corn, beans, wild tubers, antelope, buffalo, elk, and deer prepared by the capable, if unclean, hands of camptenders. He cut his food into precise bites, fed it to himself with a fork, and seemed disgusted by the common custom— which, to his dismay Whitman adopted—of picking up a strip of meat, inserting an end in the mouth, and slicing off a chunk with the swipe of a dirty hunting knife.

Yet, Parker would demonstrate that he was not frail, that in his slight frame was an amazing stamina, and that he possessed courage more than adequate to meet and overcome the demands made upon him. History would be enriched by his memoirs, reflective of cool, analytical intelligence, extraordinary powers of observation, and sagacity.

Marcus Whitman was genial, an extrovert, energetic, and untidy. Although only thirty-two, his dark hair was streaked with gray. Two descriptions of him have come down which merit repeating: "Spare, sinewy, strong features, deep blue eyes, a man made for responsibility, for overcoming obstacles, with easy manners and a *bonhomie* which recommended him to western men."[11] And "in the first journey (to the West) he is a man losing his private concerns in great cause; from now on he is completely dedicated. From now on too he is a great man. In a different way, in a way that is much more appealing, he was as much an instrument of the time-spirit as Jason Lee."[12]

The American Fur Company supply train, commanded by the veteran Mountain Man, Lucien Fontenelle, left Liberty on June 15, 1835, and about a week later reached Bellevue, a trading post on the Missouri River a few miles below Council Bluffs. There cholera struck, and quickly three men, drained of all bodily fluids as well as considerable blood, were dead. Others fell, prostrated and shrivelled in helplessness. Fontenelle was a victim, and he lay in agony, perhaps fearing death no more than the loss of a year's trade. Whitman, suffering himself with a severe pain in his groin, saved the caravan. He had the camp moved from the marsh along the river to high, dry, ground. He used what few medicines he had—undoubtedly none of them, and especially the calomel he gave the sufferers, were effective—and for twelve days kept his patients bundled in blankets, forced gruel down their parched throats, comforted them, sat with them through long nights in his pain and consoled them with quiet encouragement. He was ministering to men who had been on several occasions unkind to him and to Parker, who had ridiculed them for their ignorance of wilderness travel, thrown rotten eggs at them, and put them in danger of losing their lives by cutting loose the raft on which they were crossing a river with their horses. If the survivors of the epidemic, rough, vulgar, smelly, cruel men, concealed their chagrin and offered no apologies, they showed their appreciation by making no more trouble for the white medicine man. Parker, too, enjoyed the rewards of Whitman's unselfish, professional struggle.

The train passed Chimney Rock (western Nebraska) late in July, and shortly afterward encountered Bull Bear's band of Oglala Sioux, two thousand men, women, and children with an immense herd of horses. The Indians were going to Fort Laramie to trade, and the two groups moved on together raising a great cloud of dust over the trail along the North Platte. Parker noted that the Sioux were relatively well-dressed and clean, and thought the women better proportioned and "less pendulous" than others he had seen.

At Fort Laramie, Fontenelle, in accordance with custom, dispensed copious quantities of whiskey to his men, and they were soon lying in drunken stupors or fighting or fornicating in patches of sagebrush with squaws not unwilling to trade their charms for bright gewgaws. He sent several kegs over to Bull Bear's camp, and the Sioux staged a wild three-day-and-night dance, concluding the celebration with a sacred ceremonial in which the participants wore hideous masks and buffalo horns.

"I cannot say I was much amused to see how well they could imitate brute beasts, while ignorant of God and salvation," Parker wrote. "The impressive enquiry was constantly on my mind, what will become of their immortal spirits? Rational men imitating beasts and old gray-headed men marshaling the dance, and enlightened white men encouraging it by giving them intoxicating spirits as reward for their good performance."

His outrage drove him to march into the Sioux camp, where no one could understand what he was saying, and deliver a forceful sermon on the goodness and greatness of the Christian God. The Sioux listened respectfully, even in their hangovers avoiding offending a man who by his gestures alone they understood was saying something about heavenly supernaturals. They seemed to enjoy his rendition of *Watchman, Tell Us of The Night,* or at least his rolling deep tones and the rhythm, if not the incomprehensible words:

> Traveler, o'er yon mountains' height
> See that glory-beaming star,
> Watchman, does its beauteous ray
> Aught of joy or hope foretell?
> Traveler, yes: it brings the day,
> Promised day of Israel.

Fontenelle stayed at Fort Laramie, and the famous scout, Tom Fitzpatrick, took the packtrain on to the Green River rendezvous, arriving there to riotous shouting and gunfire and more carousing on August 12. There came sharp turns in the courses and in the lives of the Reverend Parker and Dr. Whitman.

They found awaiting them delegations of Flatheads and Nez Perces which, by some mysterious power of the wilderness telegraph, had heard that two priests were en route to visit them. Parker and Whitman were delighted and launched into exhausting conferences with their greeters, made seemingly interminable by the struggles of an interpreter who did not conceal his opinion that both the missionaries and the Indians were somewhat daffy.

What Parker and Whitman found out in the tedious powwows was much less in its context than what escaped them. They professed to be shocked by the information that Jason Lee had ignored the Flatheads and had gone on to the Willamette, but after hearing the same descriptions of the Flatheads' country that had been given Lee by Mountain Men they were less inclined to condemn the Methodist's decision. They heard again the story of how only one of the chieftains who had journeyed to St. Louis in the hope of inducing men who spoke with God to live among their people had returned. They did not learn—or if they did they chose to overlook the matter—that the Flatheads and Nez Perce, inspired by the counseling of their French – Canadian and Iroquois friends, wanted Catholic priests to enlighten them. Perhaps the Indians with whom they conferred at Green River were too polite, but more likely simply too fearful of revealing their lack of understanding about Christian customs, to ask why Parker and Whitman did not wear black robes and crosses on chains. In any case, the delegations to a man allowed them to feel assured that they would be most graciously and reverently welcomed by their respective peoples. And that was all Parker and Whitman needed to know to bring them into agreement upon a course of action involving a plan they would never carry out.

The sincerity of the Flatheads' desire to receive religious instruction could no longer be questioned. If the basis from which the desire evolved remained obscure to Parker and Whitman, they accepted the spoken words of the Flathead delegates as proof that it was genuine. In the faint light of their understanding, it probably did not occur to them that with the shadows of American intrusions growing steadily darker, both the Flatheads and Nez Perce might have seen both economic and spiritual advantages for themselves in having among them men who not only could talk with the Great Father in Washington but with the important spirits in the sky. Even if they had thought of the possibility, they would have considered it irrelevant. The Flatheads and the Nez Perce wanted missionaries and Christian enlightenment, and nothing else mattered. But Parker was realistic enough to note that their savage friends also had another motive that roused their desire to have men with magic powers among them. At the rendezvous the Indians had seen Dr. Whitman demonstrate his ability to perform miracles. He had removed with apparent ease an arrow that had been deeply embedded in the thigh of a hunter for more than two years. In another operation he had extracted an iron arrowhead three inches in length from the back of Jim Bridger with such inconceivable skill that the famous scout seemed not to suffer more than minor pain. These surgical exhibitions stirred profound wonder in the Flatheads and Nez Perce, for it was "big medicine," greater than any they had believed possible. Thoughts of enjoying its comforts increased the fervency of their pleas for teachers.

Parker and Whitman were agreed that a decisive move by them was urgent. Even before a plan had been completed, they assured the Flatheads and the Nez Perce that missions available to both tribes would be established. Then between themselves they resolved the problems facing them. Going on to the lower Columbia together would have been nothing more than a waste of valuable time. Nothing substantial could have been accomplished. Even if they sent a message back to the American Board, they would have no assurance that their needs would be properly fulfilled; indeed, they would have no assurance that the message had reached its destination. If they spent the coming winter at Fort Vancouver, or perhaps with Jason Lee—wherever he was—they could not have reached the east before the fall of 1836. At the earliest, it would have been September 1837, before they could have returned to the western slope of the mountains. By going back at once, a whole year, and possibly two, could be saved.

If the thought of repeating the ordeal now so near an end made Parker shudder inwardly, he concealed his emotions. Whitman saved him from further agony by volunteering to return. Parker could go on and take advantage of an opportunity to learn more about the country and the ways of the Indians to be saved. They prayed together, asking God to bless the decision and guide them in their respective paths. Whitman was concerned more for Parker's safety than his own, but Parker urged him to dismiss his fears, philosophically remarking that if they remained together they would need divine guidance, and if they had that it did not matter whether he traveled alone.

Late in August the two missionaries met for the last time, joining again in a prayerful plea for success, and embracing each other as they said farewell. With the permission of their fathers and mothers, Whitman took with him two Nez Perce youths to be trained as interpreters and from whom he hoped to learn something of native tongues. He would travel as far as Fort Laramie with Fitzpatrick's outfit and go on down the Platte with some homeward bound packtrain.

Parker was obliged to cast his lot with Jim Bridger's company of trappers, heading for Jackson's Hole, the Grand Tetons, and Pierre's Hole. Some of the Flatheads who had attended the annual rendezvous stuck close to him, as if fearful of losing him in the wilderness, and bringing him such delectables as wild berries and fruits and the most savory and tender pieces of buffalo tongue, venison, and antelope. His strength began to fail him, and it was only with great effort that he continued, often wondering if he was being watched over or would go to a lonely grave in the God-forsaken mountains. He managed to summon up enough endurance to preach on Sundays, and both the Indians and the trappers listened attentively. He could not bring himself to upbraid them for their sinful ways, but he did warn them in gentle terms that they could not expect to be received in the heavenly paradise without a great moral change of heart.

Bridger sent out trapping parties that would be gone for the winter and spring, and turned eastward himself, leaving Parker with a village of Nez Perce and Flatheads. They continued to provide for him, nursed him tenderly through a fierce cold, and guided him slowly on westward. He greatly augmented their faith in his supernatural powers when he fell upon his knees and prayed for buffalo at a time when their food supply was nearly exhausted. A herd miraculously appeared. However, the demands of the belly coming before all other considerations, most of the party rode off to trail the animals and secure a winter's supply of meat, and, being so sustained, engage in trapping. But enough Indians stayed with him, taking him on to Fort Walla Walla, which was reached about the sixth of October. With bread, butter, milk, sugar, things he had begun to believe no longer existed under heaven, gracing each meal at the Hudson Bay Company's station, he began at once to recover from his scrawniness and to throw off his weariness. He found another pleasure he had not known for some five months, a comfortable chair, and he sank into it, convinced that man's genius had brought forth few, if any, greater inventions.

The remainder of the trip was easily accomplished, requiring only swift rides down the Columbia as a passenger in dugout canoes to Fort Vancouver. In accordance with his famous hospitality, McLoughlin made him welcome, invited him to spend the winter as the Hudson Bay Company's guest, and directed him to a room in the McLoughlin mansion. The room had chairs and a bed with linens and clean woolen blankets.

Parker had intended to go back to the annual fur trade rendezvous of 1836 with a Hudson's Bay Company group so that he might meet the returning Whitman. He started with McLoughlin's traders, and the reason he never got there is plain enough, but why he chose to wander about the upper Columbia Valley and adjacent regions for several weeks is not a matter easily explained.

With a few Indian guides he had gone up the Columbia as far as Fort Colville and Fort Okanagan, directly away from the trail to the rendezvous. He preached and held councils with the Nez Perce, Cayuse, Walla Walla, Pend d'Oreille, Spokan, and members of other tribes. He saw a number of sites he deemed suitable for missions, but he favored most a small valley, called Waiilatpu by the Indians, near the junction of the Walla Walla River and a small creek. He would recommend it in letters to be delivered to

Dr. Whitman. Waiilatpu was in country inhabited by the Cayuse, but Parker promised the Nez Perce, Walla Wallas, Spokans, and possibly other peoples, that missions also would be located in their homelands, and they seemed satisfied with his plan. He saw no Flatheads on this journey.

He went back to Fort Walla Walla, only twenty-two miles from Waiilatpu, and secured a seat in an Indian canoe going down to Fort Vancouver. In his journal he would unhesitantly admit that he had intended to go to the Green River rendezvous to meet Whitman and from there continue on with some packtrain to the Missouri. When he reached Fort Walla Walla, however, he was unable to bring himself to face again the hardships of such a long journey on horseback across endless deserts, mountains and plains.[13]

He did not even wait for Whitman at Fort Vancouver. In the summer he embarked on a vessel bound for the Sandwich Islands. In Hawaii he was obliged to wait five months before he was able to obtain passage on a ship that would take him around South America to an American port on the Atlantic. He landed at New London in May 1837.

CHAPTER FOURTEEN

Oregon:
Promotion in the Pulpit

The rolling country surrounding French Prairie in the Willamette Valley, where Jason Lee had built the Methodist mission, was ideal for stock grazing, but the only cattle then in the lower Columbia region—a modest number of cows, young beeves, and a few bulls—were the property of the Hudson's Bay Company. The factor at Fort Vancouver, McLoughlin, refused to deplete his precious herd by selling any of the animals, although he generously supplied visitors with milk, cheese, steaks, and roasts not needed for his own table and post employees.

Jason Lee had been quick to realize the opportunity to make money by raising livestock, and when he learned from Ewing Young, a veteran Mountain Man, that horned cattle could be purchased at Spanish missions in California for three dollars a head, he organized a company for that purpose. Having no funds of his own to invest in the venture, Lee borrowed $500. French-Canadian settlers and a few Americans bought small shares, and McLoughlin was induced to contribute the munificent sum of $900. With approximately $2500 in the company till, buyers and herders were sent by ship to California. Encountering almost incredible ordeals, the drovers succeeded in reaching the Willamette Valley with some six hundred head at an overall cost of $8 each, more than twice the purchase price. But the project soon began to return large profits. The great cattle business of Oregon had been established.[1]

What Jason Lee had said to the Methodist Missionary Society in his report regarding the founding of the French Prairie Mission is not known. Obviously, however, his account was enthusiastic and encouraging, for the society voted to appropriate additional funds and to send reinforcements. These consisted of eight adults and several children, among the group being a medical doctor, a blacksmith, a carpenter, and three unattached young women of assured virtue and piety. They reached Fort Vancouver in May 1837, having been on the way from Boston for ten months. Lee wasted no time in wooing and winning the hand of Miss Anna Maria Pitman of New York, their marriage taking place about a month after her arrival. According to the physician who was with the party, Elijah White, she had dedicated her life to missionary work in foreign fields, was tall, dark of hair, gifted as a poet, fervently devout, and full of enthusiasm.[2]

The Methodist Missionary Society was plunging, spending all money collected in unending drives almost with reckless abandon, the faith of its members in Jason Lee seemingly increasing with every expenditure. In September 1837, only three months after the arrival of the first reinforcements, the ship *Sumatra* sailed into the Columbia heavily loaded with equipment and supplies for the Willamette mission. On board were two more ministers—one with a wife and three daughters — and another attractive female missionary who would manage to stave off suitors for two years while she gave all her attention to laboring in the Lord's vineyard. There were now about thirty white persons crowded into the crude mission buildings, equalling in number the Indian men, women, and children—many of whom were sickly and infested with lice, and all of whom were ragged, disdainful of

toil, and uninterested in absorbing the tenents of Christianity—
who could be induced by free food to dwell under the mission
roof.

Jason Lee sent Daniel Lee, a minister named Perkins, and Mrs.
Perkins to build a branch mission at The Dalles. With Society
funds he also acquired land owned by some Canadians in French
Prairie and obtained options to purchase other properties of considerable size. These moves were not taken to relieve the
crowded conditions at the original mission, but were steps in a
grandiose plan he had conceived. It was a scheme to gain control
of trade, transport, water power, and enormous tracts of grazing
and farm lands in the Willamette Valley and elsewhere *in the
name of but not for* the Methodist Church.

Rationalization in his own mind of his designs and contemplated acts was achieved with ease. All he needed was to ask
himself a few questions. Were not the Indians of the Willamette
Valley and the lower Columbia hopelessly diseased and de-
praved? Was it sensible to continue to spend money on a mission
at French Prairie that was in reality nothing more than an asylum
for a few, sickly, Indian orphans? Were not the Indians at The
Dalles (in the heart of an immense area with immeasurable agricultural potentialities) lazy and incurable thieves? Did not England control and intend to fight for sovereignty of the region north
of the Columbia? Was there any hope of missionary work benefit-
ing the backward natives south of the Columbia?

If the doctrines of Christianity to which he had always proclaimed allegiance weighed on his conscience, by privately pro-
pounding a few more inquiries he found a trend of reasoning that
greatly alleviated, and in some respects completely removed, the
burdensome strain. Assuredly he could serve God by ministering
to civilized man, ministering to things material as well as spiritual,
as by ministering to worthless savages. Surely it would please
God if he created a prosperous commonwealth in an untamed

wilderness.

Yet doubts continued to plague him. For he was astute enough to understand that he might have trouble persuading the people to whom he was obliged to appeal to accept his thinking—the deeply devout members of the missionary society, the good and sincere men and women who gave so much of their time to collecting coins in church bazaars, pot luck dinners, sewing and literary circles, and gathering pennies in Sunday Schools and Christian Endeavor meetings, in the deeply satisfying belief that the funds, meagre as they might be, would aid in freeing aborigine souls from the shackles of paganism.

Jason Lee prepared, with all the thoroughness and shrewdness of which he was capable, to overcome the barrier that might rise before him. If he had to be deceptive as to the true nature of his project, if he had to conceal some of its ramifications, he had convinced himself that he would be acting in the name of progress, progress that would be sanctioned by God—their God and his, ever present in the fetes and fairs of Methodist churches throughout the East. He became a one-man chamber of commerce, and went about the Willamette and Columbia Valleys getting signatures to what he termed a memorial that he declared would be presented to the Congress in Washington.

The memorial stated that settlements in Oregon had prospered beyond expectation, that the people of the United States were ignorant of the value of the land west of the Rocky Mountains, unaware of the mildness of the climate and the vast extent of natural resources awaiting development and of the unprecedented opportunity to establish profitable commercial relationships with both the west coast of America and nations of the Far East. If the government of the United States delayed longer in taking formal possession of this far western paradise the pioneers would suffer dire consequences. They had in a few years built a foundation for a great American state, and they were eager to continue the building under a code of laws, adhering to constitutional precepts and the principles of morality and justice.

Not to overlook the matter of Britain's claims in the Northwest, Lee adroitly noted in the memorial that, as one historian states, "the colony had depended to a great extent on the influence of the Hudson's Bay Company, which had preserved peace among both the settlers and the natives by its judicious management. But they could not hope, as the settlements became independent of the fur company, that this condition of harmony would remain unchanged, with a mixed population, and without a civil code."[3]

The names of the ministers and laymen attached to the Methodist mission, Lee's associates in the cattle company and other American colonists, and a number of French-Canadian settlers on the Willamette appear on the memorial. Indian chiefs, Polynesians who had deserted from ships, persons Lee described as banditti from Spanish California, American renegades, and other unprincipled adventurers were not requested to sign. The document bore the date of March 16, 1838. A few days later Lee set off with it by horseback for the East.

Perhaps to his own surprise, Jason Lee's talents as a salesman and promotor soon showed themselves to surpass greatly his capabilities as a missionary. But if development of inherent qualities can be either inhibited or advanced by environmental, social, and economic forces that inaugurate changes in thought, custom and manner, then it must be said that a man of his uncomplicated nature could easily switch his interests from one field to another. Almost suddenly Lee appeared to have come upon a course of life more appealing than any he had ever known.

He had planned well. Instead of going directly to New York and meeting with his sponsors, once he had crossed the Mississippi River at St. Louis he began a lecture tour. He addressed audiences in numerous churches, extolling the advantages of the Willamette Valley and pleading for contributions to enable him to enlarge and improve his mission and carry on his holy labors among the heathens. The response was gratifying, both in pledges of money and in an enthusiastic press. Stories preceded him, and by the time he crossed the Hudson he was being lauded as Christ's wilderness emissary.

The mission board of the Methodist Episcopal Church received him with an enthusiastic reception. His plea designed for this audience emphasized the needs of the Indians for education and spiritual guidance, goals that could be acheived only by building adequate schools and additional missions staffed with dedicated teachers and ministers. Craftsmen and farmers should also be sent out to provide the natives with practical instruction in various trades and in agriculture. Urgently required were physicians to supply medical and surgical services in the clinic he planned to establish.

Some members of the board made known their fears that Lee's recommendations involved obligations that might prove to be financially unsupportable, but they were overruled. In the end the majority voted to place a call in the *Christian Advocate* for missionaries, physicians, farmers, mechanics, and teachers. The response was greater than anticipated, thirty-six qualified adults, among them parents with a total of eighteen children, volunteering their services. The board then chartered the ship *Lusanne* and purchased necessary equipment and supplies, including quantities of medicines and surgical instruments. A sum in excess of $42,000 was expended, completely exhausting the missionary board's funds. But more money would be forthcoming in time, dribbling in coins from hundreds of meetings held in little towns and in larger lump sums from individuals of means who believed, or hoped, that they could assure themselves of tickets to heaven by philanthropic gifts to noble causes on earth. And the dollars would be sent on the long voyages or by overland wagon trains to far off Oregon—into the hands of Jason Lee.

Waiting to sail, Jason Lee carried out another phase of his colonization scheme, that of memorializing the Congress. The petition of the Oregon settlers would be printed in the record of Congressional proceedings on January 28, 1839, at the request of Senator Lewis F. Linn of Missouri. In corresponding on the subject with Senator Caleb Cushing of Massachusetts, Lee wrote:

"We need the authority and protection of the government of the United States . . . to protect the settlers from the peculations and aggressions of the Indians, and to protect the Indians against the aggressions of the white settlers.

"To secure these objects, it is not supposed that much of a military force will be necessary. . . . You are aware, sir, that there is no law in that country to protect or control American citizens. And to whom shall we look, to whom can we look . . . to regulate our infant but rising settlements, but to the congress of our beloved country?"[4]

Lee's appeal for the protection of *American citizens* and his use of the phrase *our beloved country* signify an unsuitable presumptuousness and glibness. He was a British subject. Nor would he announce his intention to become a naturalized American citizen. Perhaps Senator Cushing was unaware of these facts.[5]

The *Lusanne* sailed from New York in October 1839 and laid over seventeen days in April 1840 for repairs in Honolulu. During the wait in Hawaii, Lee negotiated a trade agreement with King Kamehameha III. It provided for an exchange of products of commercial value between the two principals. The *Lusanne* reached the Columbia late in May.

The involved commercial operations of Jason Lee during the years 1840-1844, his acquisitions of lands and agricultural developments, his building of mills, all with Methodist Church funds that had been appropriated for the exclusive support of missionary endeavors, his political machinations, his land swindles and his dishonest schemes to gain control of enterprises established by others are beyond the scope of this work. It is enough here to cite only the forces that shattered his dream of empire and that brought the house he had built with bricks of greed and mortared with subterfuge tumbling down upon him.

Not much time had elapsed after the arrival of the ministers and teachers on the *Lusanne* before they began to understand that both the mission board and they had been duped by Jason Lee. The comprehensive program for helping the Indians to become civilized, educated Methodists, which he had so eloquently and dramatically presented, was not to be undertaken; indeed, no attempt was to be made to carry out more than a few small parts of it, and these only in an insignificant manner, with little chance of having a beneficial effect.

The truth was ugly to behold and sickened their hearts. Instead of participating in an inspiring mission for God, they were nothing more than puppets dangling on strings held by the master of an ingeniously contrived colonization scheme. New mission stations, so-called, were established, but serving natives from them in any capacity would be merely incidental to the real purpose for which they were selected, for they were located in areas in which Lee and his henchmen had staked out claims on lands that could with relative ease be transformed into profitable farms and sold to new emigrants who were arriving with every ship and wagon train. Towns were being plotted, with streets and lots charted. Missionaries were being assigned to live in log and mud huts— which they were obliged to build themselves—in lonely isolation, without adequate necessities for their wives and children, without protection from Indian thieves who stole any article that could be carried away.

Several persons, including a number of children, found relief from the ordeals in death. Serious illnesses and injuries incapacitated others. And some, no less angry than dispirited and frustrated, went home. They appeared before the board of missions, spewing out grim and scandalous tales, and they were supported by the testimony of letters that came with ships from the Columbia and the Sandwich Islands.

The missionary board, although alarmed and dismayed, proceeded slowly in its deliberations, yet understanding that anguishing and delays in dealing with the problem would contribute nothing toward solving it and might well make it worse. Thousands of miles and months of travel away from the board's dilemma, Jason Lee, more than ever addicted to the opiate of his great idea, advanced relentlessly along the course he had marked out for himself. He was now possessed of a conviction that he was laying the foundation of a rich new State of the Union, a prosperous commonwealth over which the banner of Methodism and the emblem of Jason Lee would forever wave.

One matter in particular disturbed him: sovereignty. This, of course, as an unsettled issue, might well have had an adverse effect in the form of clouds on real property titles. If he had been familiar with the trend of the thinking in the British Foreign Office and the American State Department, however, he would have known that the region south of the Columbia was no longer involved in the territorial controversy between the two powers.

As long as two years might be required to send letters to Washington and receive answers to them. Impatience and concern brought him to the conclusion that it would be more advantageous if he went back to the East and conferred with senators of his acquaintance—at least doors would be opened promptly to him and he would obtain the intelligence he desired without undue delay. He gave as his chief reason for going his intention of obtaining an award from the Federal Government of $5,000 with which to equip laboratories and classrooms of a school, known as the Oregon Institute, recently organized with him occupying the office of President of the Board of Trustees. The other members of the penurious board wished him God-speed and success, and he did not reveal to them—or to anyone else for that matter—his true purpose in making the long trip. It was to attempt to obtain a Federal grant which would, in the event the United States won sovereignty over Oregon, insure a clear title to all lands he had claimed as Indian missions. Among the tracts to be enumerated in his application would be several settlements he had established, not the least of them the growing community adjacent to powerful falls of the Willamette which were already being utilized for turning flour and saw mills.

Jason Lee left the Columbia early in February 1844, on a vessel sailing for Honolulu. There he was unceremoniously handed a letter from the Methodist Episcopal Board of Missions informing him that he had been dismissed.

Already in Honolulu, waiting to embark for the Columbia, was Lee's successor, the Reverend George Gary of New York. Not only had Gary been instructed to make a thorough investigation of Lee's operations and personal affairs, but he had been empowered to close the missions forthwith if he thought that conditions warranted such drastic action.

Lee had intended to wait in the Islands for an American ship going directly to New York or Boston, but driven by mingled fury and disappointment he took passage on the first vessel available. She was the dirty Hawaiian schooner *Hoe Tita,* bound for Mazatlan. From that port he crossed Mexico to Vera Cruz and sailed for New York, arriving there in May.

No record of Lee's hearing before the mission board has come down in Methodist church history, but there can be no doubt that it was a stormy, and probably tearful, session. His pleas and protests were to no avail. Charged with misrepresenting the needs of the missions, with failing to achieve any of the goals of the society, with malfeasance, with misappropriating mission funds and using them for his private advantage, he was sent on his way, the board caring not at all where he went.

The missions were closed, the property and equipment sold. Ten years of missionary labor had been a disastrous waste of time and money. The cost to the Missionary Society of the Methodist Episcopal Church had been in excess of $25,000, a prodigious sum that had not saved a single heathen soul and had left Satan smirking in the shadows of the Oregon wilderness.[6]

CHAPTER FIFTEEN

Oregon:

Disciples in Discord

Dr. Marcus Whitman went back across the mountains and plains from the Green River rendezvous, where he and Samuel Parker had separated, with a fur trade caravan. Late in the fall of 1835 he reached New York.

The board of commissioners for Protestant missions reacted as he had believed it would, not only expressing profound satisfaction at hearing the results of the investigation he and Parker had conducted but recognizing the urgent need for establishing missions among the Flatheads and Nez Perce in the coming year. The plans he presented were promptly approved, and the funds he requested were authorized. Previously the board had not favored sending out missionaries with young children, but now it acquiesced in his recommendation that families would be preferable. Missions should not be isolated log cabins in the wilderness but part of growing settlements, demonstrating to savages the advantages and benefits of an orderly, wholesome, and Christian lifestyle.

In the winter before they had started west to judge the sincerity of the appeals of the Flatheads and Nez Perce for missionaries, Parker had happened to introduce Whitman to Narcissa Prentiss, the daughter of a Prattsburg, New York justice of the peace. Somewhat past the age when most young women of the time were either married or had resigned themselves to spinsterhood, she was exceptionally attractive, with light golden hair, large deeply blue eyes, and a fine figure. A soprano with no small talent, vivacious and spirited, she had a tendency to be more flirtatious than was considered quite proper by the stodgy society of Prattsburg. The truth was that she was not only unqualifiedly moral but was extremely devout, and her consuming ambition since girlhood had been to serve in foreign fields as a missionary to the heathen. No opportunity had come her way until the handsome young doctor had appeared before her that cold winter day of 1835. She promised that she would be waiting to marry him when he returned from the mountains, or Oregon, or wherever he was going out west, however long he might be away. But all during his absence she had waged a futile campaign to be sent out by the American Board to join him, despite the board's protestations that his whereabouts were unknown.

Whitman came back sooner than either she or the board had thought he would. They were married in New York, she and her family and attendants all dressed in black. In her black wedding dress she joined the choir in a hymn, singing the last verse alone:

> In the deserts let me labor,
> On the mountains let me tell
> How he died—the blessed Savior—
> To redeem a world from hell!
> Let me hasten
> Far in heathen lands to dwell.

In February 1836, when Marcus and Narcissa Whitman prepared for their journey of three thousand miles, and *far in heathen lands to dwell,* they had less than twelve years to live.[1]

Whitman had run into a barrier he had not expected to meet in his efforts to recruit missionaries. While every qualified person with whom he talked—that is, ministers with families—appeared to be enthusiastic about the projects, not one was willing to sacrifice the comforts and amenities of civilization.

The time to leave for the West, March of 1836, had come, and Marcus and Narcissa Whitman were faced with a crucial choice: either go on with only a hired lay assistant and the two Indian boys Whitman had brought east with him or postpone the journey for another year. If practicality touched their reasoning at all it was quickly dissolved by the state of sublime exaltation in which Narcissa had come to dwell, and the determination, laced with a generous potion of devotional brandy, impelling Whitman. They packed their luggage—enough clothing for two years and the doctor's precious medicines and surgical instruments—and started.

Cincinnati had been reached when their path crossed that of the Reverend Henry H. Spalding and his wife Eliza. The Spaldings, mourning the recent loss at birth of their first child, were en route to a mission for the Osage. Whitman looked upon the meeting as a favor accorded him by the Lord, and he urged the Spaldings to forego their assignment and accept stations in Oregon.

Narcissa had good reasons to oppose the idea, that is, she would have had grounds for objecting if she had been willing to listen to the voices of discretion and circumspection that must have spoken within her. She had not listened to them, the dream in which she lived annulling prudence, if not instinctive caution, and she did not interfere.

How much she told Marcus of her former acquaintance with Henry Spalding, of course, cannot be known, but she could not have said anything derogatory about him, simply because she had nothing of that nature to reveal, unless she chose to color her comments with the stigmatic disclosure that he had been born out of wedlock. But that bit of gossip would not have been a matter of concern to Marcus Whitman, and she was not vindictive.

Spalding had gone to school in her home town and had worshipped in the church she attended and in which she sang. If she and the aspiring young minister had anything at all in common it was their faith, but Spalding had sought to extend that relationship beyond spiritual boundaries. He had pleaded an abiding and passionate love for her, and she had sent him away.

Illegitimacy, a mental thorn from which there was no escape, had turned Spalding to the service of God, and now in performing God's work he had been led into a situation that reanimated bitter memories—the sight of the beautiful Narcissa giving her heart and her charms to another man. He deferred his acceptance of Whitman's proposal with the excuse that he feared his wife's precarious health would make it dangerous for her to undertake the long and difficult journey across the deserts and mountains.

In the tall, plain, dark-haired Eliza Spalding were a remarkable courage and an unyielding spirit, counterbalanced by an extraordinary sagacity and a religious fervor immeasurable by ordinary standards. All she asked was twenty-four hours to spend in prayerful consideration of Whitman's proposal. She emerged from her seclusion to announce that she was prepared to leave at once for Oregon. If she went without fear for her own life or any misgivings whatsoever, her attitude was not reflected in its entirety by her husband. He was not afraid of what might befall him, and he would demonstrate rare ability in understanding Indians, but he went "harrowed by humiliation and intolerance," with "a perturbed spirit that found no absolution for itself—and no charity for anyone else."[2]

In Liberty, Missouri, Whitman bought wagons, horses, and a few cows. They pressed on with all possible haste overland to Bellevue, having been unable to obtain passage to that place on the American Fur Company's steamboat. Full spring had come, and they dreaded that they would be too late to catch the caravan of Tom Fitzpatrick, with whom Whitman had arranged to travel to the annual rendezvous.

Fitzpatrick had started without them, but he was not far ahead, and in an exhausting dash they caught up with him on the Loup Fork of the Platte. The Oregon mission was rolling now, crawling along at the rear of the heavily laden carts of the supply train: three men, two women, and three youths.[3]

The lay assistant engaged by the American Board was William H. Gray, a handsome, stalwart, religious fanatic from Utica, New York, competent with carpentering tools, and farm implements, and horses. He was an egoist, supremely confident in his own importance to the expedition, and he would write a book called a *History of Oregon,* which was a gross misnomer for a dishonest narrative penned with venomous ink. He saw nothing good or praiseworthy in any of the others, but he would concede that the women were ladies—at least. The two Indian youths, now bearing Anglo names, Richard and John, seemed to have suffered nothing worse than confusion from a winter's tutoring in a genteel environment, and they had learned a few words of English and, presumably, something of the tenets, if not the mysteries, of Christianity. Somewhere on the Missouri frontier Whitman had been approached by a stray, a husky sixteen-year-old greenhorn from Iowa named Miles Goodyear. His chief ambition was to become a fur trapper, and he offered to work as a teamster and handyman if permitted to accompany them to the mountains. Whitman engaged him. At the rendezvous Goodyear would vanish, having apprenticed himself to a Mountain Man.

The passages she wrote in the light of a campfire, indicated that Narcissa enjoyed perfect health and was fully content. Eliza suffered greatly, her ailments not described to any extent in the records but obviously of a type peculiar to women, and at one time her agony was so severe that she asked to be left behind to find relief in death. Whitman ministered to her as best he could, and prostrate on buffalo robes in the bed of a wagon she went on.

Miraculously her strength returned in the gentler climate of the Pacific slope and her sickness disappeared.

Narcissa Whitman, spirited, beautiful, and carrying a knife in her belt, and Eliza Spalding, plain, gentle, and bravely bearing her pain, would be the first white women to cross the transcontinental divide in the American West.

There is another bit of history worth noting. One of Whitman's wagons was the first wheeled vehicle to be taken overland to Pacific waters. He insisted on trying to drive it westward from the Horse Creek rendezvous as an ambulance for Eliza, despite objections of Hudson's Bay Company men with whom they would travel to the Columbia, who thought that it would be a hindrance to the progress of their packtrain. But Whitman got it through with little difficulty to Fort Hall, delaying the others not at all. He turned the wagon into a cart by taking off two wheels and doggedly went on with it to Fort Boise. There it was left, the terrible reaches of sage and sand and canyons ahead being deemed impassable for anything without hooves.

Whitman would have stayed at Waiilatpu, only a little more than twenty miles from Fort Walla Walla, and have begun building, if he had had anything with which to build besides his hands. They went on down the Columbia to the hospitality and the unbelievable comforts of Fort Vancouver. And once more McLoughlin, the great gentleman and trader who would soon become a Catholic, became the benefactor of more Protestant invaders of his domain. He sold Whitman tools, food supplies, equipment, and other needed articles at fair prices. A suggestion was thrown in with the transaction purportedly as a gesture of good will: the Presbyterians might consider sending out missionaries with the Hudson's Bay Company fur brigades instead of establishing permanent stations. Whitman considered the idea, but he didn't like it any better than he liked what Jason and Daniel Lee were doing in the country. Jason came to talk with him at Fort

Vancouver, but they didn't have much to say to each other. Their paths seemed to run in different directions, but neither advocated an alteration.

Whitman, Spalding, and Gray went back up the Columbia. At Fort Walla Walla they were able to engage a few Indian helpers, and with them went up the Walla Walla to Waiilatpu. It would do very well, with fertile soil well drained and a fine stand of timber; Parker had made a wise choice. But there was another matter to be settled. Waiilatpu was in country dominated by the Cayuse, and Parker had promised the Nez Perce that they would have a mission when Whitman returned, that is, in 1836. In a letter Whitman had received from him at the Horse Creek rendezvous, Parker had recommended a place on the Clearwater River as a good site for the Nez Perce mission, for it was located in their homeland territory. [4] Whitman, Spalding, and Gray went to see it. The Nez Perce leaders with whom they talked—they had an interpreter from the Walla Walla post with them—thought a small valley called Lapwai, ten miles up the Clearwater from its junction with the Snake, a better location, and Whitman accepted their judgment. [5] The Nez Perce also had something to say about the choice of Waiilatpu. The land was good enough, but the Cayuse living in the area were unreliable and not truly friends of white people, either missionaries or fur traders. The Nez Perce were not at war with the Cayuse, but they did not trust them. Whitman would do better to build a mission for the Cayuse at Fort Walla Walla or close to some other Hudson's Bay Company post. If Whitman had heeded the advice, the story of the Presbyterian missions would have had a different ending.

They went back to Fort Walla Walla, plans settled. Spalding and Eliza would go to Lapwai. Whitman and Narcissa would stay at Waiilatpu. In the spring Gray would go back east, for Whitman was already thinking of building more missions among other Indians who had Parker's word that men of God would come to live among them. There were the mountain Nez Perce at Kamiah, sixty miles by trail up the Clearwater above Lapwai, and the Spokans and other tribes near Fort Colville, the Hudson's Bay Company post on the upper Columbia. That could be accomplished only by bringing out more ministers, more missionary families, and the assignment would be Gray's—a dedicated man at least as far as religious matters were involved.

Strangely, no plans were made for a mission among the Flatheads. Again they were forgotten, and apparently forgotten, too, were the promises of both Parker and Whitman. It might as well be set down at this juncture that no Protestant missionary ever would be sent to enlighten them with the teachings of Christ. But the Flatheads would have a missionary and a mission a decade after they had first asked for one in St. Louis, as will be seen a few pages farther on in this narrative.

By the end of 1836, Narcissa and Marcus Whitman were living in a crude structure at Waiilatpu, and Eliza and Henry Spalding were in a hut at Lapwai. Early in the spring of 1837, Narcissa was delivered of the first white child born in the American Northwest, a daughter to whom she and the attending physician, her husband, gave the name Alice Clarissa Whitman.*

Chronological order must be sacrificed for the moment to note that in the east Gray would be more successful than Whitman in the work of recruiting. But his achievement was made possible long before he got to New York by the heroic assistance of a French-Canadian Mountain Man. He had traveled with some British traders, somewhere along the route meeting a small delegation of Flatheads on their way to St. Louis in

*She would have only two years of life. Toddling out of the garden at Waiilatpu, she would disappear, and searching frantically for her, they would find her little body in a bed of rushes under a bank of the Walla Walla.

another attempt to have priests sent to them. Learning the purpose of Gray's trip, the Flatheads decided to join him. Gray rejected the advice of veteran trappers to wait for the eastbound caravan from the annual rendezvous. Impetuous, bullheaded, and arrogant, he insisted on proceeding across the plains without delay. Two American adventurers who wanted to go home, the Flatheads, and one or two other hunters decided to take a chance with him. At Ash Hollow, Nebraska, on the North Platte River, the little train was attacked by a band of Sioux. The Flatheads were slain. The white men were saved by the unidentified French-Canadian, who guided them to safety in a series of gruelling night marches. Thereafter Gray was an anathema to the Flathead people, who blamed him for the disaster, and he carefully avoided any contact with them in the ensuing years he remained in Oregon.

But in the autumn of 1838 he did arrive back at Waiilatpu with three young clergymen and their wives, an unattached missionary, and a wife of his own. The Reverend and Mrs. Asa S. Smith went to Kamiah. The Reverends Elkinah Walter and Cushing C. Eells, and their spouses, were sent to Tshimakain, near Fort Colville. Cornelius Rogers would serve as a teacher, first at Lapwai and then at Waiilatpu. The Grays stayed at Waiilatpu, where it was unlikely any Flatheads would get hold of him.

In the late summer of 1838, about the time Gray and his reinforcements arrived, the first Catholic Black Robes came down the Columbia with the annual Hudson's Bay Company express from Montreal.

Although Jason Lee always kept in close touch with the activities of French-Canadians of the Willamette Valley, most of whom seemed to him harmless, simple, people, and willing enough to cooperate with him in his programs for commercial and agricultural development, he had failed to judge correctly the degree of loyalty to their own faith that existed within them. Perhaps he had not given the matter much thought, or had been deceived by an absence of any antagonistic expressions directed toward the Methodist mission stations or the brand of gospel he and his missionaries dispensed.

Reading other people's mail, of course, was a liberty he had not gained. Thus he could not have known that even before the Methodists had arrived, the French-Canadian communities had corresponded with church officials in both Canada and the United States, asking that priests be sent to the Columbia. After the Methodists had founded their own settlement, more appeals were dispatched, revealing an increasing anxiousness to have a Catholic mission in the Willamette Valley.

Both the Methodists and the Presbyterians were entrenched— the first in the Willamette, at The Dalles, and several other places, the second at Waiilatpu, Lapwai, Kamea and Tshimakain—when the Reverend Francis Norbet Blanchet and the Reverend Modeste Demers lifted their threadbare habits and stepped ashore from a cargo bateau at Fort Vancouver. French-Canadian men and women wept as they gathered about them, and wept again before the portable altar, with its beautiful cloths and its candles and the golden cross, at the first mass ever celebrated in all the vast wilderness watershed of the Columbia.

The salients of the inter-denominational struggle to capture Indian souls were being established.

CHAPTER SIXTEEN

The Northwest:
Triumph on the Bitterroot

The Flatheads had made three attempts to induce men who spoke with the Great Spirit in the Sky to live among them. Only one member of the delegations they had sent to St. Louis had lived to return, and he had brought back information that proved to be erroneous. When at last missionaries had come over the mountains—Jason and Daniel Lee, Samuel Parker and Marcus Whitman, and others—they had spoken with two tongues, promising much and giving nothing, and had gone on, never appearing again. The Flatheads were in touch with Indians at Fort Colville and other posts, and now, in the fall of 1838, they knew that again they had been ignored, that two black gowns, Blanchet and Demers, had stationed themselves on the lower Columbia. Saddened, deeply disappointed and resentful, Flathead leaders, sitting in their snowbound council, reached a decision that would provide western history with one of its most dramatic chapters. The Flatheads would try again.

In September 1839, two Iroquois men appeared at the little log and earth building that was the Mission St. Joseph on the Missouri River near the Council Bluffs. They spoke in French, giving their names as Pierre Gaucher and Young Ignace. The priest who received them, conversing in the same language, was astonished to learn that they had not come from upper New York or Canada but from the Rocky Mountains. For more than twenty years, since they were youths, they had lived among the Flatheads and Nez Perce, working seasonally with traders. From their homes in the Bitterroot Range (western Montana) they had traveled with a small group of trappers who were going to St. Louis, over the mountains to the Roche Jaune, and by canoe down that stream and the Missouri River. Hearing that Black Robes lived near the Council Bluffs, they had left the company to visit them.

Father Pierre-Jean De Smet, at his crude desk made of Missouri River driftwood, would write in his journal of Gaucher and Ignace: "I have never seen any savages so fervent in religion. The sole object of these good Iroquois was to obtain a priest to come and finish what they had so happily commenced." He gave them letters of recommendation that would open the door of Bishop Joseph Rosati in St. Louis, and they left, as De Smet recorded, ". . .thinking nothing of adding three hundred leagues to the thousands they had already accomplished."

De Smet was not far behind them. On mule back and in a trader's wagon he made the six hundred mile winter journey to St. Louis in thirty days, arriving in November. Gaucher and Ignace were still there, and Bishop Rosati was struggling to find a way to fulfill their request, frustrated as usual by a lack of both funds and manpower. De Smet solved the problem. St. Joseph's could be well served by the colleague he had left there. He would go to the Flatheads alone, if necessary, with what small amount of money was available, or with none at all. Rosati, not by nature as daring as De Smet, but no less inspired by the thought of the rewards that could result from the project, authorized the assignment.

Although it was midwinter, Pierre Gaucher left at once, alone, on the long, perilous journey home to give his people the good news. Young Ignace would remain in St. Louis so that he might serve as interpreter and guide for De Smet, who would go out in the spring. Gaucher's journey is one of the most remarkable on record. Traveling alone on foot he crossed the plains and mountains, reaching the Bitterroot Valley late in April 1840. His word that a Black Robe was, at last and without doubt, coming in the summer caused great excitement among the Flatheads.

Pierre-Jean De Smet had arrived in America from his native Belgium as a novice of the Society of Jesus in 1821. He was ordained at St. Louis six years later. His story is not that of a brilliant scholar and linguist, a noted religious, a talented writer. He was, to be sure, all of these things, but singly or together they did not win for him the fame he would achieve. More significantly his story is that for more than thirty years he was the most influential man in the western wilderness. These were the years when the era of the fur trade drew to a close and was supplanted by the era of mass migration and settlement—the years of transition, when the juggernaut of civilization smashed across the plains, deserts, and mountains, and the calls of the wild were smothered by the ensuing uproar. During all this time no man was more trusted and revered by the western Indians engaged in their last hopeless struggles to save themselves and their homelands. It is a great deal to say that during the worst Indian wars no other white man could have gone alone among the hostile tribes and emerged alive. Yet that was exactly what was said by Army officers and scouts, by Indian agents and traders, by senators, cabinet members, and other Washington officials. Four Presidents—Pierce, Buchanan, Lincoln and Johnson—sought his services and his advice, asking him to perform tasks they knew no other person could accomplish, or even would attempt. If federal authorities had heeded his counsel, had adopted his programs and honestly executed them, many of the bloodiest western conflicts would not have taken place. But that did not happen, for there was a force greater than the power he possessed. Its components were political corruption, unbridled venality and greed, and criminal negligence.

These statements must serve merely as a brief introduction to the achievements of De Smet. There is not space in this work to recount them, nor would they, for the most part, be appropriate to its theme. He would establish only one mission in the far west, on the Bitterroot, but his activities in the Northwest placed him in a leading role in the tragic religious history of that enormous wilderness empire.[1]

Broad of shoulder, heavy, solid, standing three inches under six feet, De Smet was possessed of enormous physical strength and seemingly inexhaustible stamina. He was thirty-nine years of age in the early summer of 1840 when the American Fur Company caravan with which he and Young Ignace had traveled from the Missouri frontier crawled into the valley of the upper Green River. In the west stood the immense wall of the Wind River Mountains, and directly ahead the smoke of hundreds of campfires rose against the blazing afternoon light, pony herds drifted like shadows along the glistening stream, and ragged islands of tipis dotted the brown valley floor—the annual rendezvous of the fur traders.

A delegation of ten Flatheads was waiting to welcome him, and they greeted him "not as strangers but as friends." They had come to escort him to their country, and ". . .they told me all the little news of their nation, their almost miraculous preservation in a fight between sixty of their warriors and two hundred Blackfeet, a fight that lasted five days, and in which they had killed fifty of their enemies without losing a single man." They did not tell him, however, that at Pierre's Hole, just west of the Tetons, more than fifteen hundred Flatheads were waiting for him.

De Smet remained more than a week at the rendezvous, adding a new element to the customary brawling, fighting, wild dancing, and debauchery—that of a Chautauqua. He delivered sermons

and lectures, celebrated mass and held other religious ceremonies, and sat long hours with groups of Indians to discuss, in
something of the manner of a roundtable, current events and
various problems, both economic and social, of the moment. In
his voluminous writings De Smet never ridiculed the religious
ceremonies or the dances of Indians. At Green River, although
quite naturally opposed to the incantations and rituals, which he
considered idolatrous and paganish, he studiously refrained from
injuring the feelings of his hosts by openly criticizing or condemning the practices. He had their hearts and their faith, and that was
all he needed.

De Smet and the Flatheads would travel part of the way to the
Bitterroot with a company of trappers going to the country of the
Snakes. As they prepared to leave an event occurred that De Smet
thought most fortunate. Before his tipi appeared a big man in dirty
buckskin, with bright blue eyes peering quizzically out of shaggy
whiskers, who startled him with a greeting in Flemish. He was
Jean Baptiste De Gelder, born in Ghent and trained for a military
career. A less disciplined life had more appeal, and in 1810 he had
migrated to America. He had never gone back to Europe, and for
the past fourteen years he had been a wandering free trapper in the
Rocky Mountains. De Smet embraced De Gelder, and when the
veteran Mountain Man offered his services as a guide and adviser
he readily accepted. Although De Gelder had almost forgotten his
native tongue, De Smet was delighted to learn that he still remembered some verses of a Flemish hymn taught to him as a child by
his mother, and they sang it together.

It is improbable that a parade more colorful or wilder in its
pageantry ever wound its way through the high mountain wilderness. In Pierre's Hole, just west of the magnificent Tetons, Big
Face, "an elderly chief of truly patriarchal aspect," had pronounced eloquently the sentiments of his people. Young Ignace
gave his words, uttered with dignity and solemnity, to De Smet in

French: "Black Robe, you are welcome to my nation. Kyleeyou (Great Spirit) has fulfilled our wishes. Our hearts are big. You are among a poor and rude people, plunged in the darkness of ignorance. I have always exhorted my people to love the Great Spirit. We know that everything belongs to him, and that our whole dependence is upon his liberal hand. Now, Black Robe, speak, and we will comply with all you will tell us. Show us the road we have to follow, to come to the place where the Great Spirit resides. We will follow the words of your mouth."

During the several days spent in Pierre's Hole, De Smet had little chance to rest. Dancing and the beating of drums sometimes continued far into the night. He was presented with a small copper bell and told to ring it when he wished to call the people to prayer. Bands of Nez Perce and Pend d'Oreilles had joined the throng, and at the first sound of the bell's clapper more than two thousand Indians would rush to assemble before De Smet's lodge. If on any morning De Smet thought that he would catch a few extra winks, he was forced to get up by a zealous headman who would ride at dawn through the camp shouting: "Arise with haste! Black Robe will soon ring the bell. Open your eyes! Speak to the Great Spirit! The sun is about to appear. It is time you went to the river to wash yourselves. Be prompt at Black Robe's lodge!"

Such a great throng of men, women, and children, four thousand horses, a myriad dogs of all shapes and sizes, and long trains of pack animals almost concealed by loads of skin tipis, robes, utensils, weapons, food supplies, could not move far in a day. The horses had to be grazed, the cooking had to be done, and there had to be dancing and long talks and feasting and listening to sermons and time for just plain loafing. No man could have felt more like a conqueror than De Smet admitted he did in his diary, not a conqueror of land or of peoples, but "a spiritual conqueror, a discoverer under the banner of God." Yet there was the sensation of a geographical triumph, too, that day they camped on the shore of Henry's Lake. Its water flowed by way of the Columbia to the Pacific. And just over a ridge was Mosquito Lake, the ultimate source of the Missouri, four thousand and two hundred miles by watercourse from the Gulf of Mexico. And a few weeks earlier, climbing out of the valley of Green River, he had left waters that flowed into the Gulf of California.

. He found irresistible the urge to trudge up a shoulder of a mountain until he could gaze down upon both Henry's and Mosquito Lakes. Snowdrifts surrounded him, yet in the blinding sun the air was warm and sweet with the perfume of alpine meadows. Deeply moved by the panorama, he sat for some time in silence, and than on a rock he scratched with a knife: *Sanctus Ignatius Patronus Montium, Die Julii 27, 1840.*

The great parade crawled slowly ahead, down the Beaverhead and the Jefferson, reaching the Three Forks of the Missouri late in August, and De Smet knew a mounting concern. It reflected on the practical and economic phases of his mission. But time out now for a buffalo hunt. The Indians, too, were thinking of practical matters. About them on the valley floors "were numberless herds. Finding themselves therefore in the midst of abundance, the Flatheads prepared to lay in their winter meat supply; they raised willowy scaffolds for drying meat, and everyone made ready his firearm, his bow and arrows.

"Four hundred horsemen, old and young, mounted on their best horses, started early in the morning for the great hunt. I chose to accompany them in order to watch this striking spectacle from near at hand. At a given signal, they rode at full gallop among the herds; soon everything appeared confusion and flight all over the plain; the hunters pursued the fattest cows, discharged their guns and let fly their arrows, and in three hours they killed more than 500. Then the women, the old men, and the children came up, and with the aid of horses carried off the hides and the meat, and soon all the scaffolds were full and gave the camp the aspect of a vast butcher shop."

August passed as the meat dried, soon to be packed with bear and buffalo fat in skin sacks. The Bitterroot had not been reached, but De Smet understood that if he stayed with the Indians much longer it would be impossible for him to return to St. Louis before the mountains and plains were locked in deep snow and bitter cold. There remained not the slightest doubt in his mind that a mission in the homeland of the Flatheads would be successful, and unquestionably others could be profitably established among the Nez Perce, the Pend d'Oreilles, and adjacent tribes. He had found a vast and untouched vineyard for the Church. Was it these people whom the civilized nations cared to call by the name of savages?

In a council at the Three Forks he announced his decision. He could not go on to the Bitterroot, for it was necessary that he start back at once to obtain the tools and equipment he must have to build a mission and a church there. He also must have assistants, other Black Robes, who could carry the word of God to other tribes and build other churches. He gave them his solemn word that he would return as soon as he could after the snows had gone.

Many of the wild painted faces before him were stained with tears. The aged Big Face arose: "Black Robe, may the Great Spirit accompany you on your long and dangerous journey. When the grass begins to be green again, our hearts, so sad at present, will begin to rejoice. When the flowers appear we will set out to meet you. Farewell."

Thirty heavily armed warriors were assigned to guide De Smet and De Gelder, who elected to go with him, as far as Fort Alexander, a trading post on the Yellowstone in the country of the Crows, then allies of the Flatheads. Proceeding without an escort, De Smet and De Gelder completed a perilous journey of two hundred miles to Fort Union, an American Fur Company post a few miles from the junction of the Yellowstone and Missouri. There they were fortunate enough to meet a small company of traders en route down the Missouri Valley. The river was closed by ice when they reached Mission St. Joseph at the Council

Bluffs. It was New Year's Eve when they knocked on the door of the Father Superior at St. Louis University.

De Smet, who had a penchant for keeping detailed records, estimated that in slightly more than nine months—two hundred and forty-nine days, to be exact—he had traveled by horseback, except for short distances by canoe and wagon, somewhat more than four thousand and two hundred miles, a large part of the time through country never before visited by a man of the cloth.

He was back on the trail again in May with a westbound caravan, not only with tools and supplies for his mission, but with two priests and three lay brothers. His appeals during the winter for contributions had brought in several thousand dollars. Father Nicholas Point was experienced, having served among Missouri River Indians, and an artist of considerable talent. Father Gregory Mengarini had recently arrived in St. Louis from Rome and had been selected for the Rocky Mountain assignment because of his facility with languages and his knowledge of medicine. The brothers were William Claessens, a blacksmith from Belgium; Charles Huet, a Flemish carpenter; and Joseph Specht, a German mason and tinner. De Gelder, more than fifty years of age, had decided not to return to the mountains.

The train went to Fort Hall, and there the Flatheads were waiting with a noisy welcome. In the fall of 1841, on the Bitterroot, thirty miles above its mouth, the log buildings and the chapel of St. Mary's Mission rapidly took shape.

De Smet, with an escort of ten Flatheads, went to Fort Colville to send word of his presence and his accomplishments to Blanchet and Demers, at their own new Mission St. Paul on the Willamette, and to McLoughlin at Fort Vancouver. He also sent several long letters to his family and to his superiors down the Columbia, fervently hoping that they would catch some ship sailing for the east coast before many weeks had passed. Then he went back on snowshoes to the Bitterroot. Fires were burning in the hearths of St. Mary's.

CHAPTER SEVENTEEN

The Northwest:
Bigotry on the Columbia

They were little whirlwinds, striking spasmodically, not upon the permanency of earth but upon the fragility of human reason. Little gusting disturbances, in their transiency shadowing with hypocrisy and hate, whipping up the dust of aversion and calumny, and twisting on their erratic courses to agitate emotions and inflame convictions.

For the Indians the conflict between the Protestants and Catholics was an irremediable mental trauma, a malignancy that sapped the powers of intellect and supplanted what faith and hope they might once have possessed with distrust and confusion. Christianity, in their way of reasoning, appeared to be a religion composed of irreconcilable elements. The antagonists preached as much about the untruths purportedly inherent in the doctrines of their opponents as they did about the gospel of their own denominations. But not only Catholics and Protestants spewed out their bigotry; Protestants also quarreled with each other. The Methodists and the Congregationalists and the Episcopalians and the Presbyterians argued openly about matters that were meaningless and inconsequential to wondering red people. Everyone disputed everyone.

The Indians were brainwashed into a state of consternation, not knowing whom to believe. In the end they would believe no one, concluding that Jesus himself may have been responsible for the turmoil by failing to create harmony and order among his earthly disciples.

At this point Blanchet and Demers began to play their starring roles in the inter-faith controversy on the Columbia. The appearance of these priests in their dark robes, their mystical gestures, their apparent indifference to secular affairs, their altar decorations, at once attracted the attention of the Indians. More than being impressed, however, the Indians were puzzled. Here were men who lived without women. The Cayuse seemed particularly interested, asking the Protestants such questions as why they didn't wear gowns and didn't have such pretty things at their services—scratchy brambles of inquisitiveness and not easily soothed.[1]

With mounts and supplies furnished them by McLoughlin, Blanchet and Demers gave first attention to the French-Canadian settlements on the Cowlitz and the Willamette, a direct assault on the domain in which the Methodists had enjoyed a free hand. They did not hesitate to deliver severe scoldings to their parishioners and to condemn Wesleyans as condoners of sinfulness. The settlers of their faith with Indian wives were commanded to stay out of conjugal beds for thirty days, after which period of chastity the privileges of matrimony would be restored by holy rites. The sin of unblessed cohabitation was not absolved by marriage in the impious sanctums of Protestantism—a mistake many had made—indeed, an exchange of vows under such circumstances was meaningless in the eyes of God. Jason Lee and other ministers found themselves talking largely for their own benefit, or at best to a few ragged Indians who didn't know what to make of the situation. Catholics were forbidden to attend Methodist meetings of any type, even those of the temperance society Lee had founded, and by his own count Blanchet baptized some hundred and fifty half-breed babies who undoubtedly were less impressed by his edicts than they were terrorized by the commotion.[2]

Through the summer of 1839 Demers celebrated masses and delivered sermons to crowds of Indians in the Fort Colville region and at Fort Walla Walla, drawing throngs of Cayuses, Nez Perces, and other tribesmen, and even had the temerity to visit Waiilatpu, a social call during which the strain of ill will surfaced with the tea and cakes politely served by Narcissa.

Far down the river Blanchet was laying solid foundations for the establishments that would give permanence to the Oregon Diocese. He took craftsmen and farmers to the Cowlitz. With the permission of the Indians, a log house twenty by thirty feet in size was built, twenty-four acres were fenced with wooden rails, sixteen more were ploughed for an autumn sowing. The first crop, planted in the spring, amounted to six bushels of wheat and nine bushels of peas, hardly bountiful but enough to supplement the meagre fare Demers would have when he returned from Walla Walla. The Cowlitz would be his station.

Before the summer was over Blanchet and a crew of volunteers were building Mission St. Paul in the Willamette Valley. It was not British territory, but the Hudson's Bay Company officials at Fort Vancouver had granted the authorization he had requested. In this case Indians didn't have to be considered; there weren't any immediately adjacent; and opposition by the Methodists was ignored by Blanchet as if he were stone deaf. In his estimation, which he made no attempt to keep private, the Methodists didn't have a mission in the Willamette. What they had was a commercial conglomerate, farms, a stock-breeding business, a water-power utility, a lumber company, saw and flour mills, a land development association, a trading store, a real estate office, and a disreputable building they called a church. Jason Lee, not the Lord, was in control. And in his judgment, Blanchet was correct. Unless he was living an impossible dream, St. Joseph's Mission would have not only a church but an Indian school, hopefully with nuns as teachers, and farms to support it, not to grow crops and animals for market, and Indians would be taught agriculture and animal husbandry to make them independent. It was a dream that would come very close to being fulfilled as he had prayed it would. He would go back to Canada, even to Europe if necessary, to get the money and the people he would need. He would bring in the Indians, too.

The Protestants found some source of new spunk and bowed their necks a bit, and the troops on both sides began to fight with threats and innuendos and false charges and bitter accusations that forced their descent to levels on which the dignity of their calling lost to irrational brawling.

More priests and lay brothers, as a result of the efforts of Blanchet and De Smet, were arriving in the Northwest from both Canada and the States, and they quickly took up Blanchet's refrain that the Protestants were guilty of an impudent intrusion and crimes in the guise of religion by preaching their heretical creed to French-Canadians and attempting to convert natives. The same to you, said the Protestants, and your old man in Rome, too. One Protestant minister was trying to induce Catholics to remarry in his church, to be doubly safeguarded. No success at all, declared Blanchet, and this fanatic would burn in the fires of hell for his sacriligious designs. Daniel Lee was going about praying in the houses of Catholic Canadians, or in front of them if he coudn't get in, a pitiful spectacle of fruitless proselytism. Jason Lee had thought he was building a Methodist empire over which he would rule as an industrial mogul, but politics was all he cared about, and he was finding out whose side God was on. And Jason Lee, or one of his cohorts, had complained to the Hudson's Bay

Company that the Catholics were using their influence to keep the lambs of the flock out of the clutches of Protestant wolves, but was told that the issue was none of the company's business. No other attitude could have been expected, shouted the Protestants, for McLoughlin had always been a Jesuitical Catholic, even though he had only recently joined the church, and had always plotted against Protestantism and American progress. Blanchet boasted of his achievement of converting McLoughlin, who had once been a member of the Anglican Church. And Blanchet taunted the Methodists with the claim that in only seven days he had christianized all the Indians living at the falls of the Willamette, moreover accomplishing the feat under the very nose of the helpless Methodist minister allegedly ministering to the poor souls there.

Both Blanchet and De Smet would make trips to Europe to obtain contributions and recruits, and both would be eminently successful. Blanchet would return with eight priests, three lay brothers, two deacons, one cleric, and seven sisters from Notre Dame de Namur. De Smet sailed into the Columbia with four priests, a number of lay brothers, and six sisters of the same order as those brought back by Blanchet. The sisters were settled in a convent at French Prairie, hard by the Methodists. The coffers of the Catholic diocese in Oregon were well filled with francs, easily convertible into pounds sterling and dollars. De Smet sent his colleagues to build missions among the Kalispells, Pend d'Oreilles, Spokans, and the Indians in Colville Valley, at the Great Lakes of the Columbia, and at Flatbow Lake.

As recounted, Jason Lee would go east, his dream crumbled. Blanchet, now an archbishop, would generously offer to buy the buildings and the land of Lee's Oregon Institute and the Methodist Mission at French Prairie, but the Reverend Gary, sent out to dispose of the Methodist's holdings, refused to sell to the Catholic Church, although under such a transaction the

Methodist Board of Missions would have received more than twice what it did get for the property on the open market.

If the collapse of the Methodist organization suggests that the Catholics won a stunning victory in the Willamette and lower Columbia Valleys, the impression would be erroneous. The dominant position which the Catholics achieved was not a religious triumph; indeed, under the prevailing circumstances they could not have avoided it. Only three reasons are needed to demonstrate the inevitability of its occurrence: (a) most of the settlers at the time of the advent of their missionary endeavors, as well as most of the traders and trappers employed by the Hudson's Bay Company, were French-Canadian Catholics, thus the priests had awaiting them a faithful congregation; (b) the commercial and political operations of Jason Lee had shattered the morale of workers under his direction, precluding efficiency by forcing them into untenable positions and nullifying the inspiration that had brought them west; (c) the Methodist Board of Missions, not the Catholic Church, forced the abandonment of the Methodist establishments in Oregon by refusing to continue to support the personal greedy, if not nefarious, practices of Jason Lee and the malfunctions for which he was responsible. As for the Indians of western Oregon they benefited no more under the Catholics than under the Methodists. The Indians of the region rapidly fell into a state of degradation from which they would never recover, not only losing their homelands but all civil and legal rights, and at last, if not annihilated, being herded onto small reservations where the self-righteous emissaries of God, no matter what their persuasions, could be of no help at all to them.

The crusade of the Catholics under Archbishop-General Blanchet was executed in the guise of a religious offensive to save Indian souls from perdition. It was more than that, waged also for another purpose: to drive Protestants from the Northwest. The Catholic stations were armed camps, munitions depots, to which were sent annually shipments of guns and bullets and powder. When the upper Columbia became engulfed in warfare, Catholic priests would be charged by American Army officers with promising to furnish the Cayuse with arms to aid them in wiping out the Americans—meaning the Protestants. When a large amount of arms and ammunition arrived at The Dalles, on its way to the Jesuit missions, it was halted and held there by the American commander, Major Henry A. G. Lee.

Notified of the seizure, a Jesuit priest, M. Accolti, wrote Major Lee to remind him that the law did not prohibit the transportation of arms and ammunition through the Indian country. The exposure of the Jesuit schemes would result in a Protestant petition being placed before the Territorial Legislature advocating the expulsions of Catholics from Oregon. The appeal was rejected, but it did cause the infliction of a drastic restriction on the activities of the Jesuits: they were forbidden to enter the Umatilla country, a main theater of the war with the Cayuse.

The scene shifts now in a cut back to the spring of 1842, showing the Presbyterian missions east of the Cascades. The Indians were greatly different in character and culture from those on the lower Columbia, and it seems appropriate to say something of them here, if for no other reason than to depict briefly some of the perils and problems that faced Whitman and his colleagues in the enormous region that was still, except for a few tiny and widely separated islands inhabited by civilized men and women, the wilderness nature had created.[3]

They were the Cayuse, Nez Perce, Palouse, Walla Walla, Umatilla—these of the Shahaptin linguistic group—and only the first two would write their names indelibly in history, the Cayuse for their infamy, the Nez Perce for their integrity and courage. Then there were those speaking the Salishan tongue, the Okanogan, Colville, Sanspoil, and Spokan, the latter name to be extended with an *e* by white men, for some unknown reason.

If their languages differed, they had many things in common. They were, when the missionaries first came to know them, hardly more than a hop, skip, and a jump out of the Stone Age, their primitive instincts transformed little, their native intelligence sharpened but not yet weakened, their physical strength not yet impaired by contacts with white men, the fur traders and trappers from Canada who were not interested in changing or enlightening them but only in obtaining pelts from them in exchange for pots and blankets and worthless but bright doodads.

Speaking generally of them, their customs and habits were fairly homogeneous. They were not sedentary people, for they lived by hunting, fishing, and gathering wild plant foods, and the demands of their economy necessitated moving with the seasonal changes of their food supply. They roamed over large areas, depending almost completely on the bounties of the rivers and forests and mountain meadowlands. Attempting to instill in them the precepts of Christianity would have been difficult enough even if they had been always present for classes, but they came and went, not with regularity but with total unpredictability, much of the year vanishing, often for weeks at a time. Whitman claimed they were not only eager but were quick to learn. Perhaps that was true, but if so they had little time to study. The small number who would learn enough—prayers and psalms and biblical texts—to qualify for membership in the Presbyterian Church would not have comprised an influential nucleus—only several score still puzzled about the Crucifixion, the torturing of a God in the image of their own kind.

The missionaries and their lay assistants wanted some answers, too. Indians who agreed to cultivate crops for their own use wanted to be paid for doing the work; they maintained that they were doing a favor to Whitman by laboring in their own fields; and they wanted compensation in the form of guns and blankets and other goods for harvesting grains and vegetables they would consume. They demanded payment for permitting the missionaries to construct buildings and engage in agriculture on their lands, and when it wasn't forthcoming they stole products and equipment which had to be bought back at outrageous prices, and they let their horses trample gardens and ripening corn and wheat.

Whitman's courage appeared to be inexhaustible, his nerves of steel; but patience cracked now and then. When he delivered a tongue lashing to the Cayuse for their bad behavior, several of them covered him with mud, pulled his beard and nose, knocked him down, and threatened to burn his home. One man struck at him with an axe, but he managed to twist away in time to escape blow that surely would have killed him. Gray didn't help matters by resorting to medicinal trickery. Weary of having native children stealing his vegetables, he inserted a tartar emetic into a number of choice melons. If the resulting vomiting effectively destroyed the Cayuse's taste for melons the violent sickness also engendered the suspicion that the missionaries possessed evil powers, a suspicion that would become a conviction when other diseases struck.

Similar dangerous conditions prevailed at the other stations, at Lapwai, at Kamiah, at Tshimakain. The Whitmans, the Spaldings, the Smiths, the Eells, and all the others, were being broken in body if not in spirit. Labor confronted them in an unchanging daily pattern, and their shoulders bent with an unutterable weariness, and they grew gaunt and dried and bony. They existed in loneliness and anxiety and discouragement and bad health.

Kamiah was the first to go. The Nez Perce there were closely associated with the Flatheads and favored the Catholic missions. They gave Asa Smith permission to build a house but they refused to let him farm. When he defied them and attempted to plow, they threatened to kill him and his wife. If he dug a hole in the earth, they told him, it would be used as his grave. He gave up, and he and Mrs. Smith went down the Columbia to Fort Vancouver and sailed for the Hawaiian Islands. Smith was speaking more prophetically than he realized when he wrote the mission board: "No longer can we be borne along by the current of popular favor among this (Indian) people. The novelty of having missionaries among them is now gone . . In the future it will be uphill work."

Tshimakain did not have the same improvements nor the same troubles as those at Lapwai and Waiilatpu. The Walkers and the Eells were pestered by thieves, and frosts damaged their crops each year, but they managed to hang on. The Indians spread lies about them, but more as amusement than in animosity. And when the mission building was accidentally destroyed by fire, Indians and French-Canadians from Fort Colville came at once to help them rebuild. De Smet, enjoying his own success on the Bitter-root was not so charitable. He would write that the Walkers and Eells were "fearful that, should they cultivate more, they might have too frequent visits from the savages. They even try to prevent their encampment in their immediate neighborhood, and therefore they see and converse but seldom with the heathen they have come so far to seek." But propaganda was a weapon in the stupid war, and De Smet was not averse to taking a potshot with it now and then, although he was never as vicious as Blanchet and Demers.

If Spalding had his failings, one of them was not gutlessness. He proclaimed rules of conduct at Lapwai, and warned the Nez Perce that violators of them would suffer severe punishment. Fortunately he had leaders there—one of them was an elderly chief named Joseph whose son, taking the same name, would win undying fame as a field general in an unnecessary and unfair war against American soldiers—who saw wisdom in the rules, and they were usually obeyed—but not always. Charging that a war-rior called Blue Cloak had broken an agreement, Spalding levied a fine of a good horse on him for breach of contract. When payment was not immediately made, he ordered that Blue Cloak be whipped. Blue Cloak was siezed and bound, but one of the Indians in the large group at the scene stepped forward and told Spalding to exact the penalty himself. Spalding declared that he, like God, gave commands but did not execute them. Whip Blue Cloak, he was told, or he would be whipped instead. Spalding applied two or three lashes to the back of the bound man, then calmly reiterated his demand for the horse, and it was given to him.

There were two other incidents at Lapwai that contribute importantly to the unpleasant picture there. A chieftain inappropriately called Ellis was a troublemaker. He and a band of Nez Perce wrecked the mission mill on the ground that it belonged to them and they were receiving no benefits from it. Then Ellis and a number of his followers kept all white persons at Lapwai confined for several weeks in the Spalding home, threatening to shoot anyone, women included, who sought to escape. "I have no evidence to suppose," Spalding would write a friend, "but a vast majority of the natives would look on with indifference and see our dwelling burned to the ground, and our heads severed from our bodies." But no dwellings were burned, and no heads were lost, and the Lapwai farms produced surplus crops, and the Spaldings and their aides weathered the storms.

Whitman was mauled several times, and Narcissa, her once lovely face marred by creases increased by sun and wind, was assailed by insults whenever she was out of the hearing of her husband or other men. McLoughlin wrote Whitman to leave Waiilatpu, and knowing the way of Indians told him that if he did pull up stakes the Cayuse would soon ask him to return and would be less troublesome. Whitman took no one's advice.

The complexities of his character pose difficult problems for one writing about him. If he was a Caesar for Christ, he was no less a dedicated, kindly, unselfish man of medicine. If he was fearless, he was no less stubborn and determined to achieve the goals that inspired him. If he was gifted with a superior intellect, he was not an accomplished educator. He would row with Indians as if they were his equal in knowledge, as if they were as capable of comprehending the ways of schooled and trained white men as he himself.

He appealed often to the mission board for the means of strengthening his position, but after the year 1840 he received no encouraging responses. Independent missionaries who could have helped him deserted after short periods of service: Smith, Rogers, Gray, and others. Some emigrants paused at Waiilatpu, and he pleaded with them to remain and develop farms, but the dryness and the inclement weather quickly drove them on to the milder climate of the Willamette Valley. He showed them wheat standing seven feet high, and tall corn, and rich grazing lands, but these were not inducements enough to keep them.

The mission board had let Whitman know that it felt the Presbyterian establishments should be self-supporting. He had replied that such an idea was visionary under the circumstances of their isolation and the inadequacy of their personnel. But struggling through lonely hours with the dilemma he at last developed what he thought was a solution. A route had been discovered by which wagons could travel through to the Columbia. The number of emigrants was steadily increasing, and he reasoned that the tide of settlers would continue to grow with the passage of each year. Both Waiilatpu and Lapwai were in locations that would make it possible for them to become profitable supply stations. Commercialization would solve the problem. From his deliberations evolved prophetic scenes: long wagon trains rumbling and creaking westward, thousands of travellers, men, women and children, in need of aid and equipment, Waiilatpu and Lapwai thriving communities, surrounded by grain fields and orchards and flocks of sheep and herds of cattle. Economics in these dominating powers would have the effect of a strong Protestant influence on the Indians, and counteract, if not render impotent, the efforts of the Catholics in the upper Columbia and Snake River countries.

Whitman had resigned himself to waiting nearly two years for approval of the requests and recommendations and the comprehensive plans he had conceived. They would be started on their way east with the advent of spring, when traders began to move through the mountains and cross the plains. It was unlikely that the board would receive them before the fall of 1843, and the summer of 1844 would be nearing an end when an answer came.

But this was September 1842, and obviously the American Board of Commissioners for Foreign Missions had settled upon plans of its own nine months earlier. The board's letter, handed to him by Archibald McKinlay, the Hudson's Bay Company factor at Fort Walla Walla, contained no suggestions, only orders. Waiilatpu and Lapwai were to be closed in the coming spring. Spalding was to return to the east, his tenure terminated. Walker and Eells were to remain at Tshimakain. Dr. Whitman would advise the board of the course he desired to take—to remain or not to remain, that was the question for him to answer.

The four men sat about a stove in the grubby little parlor of the Whitman home at Waiilatpu. Struggling to conceal the sickness that weighted his heart and the rage that troubled his tongue, Whitman called the decision sheer madness. The board was proposing to keep the poorest mission, the one most difficult to maintain. As soon as they moved out of Waiilatpu and Lapwai, the Catholics would move in. Walker and Eells saw no alternative but to obey the orders. Spalding declared he would not leave Lapwai, he would not desert the friends he had made among the Nez Perce. And neither would he leave Waiilatpu, said Whitman with strained quietness. The Cayuse needed his medical ministrations, with or without the spirtual guidance he and Narcissa provided. Waiilatpu was home.

He arranged with two families to live at Waiilatpu, and his good friend McKinlay promised that they and Narcissa would be protected. October had come, too late to cross the high mountains of Wyoming to Fort Laramie and follow the trail down the North Platte. But there was a feasible route, and one might well look at a map for a moment, just to know where it went. From Fort Hall on the Snake it went south through Utah, keeping the main ranges to the left, twisting across New Mexico to Taos and Santa Fe, skirting the southern end of the Sangre de Christo Range to Bent's Fort on the Arkansas. Whitman had with him an Indian guide from Fort Walla Walla, and an emigrant, A. L. Lovejoy, who wanted to go back to Iowa.

Bent's Fort was far enough for them in one winter, but luck was with Whitman. He met a company of traders going on to Missouri, and went with them, crossing the plains of southern Kansas. On a cold day in March 1843, more than five months after kissing Narcissa good-by at Waiilatpu, he walked into the office of the mission board in Boston.

To say that the American Board of Commissioners for Foreign Missions was cold to him would be a gross understatement. The commissioners were not even cordial. He was reproved for leaving Waiilatpu without permission. They refused to pay the expenses of his journey. They bluntly rejected his requests, his recommendations, his plans. They had become convinced that the savages of the Northwest among whom their missions were located were not yet ready to receive Christ.

However, the commissioners did thaw out enough to make one concession. They told him that he and Spalding might continue to live at Waiilatpu and Lapwai if they desired, but they would receive no support of any kind. The account books of Waiilatpu and Lapwai were closed, if not in the most desirable balanced condition. The board would be represented only by the inexpensive station at Tshimakain, but even its survival was doubtful.

So Dr. Marcus Whitman, who had already given more than nine years of his life to carrying medicine and Christianity to save heathen bodies and souls in the northwestern wilderness, could go back if he wished. But the board would not pay the cost of his return journey.

Whitman went home, not this time with a fur trade supply caravan, for the rendezvous system of the Mountain Men had been abolished; the fur trade was dying. He went home with a long wagon train of emigrants, on their way, as he had predicted, to take up grants of land promised them by the United States in the Willamette and Columbia Valleys.

It was not a pleasant homecoming that fall of 1843. Narcissa had been threatened and insulted by some Cayuse, and McKinlay had sent her to safety at The Dalles. The mill and all the grain stored in it had been burned. A few emigrants had agreed to stay with him, and he left them and went down river to get his wife. Waiilatpu would not be closed.

CHAPTER EIGHTEEN

Waiilatpu:
November 1847

It ends here, building in a terrifying crescendo that could have happened only with a final thunderous collision of two worlds and two gods.

The instruments in the preceding years had played in their turns, moaning the dirges peculiar to each of them, and at last were in concert for the funereal chords that would conclude the symphony. The Cayuse were listening and thinking, disliking every note they heard, profoundly disturbed and angered by a welling conviction that the composers of the menacing music were sorcerers.

Whitman had schemed to bring more white people to take their lands, and they were coming. The Cayuse felt sure of other things: the missionaries were plotting with other Americans to bring in great herds to eat the grass they needed for their own cattle, and sheep, and horses. On Cayuse lands the missionaries were urging that farms be developed and the products grown sold to the hordes of emigrants, and that was denying the Cayuse a prosperous trade; it was stealing from them.

Greed was not a quality in Marcus Whitman. The ambitions he exhibited had other sources. He wanted to create a community that would assure the continued existence of the Protestant missions, and he wanted to prevent the Catholics from reaping the harvest of the spiritual seeds he and his colleagues had sown. The outlook was forlorn. Despite persistent efforts, in the four years that had passed since his futile journey to New England, he had been able to induce only a handful of emigrants to remain temporarily at Waiilatpu.

In the spring of 1847, Whitman had seriously considered giving up the fight. Some of the Cayuse chiefs had demanded that he pack up his little troop and depart. As far as they were concerned, he could take the Spaldings and the other white people at Lapwai with him, but that was a matter for the Nez Perce to decide. If all the Cayuse leaders had demanded that he leave, Whitman would have complied, but the Cayuse chiefs were divided on that question.

Whitman stayed, but not only because some Cayuse wanted him to remain, obviously hoping that his schemes eventually would work out to their advantage. Whitman also stayed because the Catholics were invading his domain. Father Jean Baptiste Abraham Brouillet and Archbishop Blanchet were circulating among the Cayuse in the Umatilla Valley. He saw them as vultures disguised in black robes, knowing of his plight, and waiting for him to die.

Whitman stayed, desperately searching for a means of saving Waiilatpu. It had been his and Narcissa's home for eleven years. Considerable money and no end of labor had been invested to develop a large farm, a mill, to build a school and a chapel. Yet in the summer of 1847 he knew—or sensed—in his own heart that he would be defeated in his struggle. This is indicated by the fact that he got together enough money and goods to buy the rundown buildings and farm of the defunct Methodist mission at The Dalles. He sent a nephew who had come west with him in 1843 to live there, confiding to him, to Narcissa, and perhaps to a few others in whom he had trust, that unless the Cayuse ceased their belligerent attitude toward him and more settlers could be persuaded to locate at Waiilatpu he would be obliged to abandon it. In that case, they would move to The Dalles in the coming summer.

Whitman had stayed too long.

It was not economics, not religion, not fear, not failing courage that united to write the finale. It was a scourge.

The wagon trains passing through the Cayuse country in the late summer of 1847 carried a deadly cargo in two forms— amoebic dysentery and measles. Scores of adult Cayuse sought to relieve their internal burning by plunging into cold streams and died moments later. Others lay helpless in their lodges, excrement flooding uncontrollably from their bowels. In some villages all children and many of the young people, parched in their fever and crying out their agony, perished in a few days. The measles epidemic went on down the Umatilla and the Walla Walla, leaving a trail of small bodies in its wake, all the way down the Columbia to The Dalles before it began to subside.

They were white man's diseases, weren't they? Dr. Whitman was a white medicine man, wasn't he? Then why, the Cayuse wanted to know, couldn't he cure them?

There were grounds for dark suspicions in the Cayuse. They came out of a diabolical rumor spread by a halfbreed named Joe Louis, who was sometimes engaged as a laborer at Waiilatpu[1].

The story of Louis in essence is that he accused Whitman, Narcissa, and Spalding of plotting to poison the Cayuse so that they might take possession of their lands for themselves and then sell acreage to settlers. There can be no doubt about Louis; he was a white man hater. The Whitmans must have been warned about him. It was said by witnesses that in that last hour of terror at Waiilatpu he was in the mission dooryard, and Narcissa had screamed at him from a second floor window, accusing him of fomenting the trouble.

There is strong evidence showing what Louis had done before that day of infamy. He had told the Cayuse that for two years Whitman and Spalding had been writing their friends in the east to send them enough poison to kill off the Indians at Lapwai and Waiilatpu. They had received some poison but when it was used nothing happened, and they had sent for a stronger kind, and it had arrived with a wagon train in the summer of 1847.

Louis said much more: he was resting on a settee in the mission when he overheard Whitman, Narcissa, and Spalding talking in an adjoining room. The terrible diseases had struck, and two hundred Cayuse already had died. Spalding asked why Whitman was killing the Indians so slowly, and Whitman told Spalding not to worry, that the Cayuse were dying fast enough, and the young ones would be gone before winter, and all the old ones by spring.

On Saturday, November 27, Whitman and Spalding rode thirty miles south to some Cayuse villages, Whitman to treat the ill and Spalding to conduct religious services the following day. They met Father Brouillet and Archbishop Blanchet and were invited to dine with them at the new Catholic station on the Umatilla. Some weeks after this meeting a story circulated—without proof of its truthfulness—that Blanchet had admitted to Whitman and Spalding that he knew they were contemplating leaving Waiilatpu and Lapwai, and offered to buy the Presbyterian missions. Whitman and Spalding had called the information erroneous, and nothing more was said of the matter.

On Sunday, November 28, Whitman went home alone, riding most of the night. Spalding was kept awake by Indian women chanting the melancholy Cayuse mourning song, and as he was about to leave an old Indian woman grabbed the bridle of his horse and pleaded with him not to go to Waiilatpu.

The story of the Whitman Massacre is in every history of western America and countless pioneer narratives and diaries. No purpose would be served in repeating it in all its bloody details.[2]

How many white persons, men, women and children, were at Waiilatpu or in the immediate vicinity on November 29, 1847, does not appear on any authentic record. How many died is known: eleven men, two children, and one woman.

Shortly after midday several Cayuse appeared at Whitman's office and study. Two entered and asked for medicine. As Whitman turned in his chair to reach for a vial, one of the Cayuses quickly drew a hatchet from beneath his blanket and smashed open Whitman's skull. A sick man lying on a couch nearby attempted to draw a pistol but was tomahawked to death before he could fire. More Indians entered, yowling and brandishing weapons. When Narcissa rushed in and knelt beside the dying doctor, she was shot in the shoulder. She got to the second floor with several other women, came downstairs again, and was shot twice, falling dead.

The Cayuse, more of them appearing now, hacked and shot other men and two children both outside and in the mission buildings. Several emigrant families—again the exact number is not certain—were able to get away, reaching the Hudson's Bay Company post at Walla Walla after hiding in woods through the night. At Waiilatpu the Cayuse mutilated the dead. They carried off the surviving women and children with them, to be held for ransom. Cayuse leaders took several of the youngest women, and one girl of fourteen, as temporary wives. Eventually the captives would be rescued. Henry Spalding would narrowly escape martyrdom. He was nearing Waiilatpu the following day, returning from Umatilla, when he was told by several Indians of the murders. He rode hard for Lapwai and the friendly Nez Perce.

The first rescuers to reach Waiilatpu, one of whom was Father Brouillet, found Narcissa's gold hair, now flecked with gray, matted with blood, and her face welted from the blows of a quirt. She and Whitman were laid beside each other. The other victims, cut and beaten beyond recognition, were interred in a common grave. Brouillet would write that he feared he would be assassinated by lurking Cayuse as he knelt in the little Waiilatpu cemetery and recited a prayer for the departed souls.

The war of the faiths had ended, supplanted by Oregon's first serious Indian conflict—militia not Christian soldiers were marching in the Cayuse country.

Bibliography

Ainsworth, Katherine, and Edward M., *In the Shade of the Juniper Tree*, New York, 1970

Alarcon, Hernando, (See Hammond and Rey 1940; Bolton 1949).

Allen, Miss A. J. (Compiler), *Travels and Adventures of Doctor E. White and Lady* — Ten Years in Oregon, Ithaca, N. Y., 1850.

Bagley, Clarence B., *Early Catholic Missions in Old Oregon*, 2 Vols., Seattle, 1932.

Bancroft, Hubert Howe, *History of the North Mexican States and Texas*, 2 Vols., San Francisco, 1884.
History of Oregon, 2 Vols., San Francisco, 1886.
History of California, San Francisco, 1886.
History of Arizona and New Mexico 1530—1888, San Francisco, 1889.

Bandelier, Adolf F., *Final Report of Investigations among The Indians of the Southwestern United States*, Cambridge, 1890.
and Fanny, *Historical Documents Relating to New Mexico*, edited by Charles D. Hackett, Carnegie Institution, Publication No. 330, Washington, D. C., 1923.

Bandelier, Fanny, (Translator), *The Journey of Alvar Nunez Cabeza De Vaca and His Companions from Florida to the Pacific. 1528–1536*, translated from the 1542 edition of Cabeza de Vaca's *Relacion*, New York, 1905.

Barclay, Wade Crawford, *Early American Methodism, 1769—1844*, 2 Vols., New York, 1950.

Barker, Burt Brown, *Letters of Dr. John McLoughlin written at Fort Vancouver, 1829—1832.*, Portland, Oregon, 1948.

Barrett, S. A., *The Ethno-Geography of the Pomo and Neighboring Indians*, Berkeley, 1908.

Benavides, Alonso de, *Memorial*, Madrid, 1630. English translation, Land of Sunshine Magazine, Vol. XIII, 1900, Los Angeles. Translated and privately published by Mrs. Edward E. Ayer, with annotations by F.W. Hodge and Charles F. Lummis, Chicago, 1916.

Billington, Ray Allen, *Westward Expansion*, New York, 1949.

Blanchet, F. N., *Historical Sketches of the Catholic Church in Oregon during the past Forty Years, 1838–1878*, Portland, 1878.
et al., *Notices and Voyages of the Famed Quebec Mission to the Pacific Northwest: Being the Correspondence, Notices, etc., of the Fathers Blanchet and Demers together with those of Fathers Bolduc and Langlois*, Portland, 1956.

Boas, Franz, (See *Souls* in Hodge, 1907.)
(See *Religion* in Hodge, 1907.)

Bolton, Herbert Eugene, *Spanish Exploration in the Southwest 1542—1706*, New York, 1916.
(Translator), *Kino's Historical Memoir of Pimeria Alta, 2 Vols.* Translated from original manuscript of *Favores Celestiales*, Cleveland, 1979.

Historical Memoirs of New California (English translation of Palou's *Noticias.*) Berkeley, 1926.

Fray Juan Crespi, Missionary Explorer on the Pacific Coast, Berkeley, 1927.

Padre on Horseback, San Francisco, 1932.

Rim of Christendom, New York, 1936.

Coronado, Knight of Pueblos and Plains, New York, 1949.

Bonilla-Humana (See Terrell, 1973.)

Boscana, Geronimo, *Chinigchinich* (See Robinson, Alfred.)

Brosnan, Cornelius J., *Jason Lee, Prophet of the new Oregon,* New York, 1932.

Brouillet, J. B. A., *Authentic Account of the Murder of Dr. Whitman,* Portland, 1869.

Burns, Robert Ignatius, *The Jesuits and the Indian Wars of the Northwest,* New Haven, Conn., 1966.

Burrus, Ernest J., *Kino's Plan for the Development of Pimeria Alta, Arizona and Upper California,* Tucson, 1961.

Kino Writes to the Duchess, Rome, Italy, and St. Louis, 1965-A.

Kino and the Cartography of Northwestern New Spain, Tucson, 1965-B.

Campbell, Thomas J., *Pioneer Priests of North America,* 3 vols., New York, 1914.

Casas, Bartolome de Las, *Tears of the Indians,* London, 1656.

Historia de Las Indias, Madrid, 1674.

Castaneda, Pedro de (See Winship, 1896.)

Castano (See Terrell, 1973).

Chittenden, Hiram Martin, *The American Fur Trade in the Far West,* New York, 1902.

and Albert Talbot Richardson, *The Life, Letters and Travels of Father Pierre-Jean de Smet,* S. J., New York, 1905.

Clark, Ella Elizabeth, *Indian Legends from the Northern Rockies,* Norman, 1966.

Conn, Richard T., *The Iroquois in the West,* The Pacific Northwesterner, IV, 4 (Fall, 1960).

Coues, Elliott (Editor), *On the Trail of a Spanish Pioneer: The Diary and Itinerary of Francisco Garces,* 2 Vols., New York, 1900.

Cox, Isaac Joslin, *The Journals of La Salle and His Companions* (Contains translations of accounts of La Salle's companions.) New York, 1905.

Crespi, Juan (See Bolton 1926 and 1927). Crespi's *Diarios* also were published in Palou (1874).

Cushing, F. H., *Outlines of Zuni Creation Myths,* Bureau of American Ethnology, 13th Report, Washington, 1896.

De Grazia, Ted, *Padre Kino,* Los Angeles, 1962.

Delaney, Matilda J. Sager, *A Survivor's Recollections of the Whitman Massacre,* Spokane, 1920.

De Smet, Pierre-Jean, S. J., *Letters and Sketches: with a Narrative of a Year's Residence among the Indian Tribes of the Rocky Mountains,* Philadelphia, 1843.

Oregon Missions and Travels over the Rocky Mountains in 1845–1846,

New York, 1847.
Western Missions and Missionaries: A Series of Letters, New York, 1863.
New Indian Sketches, New York, 1865.
DeVoto, Bernard, *Across the Wide Missouri*, Boston, 1947.
Diaz del Castillo, Bernal, *True History of the Conquest of New Spain*, New York, 1927.
Diaz, Melchior, (See Bolton, 1949; Hammond and Rey 1940.)
Dorsey, George A., *The Mythology of the Wichita*, Washington, 1904.
Driver, Harold E., *Indians of North America*, Chicago, 1961.
Drury, Clifford Merrill, *Francis Harmon Spalding*, Caldwell, Idaho, 1936.
  Marcus Whitman, M. D., Pioneer and Martyr, Caldwell, Idaho, 1937.
  Elkanah and Mary Walker, Pioneers among the Spokanes, Caldwell, Idaho, 1940.
  (ed.) *Diaries and Letters of Henry H. Spalding and Asa Bowen Smith Relating to the Nez Perce Missions, 1838–1842*, Glendale, California, 1958.
  First White Women over the Rockies: Diaries, Letters, and biographical Sketches of the Six Women of the Oregon Mission who made the Overland Journey in 1836 and 1838, Glendale, California, 1963.
Dubois, Constance Goddard, *Mythology of the Mission Indians*, Journal American Folk-lore, Vol. XVII, New York, 1904.
  Religious Ceremonies and Myths of the Mission Indians, American Anthropology, Vol. VII, Washington, 1905.
Dunbar, John, Letter in *Missionary Herald*, Vol. 34, Boston, 1838.
Dunn, John, *History of the Oregon Territory*, London, 1844.
Dunne, Peter Masten, *Pioneer Jesuits in Northern Mexico*, Berkeley, 1944.
Eells, Myron, *History of the Indian Missions on the Pacific Coast: Oregon, Washington and Idaho*, Philadelphia, 1882.
  Marcus Whitman: Pathfinder and Patriot, Seattle, 1909.
Eggan, Fred, *Social Organization of the Western Pueblos*, Chicago, 1950.
Elliott, T.C., *The Coming of the White Woman*, 1836, Portland, 1937.
Engelhardt, Zephryin, *Franciscans in California*, Harbor Springs, Michigan, 1897.
  The Missions and Missionaries of California, San Francisco, 1908.
Espejo (See Hammond and Rey, 1966.)
Fahey, John, *The Flathead Indians*, Norman, Oklahoma, 1974.
Fletcher, Alice C., and Francis La Flesche, *The Omaha Tribe*, Bureau of American Ethnology, Washington, 1911.
Forbes, Alexander, *A History of California*. London, 1839.
Forbes, Jack D., *Warriors of the Colorado; The Yumas of the Quechan Nation and their Neighbors*, Norman, 1965.
Gallegos (See Hammond and Rey, 1966.)
Gay, Theresa, *Life and Letters of Mrs. Jason Lee*, Portland, 1936.
Goodwin, Grenville, *The Social Organization of the Western Apache*, Tucson, 1942.
Gray, W. H., *A History of Oregon*, 1792—1849, Portland, 1870.
Hackett, Charles Wilson (Editor and Translator), *Historical Documents Relat-*

ing to New Mexico, Nueva Vizcaya, and Approaches thereto, to 1773, Washington, 1923.

The Revolt of the Pueblo Indians of New Mexico and Otermin's Attempted Reconquest, 1680—1682, Albuquerque, 1942.

Hallenbeck, Cleve, *Spanish Missions of the Old Southwest,* New York, 1926.

Hammond, George P., and Agapito Rey, *The Narratives of the Coronado Expedition,* Albuquerque, 1940.

Don Juan de Onate', Colonizer of New Mexico, 1595—1628, Albuquerque, 1953.

The Rediscovery of New Mexico, Albuquerque, 1966.

Hassrick, Royal B., *The Sioux—Life and Customs of a Warrior Society.* In collaboration with Dorothy Maxwell and Cile M. Bach, Norman, 1964.

Hemert—Engert, Adolph van and Frederick J. Teggart (Editors), *The Narrative of the Portola Expedition of 1769–1770* by Miguel Costanso, Berkeley, 1910.

Hewitt, J. N. B. (See *Mythology* in Hodge, 1907.)

Hines, Gustavus, *Oregon: Its History,* New York, n.d. (c. 1850).

Hittell, Theodore H., *History of California,* San Francisco, 1885.

Hodge, Frederick W. (Editor), *Handbook of American Indians North of Mexico,* Bureau of American Ethology, Washington, 1907.

Spanish Explorers in the Southern United States (contains the Smith translation of the Cabeza de Vaca *Relacion,* the Winship translation of the Castaneda narrative, and the Smith translation of the De Soto Account by the Gentleman of Elvas), New York, 1908.

Horgan, Paul, *Great River: The Rio Grande in North American History,* New York, 1954.

Jackson, Helen M. H., and Abbot Kenney, *Report on the Condition and Needs of the Mission Indians of California,* Washington, 1883.

Johnston, Bernice Eastman, *California's Gabrielino Indians,* Southwest Museum, Los Angeles, 1962.

Josephy, Alvin M., Jr., *The Nez Perce Indians and the Opening of the Northwest,* New Haven, Conn., 1965.

Kelley, Hall J., *History of the Colonization of the Oregon Territory,* Worcester, 1850.

Kelly, Henry W., *Franciscan Missions of New Mexico, 1740—1760,* New Mexico Historical Review, Vols. XV, XVI (1940, 1941).

Kino, Eusebio Francisco, *Historical Memoir of Pimeria Alta,* Cleveland, 1916. *Favores Celestiales (See Bolton, 1919).*

Kroeber, A. L., *A Mission Record of the California Indians,* University of California Publications American Archaeology and Ethnology, Vol. VIII, Berkeley, 1908.

Handbook of the Indians of California, Bureau of American Ethnology, Washington, 1925.

La Perouse, J. G. F. de, *Voyage Around the World,* Boston, 1801.

Lee, Daniel and Joseph H. Frost, *Ten Years in Oregon,* New York, 1844.

Lee, Rev. Jason, *Diary of,* Oregon Historical Quarterly, Vol. 17, Eugene, 1916.

Lummis, Charles F., *Fray Zarate Salmeron's Relation,* Land of Sunshine

Magazine, Vols. XI and XII, Los Angeles, 1897—1898.
Luxan (See Hammond and Rey, 1966).
Lyons, Sister Oetitia Mary, *Francis Norbert Blanchet and the Founding of the Oregon Missions, 1838–1848,* Catholic University of America Studies in American Church History, Vol. XXXI, Washington, 1940.
McLoughlin, John L., *Letters of John McLoughlin from Fort Vancouver to the Governor and Committee,* Edited by E. E. Rich, 3 Vols., Toronto, 1941—43.
Madariago, Salvador de, *Rise of the Spanish American Empire,* London, 1947.
Manje, Juan Mateo, *Luz de Tierra Incognita,* Translated by Harry J. Karns. (Contains Father Velarde's account of the Pimeria.) Tucson, 1954.
Marshall, T. W. M., *Christian Missions,* 2 Vols., New York, 1864.
Mathews, John Joseph, *The Osages: Children of the Middle Waters,* Norman, 1961.
Matthews, Washington, *The Mountain Chant,* Bureau of American Ethnology, Washington, D. C., 1887.
The Night Chant, American Museum of Natural History, New York, 1902.
Mooney, James, *The Ghost-Dance Religion,* Fourteenth Report, Bureau of American Ethnology, Washington, 1896.
Newcomb, W. W., Jr., *The Indians of Texas,* Austin, 1961.
Nunez Cabeza de Vaca, Alvar (See Fanny Bandelier; Buckingham Smith.)
O'Bryan, A., *The Dine: Origin Myths of the Navajo Indians,* Bureau of American Ethnology, Washington, 1956.
Ortiz, Alfonso, *The Tewa World,* Chicago, 1969.
Pacheco, Joaquin F., Francisco de Cardenas, Luis Torres de Mendoza (Editors), *Coleccion de Documentos Ineditos Relativos al Descubrimiento, Conquista y Organizacion de las Antiguas Posesiones Espanoles de America y Oceania,* 42 Vols, Madrid, Spain, 1864—84.
Palou, Francisco, *Life of Fray Junipero Serra,* Mexico, 1787. English translation by Maynard J. Geiger, Washington, 1855.
Noticias de la Nueva California. (See Bolton, 1926.) San Francisco, 1874.
Parker, Samuel, *Journal of an Exploring Tour Beyond the Rocky Mountains,* Ithaca, 1838.
Parsons, Elsie Clews, *Pueblo Indian Religion,* 2 Vols., University of Chicago, 1939.
Point, Rev. Nicholas, S. J., *Wilderness Kingdom; Indian Life in the Rocky Mountains, 1840—1847.* Translated and introduced by Rev. Joseph P. Donnelly, S. J., New York, 1967
Reichard, Gladys A., *Navajo Religion,* 2 Vols., New York, 1950.
Robinson, Alfred, *Life in California,* New York, 1846.
Roca, Paul M., *Paths of the Padres through Sonora,* Tucson, 1967.
Ross, Alexander, *Adventures of the First Settlers on the Oregon,* London, 1849.
Ruby, Robert H., and John A. Brown, *Spokane Indians,* Norman, 1970.
The Cayuse Indians: Imperial Tribesmen of Old Oregon, Norman, 1972.
Salpointe, J. B., *Soldiers of the Cross,* Banning, California, 1898.
Scholes, France V., *The Supply Service of the New Mexico Missions in the*

Seventeenth Century, New Mexico Historical Review, Vol. 5, 1930.
Civil Government and Society in New Mexico in the Seventeenth Century, New Mexico Historical Review, Vol. X, 1935.
Church and State in New Mexico, New Mexico Historical Review, Vol. XI, 1936, Vol. XII, 1937.
Shaler, William, *Journal of a Voyage, 1804*. Boston, 1808.
Shea, John Gilmary, *Discovery and Exploration of the Mississippi Valley*. Contains translation of Membre (1691). New York, 1853.
History of the Catholic Missions, New York, 1855.
Simpson, Alexander, *The Oregon Territory*, London, 1846.
Skinner, Alanson, *Observations on the Ethnology of the Sauk Indians*, Milwaukee, 1924.
Smith, Buckingham (Translator), *Relacion of Alvar Nunez Cabeza De Vaca*, translated from the 1555 edition, Washington, 1851.
Smith, Fay Jackson, John L. Kessell and Francis J. Fox, *Father Kino in Arizona*, Phoenix, 1966.
Spaulding, H. H., *Journal* (27th Cong., 2nd Sess., H. Rept. 830), Washington, 1842.
Sterling, M. W., *Original Myth of Acoma and Other Records*, Bureau of American Ethnology, Washington, 1942.
Stern, Theodore, *The Klamath Tribe*, Seattle, 1965.
Stevenson, M. C., *Zuni Indians*, Bureau of American Ethnology, Washington, 1901.
Swanton, John R., *The Indian Tribes of North America*, Smithsonian Institution, Washington, 1952.
Teggart, Frederick J. (Editor), *The Anza Expedition of 1775–1776*, Diary of Pedro Font, Berkeley, 1913.
Teit, James A., *The Salishan Tribes*, Bureau of American Ethnology, 45th annual report, Washington, 1930.
Terrell, John Upton, *Journey into Darkness: The Story of Cabeza De Vaca*, New York, 1962.
Black Robe, New York, 1964.
Estevanico the Black, Los Angeles, 1968.
The Navajo, New York, 1970.
American Indian Almanac, New York, 1971.
Pueblos, Gods and Spaniards, New York, 1973.
and Donna M., *Indian Women of the Western Morning: Their Life in Early America*, New York, 1974.
Thomas, Alfred Barnaby, *After Coronado*, Norman, 1935.
Thornton, J. Quinn, *Oregon and California*, New York, 1848.
Torquemada, Juan de, *Monarchia Indiana*, Madrid, 1615.
Townsend, John K., *Narrative of a Journey Across the Rocky Mountains*, Philadelphia, 1839.
Twitchell, Ralph E., *Leading Facts of New Mexico History*, Cedar Rapids, Iowa, 1911.
The Spanish Archives of New Mexico, Cedar Rapids, Iowa, 1914.

242

Ulloa, Francisco de (See Wagner, 1929.)

Underhill, Ruth, *Red Man's Religion,* University of Chicago, 1965.

Velarde, Luis (See Manje.)

Venegas, Miguel, *Noticia de la California,* Madrid, 1757, English Translation, London, 1759.

Villagra, Gaspar Perez de, *History of New Mexico,* Translated by Gilberto Espinoza, Los Angeles, 1933.

Vogel, Virgil J., *American Indian Medicine,* Norman, 1970.

Wagner, Henry R., *The Voyage of Hernando De Alarcon,* California Historical Society Quarterly, Vol. III, December, 1924.

> *Spanish Voyages to the Northwest Coast of America in the Sixteenth Century,* San Francisco, 1929.

Warren, Eliza Spalding, *Memoirs of the West* (Journal of Eliza Spalding), Portland, n.d.

White, Elijah, *A Concise view of Oregon History,* Washington, 1846.

> *Ten Years in Oregon: Travels and Adventures of Doctor E. White and Lady West of the Rocky Mountains,* Ithaca, New York, 1848.

Whitman, Marcus, *Results of the Oregon Mission,* Missionary Herald, Boston, Dec. 1866.

Whitman, Narcissa, *Journal of Narcissa Whitman,* Transactions of Oregon Pioneer Association, Portland, 1890.

> *Letters of Narcissa Whitman,* Transactions of Oregon Pioneer Association, Portland, 1893.

Winship, George Parker (Translator), *The Narrative of the Expedition of Coronado by Castaneda,* Bureau of American Ethnology, 14th Annual Report, Washington, 1896.

Wyeth, John B., *Oregon, or a Short History of Long Journey from Atlantic to Pacific,* Cambridge, 1833.

Wyeth, Nathaniel J., *Correspondence and Journals,* Edited by F. G. Young, Eugene, Oregon, 1899.

Young, F. G., *Journal and Report by Doctor Marcus Whitman,* Oregon Historical Quarterly, Vol. 27, 1926.

Zarate Salmeron, Geronimo de, *Relaciones,* Mexico City, 1790. English translation Land of Sunshine Magazine, Vol. XI, Los Angeles, 1900.

Notes

Chapter One

1. Modern place names are used throughout this work to make it easier for readers to locate geographical areas and the scenes of events.

2. In the sixteenth century, the legend of the Seven Cities had been harbored in the minds of Spanish adventurers for seven hundred years. It said that after the Moors from Africa had invaded the Iberian Peninsula, oppressed Christians led by seven bishops had sailed westward into the mysterious Ocean Sea. The fugitives had discovered an incredibly beautiful land, perhaps an island, which they had named Antilia. Each of the bishops had founded a city and together had created a utopian commonwealth that was unbelievably rich in gold and jewels, and abundantly supplied with rare foods and fine wines. Countless futile searches had been made for the Seven Cities. Still, five decades after the first voyage of Columbus, when much of the Western Hemisphere had been explored, few persons—and least of all those with an insatiable desire for enormous wealth—were willing to believe that the tale was mythical. Certainly there was no good reason to forget it, for no one had proved it false, and remembering it sustained an inspiring dream.

3. From a great ridge in the Huachuca Mountains, up where the air is thin and sweet, one may see, in a magnificent panoramic view, the place where Estevanico crossed the international border between Mexico and the United States. The area has been set aside as a memorial—but not to him. It is called Coronado National Monument. Neither Arizona nor New Mexico has troubled to erect even a modest marker to perpetuate publicly the memory of the first man of the Old World to enter their respective territories.

4. The best account of the tragic end of Estevanico was written by Pedro de Castaneda, a private soldier for three years in the army of Coronado. It appears in his narrative of the Coronado Expedition, the original manuscript of which, probably completed circa 1560-1565, is not known to exist. An English translation was made by George Parker Winship from a manuscript copy bearing the date 1596. The Winship translation and other documents pertaining to the Coronado Expedition, were published in 1896 in the *Fourteenth Annual Report of the Bureau of American Ethnology*. Later publications of the Castaneda narrative are listed in the bibliography.

Estevanico, Cabeza de Vaca, and two other Spanish officers, were the first men of the Old World to cross North America north of central Mexico. They were the only survivors of the expedition of Panfilo de Narvaez, which landed in Florida in the spring of 1528. Their journey, one of the most extraordinary in the history of American exploration, took eight years. See Terrell's *Journey Into Darkness: The Story of Cabeza de Vaca* (1962), and his *Estevanico The Black* (1968). Alvar Nunez Cabeza de Vaca's *Relacion*, his own account of the journey, was translated into English by Buckingham Smith in 1851, and by Fanny Bendelier in 1905. It appears in Hodge's *Spanish Explorers In The Southern United States*. See bibliography for other details.

5. An English translation of Ulloa's report of his voyage, made by Irene A. Wright, appears in Henry R. Wagner's *Spanish Voyages to the Northwest Coast of America in the Sixteenth Century.*

6. In his *Coronado, Knight of Pueblos and Plains,* Herbert Eugene Bolton devotes a chapter to Alarcon's vain attempt to carry supplies by sea to Coronado. Bolton's main sources were official Spanish documents, including Alarcon's own narrative written for the Viceroy of Mexico. Alarcon's report was first published in Madrid in 1601 by Antonio de Herrara in his *Historia General.*

7. A picture or a statue depicting Christ on the Cross was always incomprehensible to primitive Indians, and many narratives written by early missionaries contain comments on the subject. The following passage, proffered as an example, is found in Father Eusebio Kino's *Favores Celestiales,* which he completed late in the seventeenth century: "One day we set up in our little church a large and pretty statue of the Holy Christ (in his crucifixion), but as soon as the Indians saw it they ran away, very much afraid of it. They hardly dared to talk with us, or among themselves except in very low tones or whispers, asking who that person was and who had killed him, and if he were some cruel enemy of ours, for it worried them very greatly to think that we had treated people so. There was no way to pacify them except to tell them that he was our friend." In 1919, Herbert Eugene Bolton published an English translation made from the original manuscript of *Favores Celestiales* under the title Kino's Historical Memoir of Pimeria Alta.

Chapter Two

1. An exception to this statement must be made in the case of some tribes who dwelt in extremely barren areas, such as the Great Basin, parts of south Texas, and the deserts of eastern California. For them, because of sparse vegetal foods and little game, life was an eternal search for sustenance. They had no time to devote to religious activities, and their cultures were developed to a lesser degree than any other American Indians.

2. Regarding the religion of western Indians, works written by missionaries and other persons affiliated with church organizations are biased and therefore of relatively small value as source material. A reader interested in the subject might gain reliable information by referring to Driver (1961); Terrell (1973); Parsons (1939); Underhill (1965); Terrell and Terrell (1974); Matthews (1961); Ortiz (1969); Hewitt and Boas in Hodge (1907); Hassrick (1964). Vogel's *American Indian Medicine* is an outstanding work on the subject.

3. The name *Orenda* is from the Iroquois tongue. Corresponding with it in meaning are the Algonquian *Manito,* the Shoshonean *Pokunt,* and the Siouan *Mahopa.*

4. This material on mythology is excerpted from an article entitled "Mythology," by Hewitt, contained in Bulletin 30 of the Smithsonian Institution, Bureau of American Ethnology.

5. See Kroeber's *Handbook of the Indians of California* (1925). A famous anthropologist and ethnologist, Kroeber's enormous work remains the outstanding study of the subject.

6. Lakota Sioux religion and mythology is treated at length in Hassrick's

excellent work (1964).

7. The Tewa are a dialectical group of the Tanoan linguistic family, the others being the Tiwa, Jemez, and Piro, and are among the oldest inhabitants of New Mexico. They still live in ancient pueblos in the Rio Grande Valley and the Jemez area. Among the Old Tewa towns still inhabited are Nambe, Pojoaque, San Ildefonso, Santa Clara, Tesuque, and San Juan, all in the general Santa Fe region.

8. See Ortiz (1969), a superb study of the tribe's mythology. Ortiz, a social anthropologist, was born in San Juan Pueblo.

9. Matthews (1961) contains a moving interpretation of Osage mythology. He is an Osage, born in Oklahoma.

10. The four sacred mountains of the Navajo are known today as Big Sheep Peak in the La Plata Range on the north; Mount Taylor on the south; Humphreys Peak of the San Francisco Peaks on the west; and Pelado Mountain in the Jemez Range on the east. Some Navajo medicine men maintain that the eastern sacred mountain is Sierra Blanca Peak in Colorado; thus the names of both eastern mountains appear in Navajo mythology.

11. The literature on Navajo mythology, religion, and ritual is extensive. Reference is made here to *The Navajo*, Kluckhohn and Leighton (1946); *The Mountain Chant* (1887); and *The Night Chant* (1902), Matthews; *The Dine: Origin Myths of the Navajo* (1956), O'Bryan; *Navajo Religion* (1950), Reichard; *The Navajo* (1970), Terrell. Additional sources appear in the bibliography.

12. Frank Hamilton Cushing lived for many years among the Zuni, and the lightning example is paraphrased from his *Outlines of Zuni Origin Myths* (1896). His works are of inestimable value. Although he wrote chiefly about the Zuni, much of the Zuni religious doctrine is applicable to the beliefs of other Indian peoples.

13. The paragraphs treating of souls are in large part a paraphrase of the brief article written by Dr. Franz Boas of Columbia University, which appeared in Hodge (1907) under the heading *Souls*. See bibliography for other sources on the subject.

14. A line from a Potawatomi hymn, translated by Skinner (1924).

Chapter Three

1. Indians allotted in *encomienda* were in reality workers in bondage, and usually poorly fed and clothed. The *encomiendero* was required under the law to provide his native laborers with all necessities and to insure that they were converted to Christianity. Abuses wre more the rule than the exception.

2. The manuscript of Gallegos's *Relacion* is preserved in the Archives of the Indies, Seville, Spain. An English translation appears in Hammond and Rey (1966). See also Bancroft, *History of Mexico* (1883); Terrell (1973).

3. Accounts of the Espejo Expedition have appeared in many histories in several languages. Lusan's journal was submitted to the Count of Monterrey, Viceroy of Mexico, but like so many invaluable documents of the time, it was buried among masses of state papers that accumulated in the archives of Mexico City and Seville. It was resurrected circa 1602, and copies were made of it. An English translation by Hammond and Rey was published by the Quivera Soci-

ety in 1929. A revised English translation by the same scholars is contained in *The Rediscovery of New Mexico* (1966). Espejo also wrote a report of the expedition, as well as letters regarding it to church and royal officials. The Espejo account was published in Pacheco and Cardenas (1864). English translations appear in Bolton's *Spanish Exploration in the Southwest;* and in Hammond and Rey *op. cit.* Of the two accounts, Espejo's is more in the nature of a propaganda document, and therefore Luxan's is the more reliable.

4. Espejo made several remarkable discoveries and traversed country never explored by white men. The accounts of the expedition are well worth reading, for he was a daring adventurer. However, only matters pertaining to the missionaries killed at Puaray and to Fray Beltran are included in this work.

5. Fray Beltran's party reached Mexico in safety. No account of their homeward journey is known to have been written, but it was reported they took "a more direct route." In order to avoid the unfriendly people of Puaray and other pueblos they probably turned down the Rio San Jose in the vicinity of McCartys, New Mexico, to its confluence with the Rio Grande. Espejo and his men returned to their starting point in September, 1583.

6. Two other expeditions, both illegal and both ending in disaster, would come north from Mexico after Espejo, but no priests would be with them, and, therefore, they are not described in this book. Accounts of them appear in Terrell (1973), which also contains a bibliography of sources and documents pertaining to them. They were the Castano and the Bonilla-Humana Expeditions of 1590 and 1593, respectively.

Chapter Four

1. Pertinent material on the colonization of New Mexico by Onate' and the contemporary work of the friars with him is to be found in numerous histories and narratives. Some of the most useful follow: Bandelier and Bandelier (1923); Bancroft (1883); Bolton (1916); Pacheco and Cardenas (1864); Horgan (1954); Scholes (1930), (1935), and (1937); Twitchell (1914); Villagra (1933); Terrell (1973).

The most comprehensive collection of material on the subject, and undoubtedly the most complete ever published, is contained in Hammond and Rey, *Onate': Colonizer of New Mexico,* (1953). They made English translations of a great many original documents owned by government archives in Spain and Mexico.

2. Farfan had found the deposits that Espejo had discovered, and which his diarist, Luxan, had reported as being worthless. In reality they were the great mines near Jerome, Arizona, which in later years would yield immense fortunes in copper and silver.

Chapter Five

1. Paul Horgan (1954).

2. Scholes (1930).

3. Both Scholes (1936) and Beck (1962) treat the Peralta-Ordonez affair. See also Terrell (1973).

4. Bancroft (1889); Scholes (1936); Terrell (1973).

Chapter Six

1. The earliest publication date known for Zarate's *Relaciones* is 1790, but

undoubtedly copies of his manuscript were widely read soon after it was written. See bibliography.

2. The Spanish judicial league was the equivalent of 2.634 English miles. Thus, fifty leagues would be approximately one hundred and thirty miles.

3. Tying knots in a thong was a method by which Indians kept account of time, such as the number of days spent on a journey or on a long visit away from home. A knotted thread would be an important symbol in the great Indian rebellion against the Spanish in 1680, as will be seen.

4. F. W. Hodge in a comment in the Ayer translation of Benavides's *Memorial*.

5. Fred Eggan (1950).

6. Fanega: Varied in times and places from approximately 1½ to 2½ bushels. If a fanega approximated 2 bushels in New Mexico when Benavides was there, the wheat harvest was hardly less than miraculous.

7. Benavides's *Memorial* was published in Spain in 1630, but the first English translation appeared in *Land of Sunshine* magazine, under the editorship of the noted scholar and writer, Charles F. Lummis, in 1900. Ever since it has been cited and quoted in every history of Mexico and Southwestern America.

8. Speaking of Benavides's inaccuracies regarding Indian populations, Badelier (1890) states that his *Memorial* was "in many respects a campaign document. Its purpose was to induce the King to favor the missions, to create a better impression of the missionaries than the Spanish government had at the time, after their constant quarrels with the Governors of New Mexico, and to obtain the establishment of a bishopric at Santa Fe."

Chapter Seven

1. Horgan (1954).

2. Rosters of New Mexico Governors differ somewhat in varied works. I have followed Bancroft (1889), which is the most complete I have seen, and probably more accurate than others, as he had available to him a mass of early Spanish documents. See Terrell (1973) in which I made an effort to locate all pueblos of prehistoric and historic times that can be identified by name.

Chapter Eight

1. Madariago (1947).

2. The most detailed account of the Pueblo revolt is Hackett (1942); especially dramatic is his account of events occurring during the final days of the uprising and immediately thereafter.

Chapter Nine

1. See Chapter One.

2. Alarcon called the Rio Colorado the Rio Buena Guia (Good Guide). Diaz gave the stream the name of Rio del Tizon (Firebrand River), because of the Indians' custom of carrying burning pitch torches to warm themselves.

3. In northern Sonora, southeast of Magdalena.

4. Unless otherwise stated, quotations in this part are excerpted from Kino's own writings. His books, letters, and reports, as well as the translators of them, are cited in the bibliography. Herbert Eugene Bolton's *Rim of Christendom* is by far the best and most complete biography of Kino.

Chapter Ten

1. With two vessels under his command, Juan Rodriguez Cabrillo, a veteran Portuguese mariner, had sailed northward from Mexico into a sea unknown to the civilized world. He had discovered San Diego Bay, San Pedro Bay (Los Angeles harbor), and the Channel Islands. He died following an accident on San Miguel Island. Other ships, some returning from the Orient, passed along the California coast between 1543 and 1596. For the history of these expeditions the best work is Henry R. Wagner's *Spanish Voyages to the Northwest Coast of North America in the Sixteenth Century.*

2. Fr. Ascension's accounts appeared in Torquemada (1615) and in Venegas (1757). From Venegas it was translated into English, French, Dutch and German circa 1759. An early copy of the original manuscript is the property of the Edward E. Ayer collection in the Newberry Library, Chicago. An English translation also appears in Wagner (1929).

3. Sixty years earlier, Cabrillo had written an almost identical report. A tempest had struck while he was anchored in San Diego Bay (to which he gave another name), but his ships suffered no damage. Ascension made no mention of Cabrillo.

4. Bancroft's *History of California* (1886). The sources cited in Bancroft's works are an invaluable guide for scholars. Indeed, while later research has revealed some minor errors in his writings, they were honest mistakes, no fault of his own, and his State histories remain incomparable, nearly a century after he completed them. His vast accumulation of material, in the Bancroft Library of the University of California, is recognized as one of the world's great historical collections.

5. The governor to whom reference is made by Grimaldi was Gaspar de Portola. Grimaldi's letter is quoted in Engelhardt (1897).

6. Palou, Serra's colleague and biographer, said little about his physical appearance. The Ainsworths (1970) describe him at various periods of his life, utilizing with good effect the sparse material they found in Mexican, Spanish, and American archives.

7. See Ainsworths (1970) for an excellent account of Serra's self-discipline. I have paraphrased some of their statements on the subject. As they note, Serra's "spiritual exultation and his appreciation of the dramatic never left him, just as his religious fervor remained fresh and vital all the days of his life."

8. Engelhardt (1908) states: "The fact that no provisions were made from the government treasury to aid the friars . . . and the further fact that no expenses were incurred save for political objects . . . proves that the Spanish Government would not have sent ships and troops to the northwest if the Russians had not crept down the Pacific coast. The men who presumed to guide the destinies of Spain, down to the year 1821 (when Spain met defeat in the Mexican revolution), cared naught for the success of Religion or the welfare of its ministers, except in so far as both could be used to promote political schemes."

9. The story of Serra's cure appears in Palou (1874), Bolton (1926), Bancroft (1886), Ainsworth (1970).

10. Kroeber (1925) is by far the most authoritative and most detailed work on California Indians. Bancroft (1886) is the most reliable and complete source for

dates, names, and significant events in the early history of California. Important details also are to be found in Bolton (1926 and 1927), and a few in Englehardt (1908).

Chapter Eleven
1. Mooney under *California Missions* in Hodge (1907).
2. Engelhardt (1908). A Franciscan priest, Engelhardt violently denounces all historians who do not treat with unqualified praise the work and practices of the missionaries. He excoriates with such words as vile, bigoted, superficial, shallow, and dishonest all writers who criticize the padres. His work is useful only for religious material pertaining to the California conquest, and in actuality is a long and boring brief in defense of Franciscan policies.
3. For tribal population estimates I have relied on Mooney (1928), Swanton (1952), and Kroeber (1925). The latter sets the total at 64,000. It is obvious, of course, that not all members of a tribe were affected by the missions.
4. See Terrell (1971) and sources listed therein for more information on the linguistic groups.
5. Kroeber (1925) under *Pomo*.
6. Kroeber (1925) under *Chumash;* Terrell (1971) under *Pacific Coast.*
7. Barrett (1908); Kroeber (1925).
8. Kroeber (1925) under *Yokuts;* Swanton (1952) under *California;* Terrell (1971) under *Pacific Coast.*
9. Johnston (1962)
10. Kroeber (1925)
11. Swanton (1952) is the most concise reference work for the names and location of mission Indians. Also listed are the names and locations of hundreds of villages, the existence of which has been established by archaeologists.

Chapter Twelve
1. Both Bancroft (1886) and Engelhardt (1908) write at length on Serra's *Representacion.*
2. Engelhardt (1908).
3. Material on the daily routine of the missions has been gleaned from numerous sources, among them Forbes (1839); Bolton's translation of Palou's *Noticias* (1926); Bancroft (1886); Hittell (1885); Mooney under *Missions* in Hodge (1907); Kroeber (1925); Engelhardt (1908). The latter work contains English translations, presumably made by Engelhardt but not stated, of some of the regulations issued by Serra.
4. This is an interesting historical note by Engelhardt (1908), for in the annals of the Catholic Church Fr. Salvatierra is proclaimed as one of the most successful missionaries to the Indians of Mexico. He was a colleague and close friend of Fr. Kino, but there is no evidence to show that Kino approved of his system of punishing Indians, or ever employed it either in Baja California or Pimeria Alta.
5. The rare volumes of La Perouse's narrative were not readily accessible to me at the time I needed them, and the quotations from his work I have used are contained in Bancroft (1886).
6. Mooney under *Missions* in Hodge (1907).
7. Kroeber under *Mission Indians of California* in Hodge (1907).
8. Shaler (1808).

9. A *fanega* approximated a bushel, but grains were often measured and sold by hundred weight. A Spanish *aroba,* by which such products as tallow, flour, lard and cured meat were usually priced, weighed about twenty-five pounds.

10. Few narratives, reports, diaries, etc. of the California mission period do not contain some statistical information. The most comprehensive compilation of this material was made by Bancroft, who presents an analysis of production for each decade between 1769 and 1833, in his *History of California.* Engelhardt (1908) publishes a long price list of commodities that was issued by Governor Felipe de Neve at Monterey in 1781. The prices on it are considerably lower than those prevailing twenty years later, yet during his tenure Neve complained that the friars were attempting to over-charge presidios. Indeed, every California governor and military commander registered similar complaints. It would be impossible to learn the differences between prices asked and prices paid in any year.

Chapter Thirteen

1. There are conflicting statements regarding the identities of the chiefs in the delegation, some reports declaring two of its members were Spokan. The most reliable account seems to be that of Bishop Joseph Rosati, who talked with them and wrote of their visit in official Catholic publications in the same year.

2. J. Quinn Thornton (1848).

3. Of all the Indians in the northwestern plateau region who belong to the inner division of the large Salishan Linguistic Family the best known are the people erroneously called Flatheads. their proper name is Salish, meaning simply "people." It is popularly thought that they were given the name Flatheads by other Indians because they followed the practice of deforming the heads of infants. The opposite is true. They were called Flatheads because, unlike some of their congenitors living farther to the west, they left their heads in a normal condition, that is, flat on top, instead of deforming them by pressure to slope toward the crown. Their earliest known homeland was in the mountains of western Montana, extending into Idaho, southward to some of the Missouri River headwaters, and centering in the vicinity of Flathead Lake. There were nine other tribes of some importance in early historic times who spoke dialects of the Salishan tongue, spread all the way from Montana to British Columbia and the coast of Oregon. The Flatheads of western Montana were both plains and mountain Indians, for they regularly journeyed east of the mountains to hunt buffalo.

4. Condensed from Bancroft's *History of Oregon* (1886), as is the description of Daniel Lee that follows.

5. See *Oregon Historical Quarterly,* Vol. XVII, 1916, cited by Fahey (1974).

6. Near the present Pocatello, Idaho.

7. "He was simply a carrier of the Zeitgeist. Here in 1834 it can almost be seen running in his veins. By another three years it spoke with his voice." De Voto (1947).

8. Chapter on Lee in *Across the Wide Missouri,* in which De Voto also says that on the way west Lee had learned enough to know that Indians could not be made into white men in such forbidding lands as the deserts of western Wyoming and southern Idaho. I think Lee must have felt the same about the Flathead's

country, which was much farther to the north, after his conferences about it with the Mountain Men. It was better in most respects than valleys of the Green and Snake Rivers, but he didn't go to see for himself.

9. Parker wrote an excellent book about his experiences (Parker 1838), which remains the most reliable account of his role in western history. Whitman wrote no books, his literary contributions comprising numerous letters and reports. These communications have been widely used by historians, and while lacking desirable details throw considerable light on the trend of his thinking. See Drury (1937); Gray (1870); Bancroft *Oregon* (1886); Delaney (1920); Eellas (1882); Ruby and Brown (1972); Whitman (1866); De Voto (1947).

10. Parker would attempt to journey to the Northwest in 1834, a year before he knew Whitman. With two other missionaries, John Dunbar and Samuel Allis, he arrived on the Missouri frontier about a fortnight after the supply train with which they were to travel had departed. Parker returned to his New York home. Dunbar and Allis elected to set out with a large band of Pawnees and would establish an earth lodge mission in the country of this tribe.

11. Bancroft (*Oregon* 1886).

12. De Voto (1947).

13. Unlike Lee, Parker not only liked the Indians but made a serious effort to understand them. Probably more than any other early Protestant missionary to reach the Northwest, he sensed the tragedies to come, and predicted them in his Journal (1838). He considered the Indians fully capable of receiving civilization, and thought that a consistent and persevering attempt to enlighten and train them would bring great rewards. De Voto (1947) expresses the opinion that Parker "saw the country, the Indians, and the future of both as clearly as anyone who went West during the first half of the nineteenth century . . . and in particular was so much more intelligent about them than the other missionaries that he is in a class by himself. He was wrong in only one important judgment. It was not the Mountain Men in whom the threat of destruction lay. It was in the emigrants. . . whose coming was so notably facilitated and in great part procured by the missionaries—not least by Parker himself."

It is well to note Father De Smet's feelings with regard to the mass migrations of miners and settlers, as related in pages ahead. De Smet followed Parker and Whitman by only a few years.

Chapter Fourteen

1. An excellent account of the Willamette Cattle Company is contained in Bancroft (*Oregon,* 1886). The brutality of the drovers is sickening.

2. White (1848). Anna Pitman Lee would be the first white woman to die in Oregon, her demise taking place in June, 1838, only a year after her marriage to Lee. A son to whom she had given birth three weeks previously also had died.

3. Bancroft (*Oregon,* 1886) was my main source regarding Lee's plot, and I consider this work a most reliable history of the subject. He expresses the opinion that Jason Lee "had marked ability in using others for his own advantage." See also H. R. Report 101, Twenty-fifth Congress, Third Session.

4. Report 101, 25th Congress, Third Session.

5. McLoughlin had sent a letter to Lee advising him of the death of his wife and infant son. In the East Lee married again, taking his second wife back to

Oregon on the ship *Lusanne*.

6. The cost figure appears in Bancroft (*Oregon*, 1886) and he in turn quotes Hines (1850).

Chapter Fifteen

1. Drury (1937) is the best and most comprehensive biography of Whitman. The stanza quoted is from a hymn written by Reverend Samuel F. Smith. Drury states that Narcissa Whitman had made a number of calico dresses which she thought would please the Indians. Highly recommended in connection with the history of the Protestant missions of Oregon are Drury's works of 1936, 1940, 1958, 1963, all listed in the bibliography. See Eliza Spalding Warren (n.d.); Narcissa Whitman (1890) and (1893); De Voto (1947); Gray (1870); Elliott (1937); Bancroft (Oregon 1886); Eells (1909).

2. De Voto (1947). Bancroft (Oregon 1886) states that Eliza Spalding was skilled in painting with water colors and an adept linguist who learned to speak Indian tongues.

3. Details of the journey of the Whitman group have been omitted. They will be found in profusion in the books cited in Note One above. Only essential events are recounted in this work, my express purpose being to show why the Protestant mission founded by Whitman was doomed to failure even before the occurrence of the tragedy of 1847.

4. Near Lewiston, Idaho.

5. Lewis and Clark called the Clearwater the Kooskooski, as the name given them by the Indians sounded to their ears.

Chapter Sixteen

1. The richest mine of material about De Smet is in the innumerable letters he wrote to friends, members of his family, colleagues and superiors over a span of forty years from various parts of the American West. It was his way, undoubtedly because of an uncertain supply of paper and ink in the wilderness, to write long letters when the materials were available to him. With very little editing these could be transformed into articles for magazines and newspapers, or adapted for inclusion in a book. His published works, therefore, are largely compilations of his correspondence, and of enormous value to historians. They are listed in the bibliography.

The quotations in this chapter have been excerpted from De Smet (1843 and 1845), largely from his personal letters.

Chittenden and Richardson (1905) is the most comprehensive work on De Smet, four large volumes containing his letters, articles, scientific papers, religious treatises and essays—as well as a number of poems of dubious quality—carefully organized and well annotated.

Chapter Seventeen

1. Church histories and narratives by missionaries should be treated with caution, for most of them are prejudiced, omitting or glossing over faults and spotlighting commendable qualities of principals. Religious magazines and newspapers are largely propaganda designed to inspire increased activities on the part of the faithful and attract monetary contributions. In all these publications critical material that would be of great value to objective historians is concealed. General histories should be studied first, after which accounts deal-

ing with particular issues, events, and denominations should be weighed against them. See Billington (1949); Bancroft (Oregon 1886); Ruby (1970, 1972); Josephy (1965); Chittenden (1902); De Voto (1947); Fahey (1974).

2. Literature regarding Catholic missions in the Northwest is voluminous. The following will serve as guides to other sources: Bagley (1932); Blanchet (1878); Chittenden (1905); De Smet (1843, 1847, 1863); Lyons (1940); Point (1967); Terrell (1964).

3. Scholarly works regarding Protestant missions of the Northwest are Drury (1936, 1937, 1940, 1958). See also Eells (1882, 1909); Gray (1870); Delaney (1920); Allen (1850); Barclay (1950).

All the citations in the above three notes include material drawn upon in this chapter.

Chapter Eighteen

1. Bancroft (*Oregon, 1886*) says: "The story of Joe Louis is given by several witnesses. One of these, William Craig of Lapwai, no one would dispute." It must be assumed that if Craig was associated with Spalding at Lapwai he was a Protestant devoting himself to mission work. Bancroft quotes Craig's testimony as it appeared in an account written by a Catholic missionary, Brouillet (1869).

2. The Catholics, especially Archbishop Blanchet, were accused of urging the Cayuse to kill Whitman and Spalding, but no evidence to support such charges has ever come to light, and they are undoubtedly without any foundation whatsoever. For readers who may wish to acquire more knowledge of the tragedies at Waiilatpu I suggest the following works: Drury (1936, 1937); Bancroft (Oregon 1886); Delaney (1920); De Voto (1947); Eells (1909); Gray (1870); Ruby (1972); Brouillet (1869).